Urban Headway and Upward Mobility in India

This book addresses a wide range of issues relating to urbanization in India. It reflects on the conceptualization of well-being, the association between urbanization (city size) and well-being, the new initiatives such as the smart city programme adopted by the government, new changes such as the growth of census towns in the context of urbanization, rural–urban migration and the possible benefits the migrants reap in terms of work accessibility and poverty reduction, relevance of caste in accessing jobs in the urban labour market, and other social transformation issues relating to gender equality in particular.

What motivate workers to experience upward mobility and pull them back are important questions which are examined on the basis of the network literature. How the nature of activities varies in relation to the nature of the city and its economy and how the well-being level changes across space are examined meticulously. The macro impact of urbanization is complemented by micro studies to offer additional explanation in the context of poverty mitigation. This book brings to the fore the rigidity of the social system that can be mitigated through significant interventions into some of the economic variables. Various policy implications of the evidence-based research are discussed at the end of each chapter.

Arup Mitra is Professor of Economics at the Institute of Economic Growth, New Delhi. He currently holds a joint position as the Dean of the Faculty of Economics at the South Asian University, New Delhi. He has been a senior researcher at the ILO, Geneva, and has held the Indian Economy Chair at Sciences Po, Paris. His research interest includes issues in development, urbanization, labour, corruption, industrialization and productivity, services sector and gender inequality. He co-authored, with Chandan Sharma, *Corruption and Development in Indian Economy*, which was published by the Press in 2016.

Urban Headway and Upward Mobility in India

Arup Mitra

CAMBRIDGE
UNIVERSITY PRESS

CAMBRIDGE
UNIVERSITY PRESS

University Printing House, Cambridge CB2 8BS, United Kingdom

One Liberty Plaza, 20th Floor, New York, NY 10006, USA

477 Williamstown Road, Port Melbourne, vic 3207, Australia

314 to 321, 3rd Floor, Plot No.3, Splendor Forum, Jasola District Centre, New Delhi 110025, India

79 Anson Road, #06–04/06, Singapore 079906

Cambridge University Press is part of the University of Cambridge.

It furthers the University's mission by disseminating knowledge in the pursuit of education, learning and research at the highest international levels of excellence.

www.cambridge.org

Information on this title: www.cambridge.org/9781108496360

© Arup Mitra 2020

First published 2020

Printed in India by Nutech Print Services, New Delhi 110020

A catalogue record for this publication is available from the British Library

ISBN 978-1-108-49636-0 Hardback

Contents

Tables

Acknowledgements

The volume entitled *Urban Headway and Upward Mobility* reflects on a wide range of theoretical, empirical, and policy issues with a strong reference to the contemporary situations, particularly in India. Urbanization as a process of demographic and socio-economic transformation can be better understood in the backdrop of a number of changes occurring at the macro level within the domestic economy and also the shifts that are envisaged in the course of rapid globalization. While the older tenets still lend support to the growing phenomenon, new dynamics and interactions are emerging fast to offer fresh explanations and interpretations. The present volume is a modest attempt in this respect.

It cogitates the arena of well-being, the association between urbanization and well-being, new initiatives such as the smart city programme adopted by the government, the growth of the census towns in the context of the changing pattern of urbanization, rural–urban migration and the possible benefits the migrants reap in terms of work accessibility and poverty reduction at the place of destination, relevance of caste in accessing jobs, and other outcomes related to social transformation, such as gender equality. The macro impact of urbanization is complemented by micro studies to offer additional explanation for poverty mitigation and upward mobility. Economy, geography, society, and polity—all seem to be in interplay in shaping the outcome variables.

While the organization of the work bears a great deal of novelty, some of the ideas and their empirical supportbase happen to deduce their roots from a couple of my earlier writings and co-publications at various fora. In particular, I am grateful to S. Chandrassekhar, Rajnish Kumar, Satendra Kumar, Jay Prakash Nagar, Aviral Pandey, and Yuko Tsujita. Some of the journals and books from which excerpts are drawn include the *Economic and Political Weekly, Environment and Urbanisation Asia, Habitat International, Indian Journal of Women and Social Change, Journal of Developmental Entrepreneurship, Urban India, Urban Research and Practice, World Development*, and *Insights into Inclusive Growth, Employment and Wellbeing in India*. I am grateful to all of them for allowing the reuse of some materials which provide a strong basis to the current volume to offer a fresh perspective and in-depth analysis in a holistic manner. The gaps in our understanding of the urban issues are enormously large; the current work only tries to fill them in to a partial extent. Much more still remains to be done than what could be addressed here.

Acknowledgements

CHAPTER 1

Analytical Frame

Urbanization in development economics literature is expected to bring in a spectrum of social and economic transformations. In the backdrop of this understanding, the volume on the one hand focuses on various aspects of urbanization in India and on the other, analyses its impact on different socio-economic variables. Urbanization envisaged as a process in a developing-country context is then able to decipher a wide variety of positive changes which are occurring, though mildly. On the flip side, the rigidity of the social system is also on display, which possibly can be mitigated through significant interventions in addition to the rapid changes in some of the economic variables. The policy implications of evidence-based research are unfolded at the end of each of the chapters.

The volume begins with an analytical frame encompassing various factors that not only lead to urbanization but also unequal urbanization in particular. As per the received theory on urbanization, particularly in the conceptualization of modern economic growth by Kuznets (1966), industrialization per se is the driver. The 'overurbanization' thesis of Hoselitz (1953), on the other hand, looked at the urban phenomenon in the absence of adequate industrialization and opportunities for the rural population to shift to productive activities while agriculture pushed them out from the rural areas. The transfer of rural poverty to the urban space with the urban informal sector being the outlet for a residual absorption of labour stands central to this argument. However, with large-scale labour-intensive industrialization, the mobility of population is seen to be accompanied by a reduction in poverty as Lewis (1954) and Kuznets (1966) both had envisaged. Thus, the entire evolution of development was centring round the growth of factory. Since then the urban changes have taken place on a massive scale and the drivers of urban growth have deviated significantly from the traditional conceptualization. The growth of the services sector, international trade, infrastructural hubs, and, more importantly, even activities without much scope for labour-intensive methods have played a strategic role in the urbanization process, highlighting the mutual reinforcements between urbanization and economic development. As Hardt and Negri (2009) suggested, the contemporary metropolis has become a locus of socio-political mobilization analogous to the role of the factory during the initial phases of industrial epoch. They noted that the metropolis has become the 'space of the common', the territorial basis for collective action under conditions of globalizing capitalism, neoliberalizing states, and reconstituted Empire, as observed by Brenner (2013). There is now a huge amount of research available on migration and urban poverty, the impact of globalization on urban poverty, de-industrialization in cities of the global south leading to a decline in employment opportunities for unskilled migrant workers, and so on (Ugur and Mitra, 2017; Mitra, 2013). Effective land, housing, transport, and local labour market policy in cities and their implications for economic development and social inclusion constitute an endemic part of urbanization and poverty studies. Forhad (2019) discusses recent research on the interactions between spatial and structural transformation. Areas across space are interlinked through transport and migration, and a change in transport costs due to infrastructure projects can affect spatial specialization though migration may not solve all the problems of regional inequality. A temporary transport cost shock can result in persistent regional inequality, suggesting that the problems in a city cannot be solved by focusing on the city alone. It requires a spatial general equilibrium perspective without which there can remain a significant gap in the policy dialogue. Similarly, to ensure that the benefits of urbanization are shared by all, policies for infrastructure and services will have to emerge to provide access to both the urban and rural population, particularly the urban and rural poor. Sustainable development depends increasingly on successful management of urban growth, especially in low-income and lower-middle-income countries where the pace of urbanization is projected to be the fastest (United Nations, 2018). In such situations, how urbanization and migration respond and how labour market functions and poverty configurations change are some of the crucial issues which are worth revisiting. Growth of cities can derail economic growth and, therefore, the biggest challenge is not to reduce rural–urban migration but to work out strategies without paying too high a cost to make cities inclusive and the beneficial effects of urbanization wide and long lasting (Spence, Annez, and Buckley, 2009).

Moving on to spatial inequality, it may be noted that agglomerations economies contribute to productivity growth but on the other hand they result in concentration of economic activities and population on a large scale. Such unequal distribution of activities and investment keep mutually reinforcing on each other as a result of which economic growth across space tends to become highly unequal. On the one hand, while the globalization forces try to integrate the economies, on the other hand the same forces initiate divergence within a given economy which is particularly large in size (Fujita and Hamaguchi, 2008; Nishikimi, 2008). Outflow of rural population then naturally gets directed to large urban settlements in an attempt to take advantage of the large labour market and its associated benefits such as lower job search cost and better infrastructural facilities. How the individual efforts to escape deprivation and poverty respond to the macro changes and in what way urbanization as a concomitant of development and modernization offers opportunities to facilitate upward mobility are some of the key questions that stand out for an in-depth empirical research. The optimism resounds that emerging inequality in the process of economic growth may still hold possibilities of resulting in economic betterment of those located at the lower echelons.

This chapter focuses on various factors which give rise to large urban agglomerations. From one point of view agglomeration economies contribute to productivity growth but from another angle it involves gross inequalities. Regional integration can result in inter-country disparity, intra-country spatial inequality, rise of large agglomerations, and so on. The new factors which may have cropped up as a post-globalization phenomenon also need to be investigated. In the backdrop of these changes, how rural–urban migration takes place and what efforts the poor make for their survival are some of the critical issues. Whether upward mobility can actually take place and urbanization can be termed as inclusive is one of the key questions. Whether urbanization is able to usher in economic, social, and cultural changes in the direction of modernization is the larger issue which sets the perspective. This chapter, in fact, provides an analytical frame for the empirical analysis carried out in the subsequent chapters.

The agglomeration literature building on Henderson (1974) and Sveikauskas (1975) (as surveyed in many other studies, for instance, Duranton and Puga [2001], Rosenthal and Strange [2004], and Head and Mayer [2004]) argues that firms in large cities are more productive due to the advantages that large cities enjoy from a number of factors such as indivisibilities in investment, huge infrastructure base, large market size, lower labour turn-over cost, and easy information-sharing. The study by Combes et al. (2012) extended it by considering an entirely different reason for the higher average productivity in larger cities. It refers to stronger selection in larger cities, which would mean though there are some productivity advantages for all firms from being located in denser areas, the rewards are particularly strong for those firms that are per se more productive. In the new economic geography (NEG) literature the trade-off between increasing returns and mobility costs encourages migration and population expansion in cities. Though the modern sector in the historical sense was manufacturing, in the present context the services sector falls within its scope and firms in this sector not only supply to consumers and manufacturing firms but also serve each other (Ottaviano and Thisse, 2004). In the NEG framework of industry location (Krugman, 1991), external-scale economies make people and companies more productive through the following mechanisms, as pointed out by Frick and Rodriguez-Pose (2017): (*a*) knowledge spill-overs between workers enabling learning and spur innovation; (*b*) forward and backward linkages between companies, suppliers, and buyers, making interactions between economic actors more efficient; and (*c*) a pooled labour market allowing for an easier matching between firms and employees. They indicate that a high share of industries, a well-developed urban infrastructure, and an adequate level of governance effectiveness allow countries to take advantage of agglomeration benefits from larger cities. Besides, the productivity impact of metropolitan governance structures is well documented by Ahrend et al. (2014) while estimating agglomeration benefits across five Organisation for Economic Co-operation and Development (OECD) countries. The difference between the NEG literature and the urban economists' approach is that the former analyses the impact of city size or agglomeration on economic growth at the national level, while the latter is concerned with the impact of city size on the productivity of urban workers at the city level though the mechanisms which determine people's productivity are similar (Castells-Quintana and Royuela, 2014). Criticizing the existing literature on static agglomeration economies, Camagni, Capello, and Caragliu (2016) abandon the agglomeration-growth shortcut and unravel the role of dynamic agglomeration economies and their determinants. The quality of the activities, the quality of production factors, the density of external linkages and co-operation networks, and the characteristics of the overall urban system in which the city is located are some of the major factors which are expected to increase productivity and long-term 'structural dynamics' processes of urban transformation (Camagni, Capello, and Caragliu, 2016).

Zipf's law in city size distribution literature which implies that, in a system of cities, the largest city is roughly twice the size of the second largest city, about three times the size of the third largest city, and so on (Arshad et al., 2018) can also be rationalized in terms of this inverted U-shaped relationship between city size and productivity/growth, indicating that as one city saturates the second one comes up, and so on.

If the size–productivity relationship, demonstrating an inverted U-shaped curve, is extended in literal sense to capture size–deprivation relationship, the implication is that the latter would unfold a U-shaped curve. But the size–deprivation relationship may not demonstrate such a pattern—rather deprivation could be a monotonically decreasing function of size. Even when productivity starts declining in relation to city size beyond a certain threshold level, deprivation may not be rising as people's income and affordability have already gone up. Once wages have increased, further decline is difficult given the downward stickiness. Similarly, access to amenities, investment in housing, and purchase of assets which have already taken place cannot undergo a decline. The fall in productivity beyond a certain threshold limit in the city size would mean that new urban space elsewhere will have to be explored by firms for new investment. Similarly, new migrants may not find it profitable to move into the cities which have already reached an optimum size. But that does not mean that deprivation actually starts rising for those who have already settled in though quality of living in terms of pollution and other negative externalities may decline. However, inequality in terms of resource allocation as per city size has been an age-old issue (Kundu, 1989), which may further justify a rising relationship between size and deprivation before the falling part of the curve becomes evident.

The increasing inequality accompanying economic growth is a major concern in the Indian context (Mitra, 2013). A large percentage of the workforce is engaged in low productivity activities within the realms of the informal sector. Even the formal sector is recruiting labour in informal capacity in order to avoid regulations and reduce wage cost. Besides, migrant workers from rural areas and workers from low income clusters within cities do not often have the requisite skill to seek employment in high productivity activities. In the face of all this employment growth in general has been sluggish as the new technology is both capital and skill intensive. It is, therefore, unlikely that growth will percolate down to benefit all sections of the society in a given city even when agglomeration economies are in operation on a large scale. Thus, neither the size–deprivation relationship may be strong nor the other indicators of development (socio-economic characteristics) may improve in relation to city size. As a result upward mobility conceptualized in terms of higher educational attainments and workforce participation rates, greater inclusiveness and quality employment may not actually materialize in a significant manner. On the whole, unequal distribution of the benefits of agglomeration may not result in a strong association between city-size and various other indicators of development.

The concept of agglomeration economies which leads to productivity gains is associated with unequal urbanization but that may be desirable from the point of view of resource conservation or optimal use of resources. As cities get exhausted in terms of productivity gains, the city limit expands further in order to minimize the negative externalities on the one hand and continue to reap some of the benefits associated with largeness on the other. Since agglomeration economies attenuate across geographical space the cities expand to cover the rural hinterland. Can the phenomenon of urban sprawl be rationalized with such advantages associated with the urbanization process? Perhaps yes because agglomeration economies, as mentioned earlier, enhance productivity; consequently, productive regions grow more rapidly. Glaeser and Kahn (2004) argue that sprawl is not the result of government policies or the lack of good planning; rather, it is the outcome of people's preference to reside in faraway localities in the midst of green environment and commute to work places using their own transport. As commuting costs fall, the edge of the city expands. The new economic geography uses general equilibrium models with monopolistic competition and the existence of two sectors (modern and traditional). Though the modern sector in the historical sense was manufacturing, in the present context the service industry falls within the scope of the modern sector because the firms in this industry not only supply consumers and manufacturing firms, but also serve each other as highlighted by Ottaviano and Thisse (2004). The trade-off between increasing returns and mobility costs, as envisaged in new economic geography framework, also generates limits to the growth of the existing cities. People from rural areas at times migrate to nearby towns even if a great deal of opportunities do not exist in comparison to the large centres, which are attractive in terms of agglomeration economies manifested not only through higher productivity growth but also higher wages and better well-being levels. High cost of land, difficulty to access housing, high transport cost, overuse of existing amenities, and other kinds of struggles set limits to migration into large cities. Further, with agglomeration economies economic growth is positively associated but regional divergence tends to increase, as mentioned earlier. Even when countries tend to experience growth and convergence, divergence within a given country is most likely to occur as agglomeration benefits are exploited to raise the non-input-driven component of growth. In such a situation the government policy at times deliberately chooses to create new urban centres so that with more growth centres divergence and related problems of inequality and social and political unrest may decline. As Mohan (1993) pointed out, most of the governments in developing countries, in fact, tried being against the principle of concentration though it actually could benefit them to experience higher growth without proportionate increase in resource use. Thus, in the face of under-capacity utilization fresh capacity is created to curb inequality.

The other important source of new urban centre can be found in the rural transformation literature, with little difference between the rural and urban divide and the spatial difference being articulated through an explosion of developmental patterns and potentials within a thickening fabric of worldwide urbanization (Brenner, 2013). The demand-induced explanation would rationalize rural transformation in terms of population shifting from agricultural to non-agricultural activities in response to growing demand in the latter, resulting in the change in the designation of the same areas from rural to urban. On the other hand, the supply-push theory perceives excess supplies of labour in the agriculture sector being absorbed residually in low-productivity non-agricultural activities such as petty trade and services. In such a situation though urbanization of the area takes place from a definitional point of view, it is not generative in nature, meaning it does not lead to economic growth and poverty reduction. The agglomeration economies in large cities not only benefit business firms but also consumers. For example, in large cities there are usually a number of labour recruitment centres (informal), and as the new contacts develop, individuals tend to access more than one labour recruitment centres simultaneously, which in turn raises the options leading to occupational mobility and the possibility of accessing higher incomes (Mitra, 2010a, 2010b). Better connectivity, cheap transport system, and the availability of alternative modes of transport help individuals commute faster, which does not restrict them to secure jobs in the neighbourhood of where they reside. Further, labour exploitation in large cities is less as unions and various voluntary organizations in some form or the other safeguard the interest of the general public. The anonymity of individuals, particularly from the point of view of those who belong to disadvantaged castes, helps break the legacy of the caste-based occupations (Kumar, Kumar, and Mitra 2009). The sense of urbanism is supposedly more prevalent in large cities, which helps people overcome the barriers of caste and other social hindrances and follow a more market-oriented approach. From all this it may be inferred that individuals across various socio-economic sections benefit in terms of accessing sustainable livelihoods in large urban settlements vis-à-vis small towns.

On the whole, regional integration can result in inter-country disparity, intra-country spatial inequality, and rise of large agglomerations. New urban settlements emerge in the neighbourhood of such large agglomerations and help them expand further. Industrial regulations relating to the spatial aspect may reduce the entry of firms to large cities but eventually the peri-urban areas and other satellite towns may grow. Migrants from rural areas target large cities as destinations in order to escape poverty. But even in such islands of prosperity poverty can co-exist because of excess supplies of labour and emergence of a huge informal sector. Particularly with shortage of land, housing poverty may grow significantly. However, the informal sector may also grow due to the complementary relationship between large firms and small entrepreneurs. Informal–formal connections in a globalizing context are important as big companies, including those owned by foreign nationals, use local resources and labour following the sub-contracting routes.

At the outset of globalization, innovation and technology acquisition have become the key drivers of growth and prosperity. Various firms are in a race to import technology and adapt them in the domestic context, while some of the firms are actually expanding their collaborative activities with a view to creating technology. It is also a fact that new processes of technology designing involve information and communication technology (ICT) and related services in a significant manner, and for all this location plays an instrumental role. Technology innovation centres in large cities and their contribution to city growth are phenomenal. The upcoming education hubs in large cities also make their contribution to further growth. Even the massive construction activities and the surge in labour requirements have accelerated migration to large cities. In spite of layers of intermediaries and the associated commission agents, real wages are higher in large cities and, more importantly, the magnitude of job vacancies acts as a major pull factor. Emergence of new services supported by the changing demand pattern of the consumers has created new openings and revived aspirations.

The changing human behaviour in large cities, manifested in terms of less interaction between different sections of the society, results in polarization and segmentation. Larger income inequality expresses itself in terms of money laundering, purchase of luxury goods, and further aggravation in the unequal distribution of space in large cities. Corruption among the production units for the survival of the inefficient units and for accessing greater advantages by the better performers tends to affect the labour share adversely. Excess supplies of labour due to poor agriculture and the prevalence of networks among the low-income households keep the bargaining power of labour weak, not allowing the inequality to reduce. Even the phenomenon of town agglomeration (not city agglomeration) resulting from inadequate productive employment opportunities in agriculture, that is, supply-push effects, and low productivity activities in the rural non-farm sector can lead to transfer of rural poverty to urban poverty.

In the backdrop of these issues, the present volume covers certain aspects as described in the following sections.

Specific Aspects

Based on a number of attributes such as housing characteristics, basic amenities, and assets in possession, the study estimates the deprivation index across different types of cities. Whether large cities due to their agglomeration economies benefit all to reduce deprivation is a critical question. Rising inequality in terms of opportunities may not allow the deprivation index to fall sizably in relation to city size though it may be equally erroneous to reject the existence of agglomeration benefits. The relationship of this deprivation index with a number of other indicators of development is also under scrutiny. A large number of new towns are in the process of emergence without even getting the recognition from the government in terms of a sanctioned statutory local body. Is their materialization related to the spillover of the agglomeration economies existing in the large cities? Or do they reveal hard facts of remote rural areas being in the process of change in the presence of shrinking productive activities in agriculture? Whether such towns hold enough infrastructural base to keep pace with such transformation processes is another key issue. Rapid changes in terms of land use patterns in the neighbouring rural areas of the big cities pose threats to livelihood sources of agriculture-dependent households. What long-term strategies need to be adopted to counter such pressures of urbanization processes is another key question which must shape the urban development paradigm in India. The government on the other hand is keen on nurturing a handful of cities with a view to creating world-class centres so as to invite foreign direct investment (FDI) and domestic investment, all of which in turn may enhance growth. Are such initiatives of smart cities likely to result in greater inequality and, if so, what interventions are on move to balance these unequal outcomes?

The complex relationship among economic growth, inequality, poverty, and urbanization are captured through econometric models at various levels. In the process of urbanization how the standard relationship may change is explored. The interconnections between growth and urbanization are important and the impact of the latter on poverty may still be positive, mitigating the adverse inequality effect. However, urbanization may help reduce poverty only when the poor are in the close vicinity of urban space, with access to better labour market opportunities. On the other hand, the poor in the remote areas may not receive the positive spillover effects of urbanization. As we move from bigger units of analysis (such as state) to the smaller ones (district or city), attempts are made to verify the uniformity in the findings.

If we focus on the urban labour market, we see that the informal sector obviously occupies a key position within its ambit. The aspirations of the rural migrants and the possibility of realizing them with the available sources of livelihood within the informal sector in the face of sluggish growth opportunities within the formal sector are some the issues which are analysed with quantitative rigour. The emergence of a dynamic informal sector due to a vibrant formal sector and its beneficial impact on poverty are noteworthy. Greater urbanization, creating better livelihood opportunities, is therefore expected to reduce poverty, benefitting the migrants. However, such patterns can be nominal and need to be strengthened through effective interventions.

In order to deal with the issue of upward mobility with greater profundity, the study analyses micro data from urban slums. Different concepts of mobility are envisaged through occupational and income changes. Even within informal-sector activities workers may experience upward movement, though cases of downward mobility need not be negligible. What motivates workers to experience upward mobility and what pulls them back are, therefore, binding questions from the policy point of view. How the nature of activities varies in relation to the nature of the city and its economy and how the well-being level and changes in it differ across space then become crucial for a thorough analysis. The role of asset formation and efforts to diversify the modes of accessing information on the job market are important. The macro impact of urbanization on poverty is complemented by such micro studies to offer additional explanation in the context of poverty mitigation. Economic factors, education, location characteristics, and social interactions determine the pace of mobility. Economy, geography, and society all seem to be in interplay in shaping the outcome variable.

An important aspect of change that urbanization is likely to bring in is related to ideology and modernization of practices. Moving on to the caste dimension, which in the Indian context has been a matter of concern for long, the study based on micro data tries to verify if the lower castes are actually able to reduce their poverty by migrating out as frequently as the higher castes. Other than the macro data we need to explore on the basis of primary surveys whether the lower castes have a lower propensity to migrate. In addition, are their well-being levels poorer in comparison to the higher castes? These investigations are, however, based only on slum surveys and not on the aggregate economy which may comprise instances of positive outcomes for the lower castes. Nevertheless it is important to combine the analyses based both on secondary and micro survey data. Within a more or less homogenous set-up (slum) are the relatively backward castes worse off? Is their ability to migrate less and, even after migrating, is their access to opportunities somewhat lesser than their counterparts from higher social categories? It is possible that the caste factor matters even among the low-income households in their struggle to escape deprivation? The network-based migration and its outcome in terms of job accessibility and earnings cannot be independent of the caste category that one belongs to. Though at the aggregate level the reservation policies are in practice, in the lower echelons income support measures may have to go beyond caste boundaries to avoid caste war and conflict.

Finally, the impact of urbanization is assessed on a variable which is greatly influenced by cultural practices. If urbanization is expected to improve the cultural practices and transform behavioural pattern then women work participation is seen to be the right indicator as it is more sensitive to cultural variables. Even other development indicators such as education and income are not able to counter the adverse impact in terms of attitude towards female sexuality and stigmatization associated with women's participation in the job market. The study selects a relatively backward area (Odisha) and tries to examine the impact of urbanization both in rural and urban areas at the district level. The nature of the findings can be important from the policy point of view: whether there are signs of positive change and whether the urbanization headway has to go a long way before any significant change can be discerned are questions that need in-depth research.

The analysis is carried out at various levels of disaggregation such as state, district, city, and household. The database is drawn from a number of sources including population census, the National Sample Survey Office's (NSSO's) surveys on employment–unemployment and consumption expenditure, and primary surveys on slum households.

Chapter Layout

In Chapter 2, on the quality of cities with a focus on deprivation and various other indicators of development, we extend the size–productivity framework and examine the nature of relationship between city size and the deprivation index developed at a highly disaggregate level of urban centres (city/town) on the basis of dwelling conditions, basic amenities, and assets in possession. Further, the demographic and economic characteristics in relation to the deprivation index and city size are analysed in detail. Very large cities are seen to be endowed with better living conditions and infrastructural facilities, displaying lower magnitude of the index, though this relationship is not very strong, suggesting the importance of other variables such as income, location, and the overall level of urbanization impacting the index value. Large cities experience agglomeration economies but they do not benefit all sections of the population equally, which in turn does not necessarily bring in proportionate decline in the deprivation index with a rise in city size. Further, other demographic and economic variables are examined in relation to the deprivation index and city size. The findings show that there is no marked improvement in these other indicators of development as city size increases. Greater intervention is called for to provide support in terms of housing, sanitation and water, and for the improvement of other indicators of development.

Chapter 3 deals with new initiatives to create smart cities and also reflects on new areas emerging as urban. It examines the quality of life in smart cities versus the other cities and towns in India. Though within the group of the smart cities the deprivation index does not indicate wide variation compared to all urban centres, the objective of inclusive urbanization does not seem to have been achieved significantly. What forces are involved behind the growth of new towns is an important question and this is what this chapter tries to explore. The regional spread of these census towns is examined and, based on the district-level data, the growth dynamics of such reclassification of areas from rural to urban status is brought out through factor analysis. Further, the viability of such new towns to sustain economic activities and population growth is also discussed. Findings suggest that activities in areas which were already urban tend to spill over to the rural hinterland and then usher in a change in their classification status, in a limited sense though. On the other hand, the shift of labour to non-farm activities due to the lack of productive sources of livelihood in the agricultural sector is also a strong possibility. Finally, the policy implications are brought out.

Chapter 4 on growth, labour market, and poverty carries out the analysis in relation to urbanization. Urbanization does not show any significant impact on rural poverty though it tends to reduce poverty in the urban areas. Growth influences urbanization positively, while urbanization and expansion in non-agricultural activities both contribute to economic growth. Although urban inequality is not strongly correlated with urbanization and growth, the relationship is distinct. While poverty tends to decline evidently, inequality rises in the process of growth and urbanization. Even the urban informal sector activities are able to provide relatively better job opportunities and higher living standards. On the whole, urbanization and migration show beneficial effects in terms of reduction in both rural and urban poverty as labour market outcomes tend to improve. However, this process is not strongly evident and hence more policy interventions are required to boost the beneficial effects of urbanization.

Chapter 5 on upward mobility based on primary surveys of the same households in two different time points assesses the extent of inter-temporal change in income of the individual workers from slum households and makes an attempt to identify important correlates of upward mobility in econometric models without ignoring the endogeneity problem. The findings are indicative of a rise in the income of workers across a sizeable percentage of households though many of them remained below the poverty line notwithstanding this increase. Inadequate education reduces the probability of upward mobility while education above a threshold level raises it. Savings are crucial for upward mobility, emphasizing on the importance of asset creation. Views that entail neighbourhood spillover effects also received validation. This chapter also examines the importance of networks in pursuing job search and indicates that network concentration reduces the probability to experience upward mobility.

Chapter 6 based on a primary survey of slum dwellers in four Indian cities examines the caste dimension of migrants and the nexus, if any, between caste and job market participation. Based on the quantitative exercises, it notes overlaps between social and economic status. A higher propensity to migrate is evident among the population belonging to the General category and Other Backward Castes in comparison to the Scheduled Castes and Tribes who are at the bottom of the caste hierarchy. The disadvantaged castes are not even in a position to take the benefits of migration. Vulnerability conceptualized in terms of several socio-economic and demographic indicators exists among most of the social categories though the relative extent of deprivation varies across social groups. In a binomial logit framework, based on the pooled sample, the extent of decline in the probability of experiencing well-being beyond a threshold limit is sharper for the socially backward classes than the others. However, in individual cities such a pattern is not so conspicuous, implying that all the social categories are equally vulnerable. These findings have important policy implications, indicating that policy initiatives for deprived areas irrespective of the caste factor are more important than caste-based support measures.

Chapter 7 examines the impact of urbanization on the workforce participation rate of women which is taken as a cultural variable. Urbanization and women work participation based on district level data show a negative association both in the rural and urban areas though urbanization is expected to raise work opportunities. Women from poor households due to compulsions seem to be working more, translating into a positive relationship between poverty and female work participation rate. Also, economic growth and women work participation are negatively associated which may be indicative of a backward sloping supply curve of women at higher levels of per capita income. Or it may suggest that growth being non-inclusive is unable to create productive work opportunities, which in turn lead to the phenomenon of 'discouraged dropouts'. Policy interventions to counter such distortions are essential so that women access higher levels of skill and education and subsequently participate in the job market instead of withdrawing.

CHAPTER 2

Assessing the Quality
of Cities and Towns

Introduction

The agglomeration framework suggesting higher productivity gains in larger cities can be extended to argue that part of the productivity gains benefits workers in terms of higher wages (Duranton, 2016) compared to those in small towns. Higher economic growth originating from large cities is likely to have some percolation effect even when it is accompanied by a sizeable increase in inequality. Increased earnings may result in better living standards in terms of food as well as non-food consumption and also through enhanced investment in dwelling conditions and basic amenities. Thus size, productivity, and amenities all three can be in relationship. Also, in the size–productivity literature, infrastructure is seen to be a major driver of agglomeration economies. One may then argue further that infrastructure enhances the quality of living in large cities. Initially, government investment encourages concentration of activities which in turn motivates private investment and expands the city size further, unfolding simultaneity between investment and city size. Enhanced investments coming from the government, private sector, and households result in improved living standards including accessibility to various amenities. This would mean that deprivation defined in terms of the lack of access to assets, amenities, and quality housing would be in relationship with city size.

On the whole, the agglomeration economies in large cities are seen to benefit not only the business firms but also consumers. In large cities there are usually a number of labour recruitment centres (informal), and as new contacts develop, individuals tend to access more than one labour recruitment centre simultaneously, which in turn breaks the labour market segmentation and raises the number of options, leading to occupational diversification and upward income mobility (Mitra, 2010a, 2010b). Skilled workers are more likely to prefer megacities than the unskilled ones (Glaeser, Ponzetto, and Zou, 2016). Better connectivity, cheap transport system, and availability of alternative modes of transport help individuals commute faster, which does not restrict them to secure jobs in the neighbourhood of the place of residence. Further, labour exploitation in large cities is less as unions and various voluntary organizations in some form or the other safeguard the interest of the general public. The importance of urban networks and increasing geographical scope of agglomeration externalities are reflected in the new terms such as 'urban network externalities', which means firms and households are benefiting by being located in agglomerations that are well embedded in networks and that connect with other agglomerations (Burger and Meijers, 2016). Besides, as Fujita and Hamaguchi (2016) argue, supply chain internationalization is promoting a new cascade of agglomeration and dispersion as labour-intensive tasks in developing countries are geographically concentrated. Also, the anonymity of individuals, particularly from the point of view of those who belong to disadvantaged castes, helps break the legacy of the caste-based occupations (Kumar, Kumar, and Mitra, 2009). The sense of urbanism is supposedly more prevalent in large cities which help people overcome the barriers of caste and other social hindrances and follow a more market-oriented approach. From all this it may be inferred that individuals across various socio-economic sections are likely to benefit in terms of accessing sustainable livelihoods in large urban settlements vis-à-vis small towns.

While drawing a one-to-one relationship between city size, and productivity and then extending it to relate city size with deprivation via productivity, it is pertinent to acknowledge that high cost of land, difficulty to access housing, high transport cost, and various other negative externalities rise as cities expand beyond a certain threshold limit. This would mean that productivity levels do not increase monotonically with respect to city size. In fact, Williamson's (1965) inverted U-shaped curve in the size-growth constellation, that is, economic growth initially rises with geographic concentration and later declines due to a combination of agglomeration diseconomies and the transmission of growth impulses to the lagging points, as described by Chakravorty (1993), captures this non-linearity aspect. Frick and Rodriguez-Pose (2017) employ data for a panel of 113 countries between 1980 and 2010 and suggest a non-linear relationship in contrast to the prevailing view that large cities are growth-inducing. The centrifugal forces, that is, high land rents, pollution, and congestion, as the study points out, work in the opposite direction as population concentration grows, thus reducing productivity. Further, municipal size and the efficiency of the delivery of municipal services are seen to follow an inverted U-shaped relationship from the extensive review carried out by Holzer et al. (2009).

In the backdrop of these views it will be interesting to estimate the deprivation index in various cities and towns in India. Whether large cities have better infrastructure, living amenities, and a higher asset base at the household level, resulting from higher public as well as private investment, is a pertinent research question. Higher public investment might have been incurred to create agglomeration economies while higher private investment could be related to the productivity gains. Whether these improved living conditions and earnings also reflect in better demographic and economic indicators is the other question which we investigate in this chapter. And that justifies why we first estimate a deprivation index and then relate it to other demographic and economic variables corresponding to the urban settlements.[1]

Methodology

Why large cities can offer better living amenities and lower levels of deprivation is a less researched question. Possibly for the first time an explicit mention of cities with greater amenities being large in size is made in the study by Combes et al. (2012), which is reinforced by Glaeser, Ponzetto, and Zou (2016), arguing that megacities can prevail due to amenities as scale overwhelm the costs of density. Why large cities are more productive has, however, been researched extensively, both in theoretical and empirical terms. And, interestingly enough, this framework based on agglomeration economies can supply a rationalization, indirectly though, to the negative relationship envisaged between city size and deprivation. Defining deprivation in terms of amenities, assets, and dwelling conditions (materials used for housing), this chapter develops an index for each of the urban settlements in India and examines its relationship with city size. Whether improved living conditions are also associated with better demographic and economic indicators is the other key question which this chapter focuses on.

Two sets of data from the population census 2011 (Government of India, 2011) are considered: (*a*) data specific to amenities, housing quality, and assets and (*b*) the demographic and economic data. The second set is quite limited in terms of the number of variables. Nevertheless, it provides a basis to focus on some of

---

[1] Materials have been drawn from an earlier paper of the author (Mitra and Nagar, 2018a, 2018b).

the issues related to urban development. These two sets of data are given separately by the census authorities. Under the head 'housing statistics' the information on households with different types of houses (materials used for construction), various living amenities and assets are reported by the office of the Registrar General (population census). On the other hand, the second set on demographic data includes sex composition, age distribution, caste composition, working persons and their classification across broad economic activities.[2]

The methodology of the study is as follows: First, based on certain attributes such as quality of housing, basic amenities, and assets of the households, the deprivation index at the level of cities and towns is developed. The method of factor analysis is used for developing a combined index. The details of the variables are listed in the next section. Since there are a number of indicators representing the quality of housing, access to sanitation, and different types of assets, it is important to first examine the nature of association among these variables. If the results are not counter-intuitive only then is the index formation sensible and the low and high values are unambiguously interpretable. Otherwise, any increase or decrease in the index value may not represent an unequivocal change in the deprivation or well-being level. The lower values of the index are supposed to indicate lower levels of deprivation (or better well-being), while the higher values reflect a higher percentage of households without adequate amenities, assets and proper dwelling conditions, provided the variables are associated coherently. For example, if all the variables representing poor quality of housing are interrelated positively and also bear a positive association with variables representing poor amenities and asset base of the households, it would then make sense to draw inference from the magnitude of the index.

Second, given the theoretical underpinnings that large cities are in possession of agglomeration economies, we try to examine if city size can explain much of the variations in deprivation index. Our hypothesis is that city size reduces deprivation index. On the other hand, if agglomeration benefits accrue inequitably then city size and deprivation index may not unfold a strong association. The association between size and deprivation is captured through regression framework. However, other relevant variables such as per capita income, location-specific characteristics, and the spread of the urban areas measured on the basis of the overall level of

---

[2] Though the soft version of these data files is available with the census office, the variables were not reported at the level of cities/towns. For a given city/town, data are reported at a disaggregated level of spatial units which had to be combined to arrive at the city specific figures.

urbanization of the regions to which cities belong, also need to be controlled for because across space different factors other than size may be impinging on deprivation. Similarly, across low- and high-income regions the nature and extent of association between size and deprivation may be different which may be captured through dummies, representing unknown variables.

In the next step the relationship between deprivation index and a number of demographic and economic attributes including city size is assessed. This is again pursued on the basis of factor analysis. While the correlation matrix is the basic input to the factorial analysis, the latter is considered to be appropriate as it allows the assessment of the extent of co-movement of a number of variables with precision. On *a priori* basis large cities are expected to correspond to better indicators as largeness not only results in economic gains but also initiates social and demographic transformations. Consequently, large cities are likely to display a higher literacy rate, higher work participation rate especially among females and greater presence of economic activities which are dynamic in nature. Prevalence of higher wages in large cities can be, in part, traced back to city education and industry shocks (Duranton, 2016). Similarly, inclusiveness would require greater presence of low caste population or a lower incidence of poverty for which the percentage of Scheduled Caste and Scheduled Tribe population is taken as a proxy in our analysis. The sex composition of the population or the workforce is also a development indicator. The fertility behaviour which is captured through child–woman ratio in this chapter also tends to decline with city size. The details of these variables are provided in the fourth section. The rest of the chapter is structured as follows. The third section covers the estimation of deprivation index and its relationship with city size. The fourth section examines the association between deprivation index and other demographic and economic variables, and the last section summarizes the major findings with policy implications.

Deprivation Index

We begin our analysis by estimating the deprivation index for each of the urban centres (statutory and census towns) based on the variables given in Table 2.1. These variables cover dwelling conditions, access to basic amenities, and certain assets which are important for well-being, awareness, and mobility in the labour market. The poor quality of houses people reside in naturally reflects on poor levels of living and their vulnerability in relation to a number of uncertainties and difficulties. Similarly the lack of safe drinking water, electricity, and sanitation make them more susceptible to ill health and poor productivity. On the whole, these indicators give us a broad idea of the quality of life the residents lead in a particular urban settlement.

Table 2.1 List of Variables Used for Estimating the Deprivation Index

Variable	Definition
Condition of census house	% of households with dilapidated census houses
Material of roof	% of households with house roof made of grass/thatch/bamboo/wood/mud/plastic/polythene
Material of wall	% of households with house wall made of grass/thatch/bamboo/plastic/polythene/mud/un-burnt brick
Material of floor	% of households with house floor made of mud/wood/bamboo
Number of dwelling rooms	% of households with no exclusive room or one exclusive room
Ownership status	% of households living in rented house
Source of drinking water	% of households using untreated tap water or water from untreated source/un-covered well/spring/river/canal/tank/pond/lake, etc.
Main source of light	% of households without electricity connection
Latrine facility	% of households who do not have latrine facility within premises
Waste water outlet	% of households without connection to closed drainage
Type of fuel used for cooking	% of households who use cooking fuel other than LPG/electricity/biogas
Banking service	% of households without availing banking services
Availability of television	% of households who do not own television
Number of specified assets	% of households who do not own radio/transistor, television, computer, telephone/mobile phone, bicycle, scooter/motorcycle/moped, car/jeep/van

Source: 'Primary Census Abstract', population census, 2011 (Government of India, 2011).

Note: All variables are in percentage terms.

Since the variables are highly heterogeneous, combining them to form a single index poses certain challenges. In order to avoid the problem of assigning weights on subjective basis factor analysis has been carried out on the variables, and then, using the factor loading as weights, a single index value for each of the urban centres has been worked out. The results of factor analysis presented in Table 2.2 are not counter-intuitive. Hence, the results can be used to construct a meaningful index. Factor 1 and factor 2 are the two groups which are statistically significant and, corresponding to these factors, the variables which have significant factor loadings also have the right signs, indicating the fact that the movement

Table 2.2 Factor Loadings of Variables Considered for Deprivation Index

Variable	Factor 1	Factor 2
Condition of census house	0.4105	0.3019
Material of roof	0.1927	0.2320
Material of wall	0.1484	0.7966
Material of floor	0.05833	0.6846
Number of dwelling rooms	0.2299	-0033
Ownership status	0.6279	-0.0698
Source of drinking water	-0.0817	0.1124
Main source of light	0.7797	0.1765
Households latrine facility	0.4059	0.0927
Waste water outlet	0.2253	0.3128
Type of Fuel used for cooking	0.7264	0.2293
Banking services	0.4027	0.0992
Availability of television	0.9365	0.1658
None of the assets specified	0.7488	0.1877
Eigenvalue	5.06	1.25
Percentage Variation explained	0.67	0.17

Number of observations: 6,279

Source: Based on population census, 2011 (Government of India, 2011).

Note: There are a total of 7,935 urban centres in India classified as statutory and census towns, as per the 2011 census. In total, there are 4,041 statutory towns and 3,894 census towns. In our dataset we have considered urban agglomerations, that is, all urban towns which are part of the urban agglomeration are taken together. (Besides six census towns are missing in our dataset.) Finally, we get a total of 6,279 urban centres of which 2,563 are census towns and are not part of any urban agglomeration.

in the set of variables representing vulnerability at the city or town level unravel a consistent relationship. In factor 1 all the variables have the same sign except one (% of households exposed to unsafe drinking water). The positive sign would have meant that as the magnitude of this variable increases, deprivation rises. But the sign being negative tends to be counter-intuitive. However, the magnitude of factor loading corresponding to this variable is very low, implying that it has a very low correlation with the other variables and the index constructed on the basis of these variables Similarly, in factor 2 the households with inadequate space and percentage of households living in rented units take negative signs, indicating inverse relationship with the index value though *a priori* expectation could be otherwise. But again the magnitudes of factor loadings are highly negligible. On the whole, findings suggest that cities/towns with a high percentage of bad dwelling units are also seen to have a high percentage of households without basic amenities and households with relatively poor asset base, suggesting considerable overlaps among the attributes, that is, households deprived of one particular facility are also deprived of another.

As mentioned earlier, using the factor loadings the index has been formed at the city/town level. Since there are two factors which are statistically significant, two sets of indices have been generated and both have been combined using the eigenvalue of each of the significant factors as weight. Factors 1 and 2 are said to be statistically significant because each of the two has an eigenvalue greater than 1.

The findings suggest that a large percentage of urban centres, particularly the ones which are small in size, correspond to a high level of deprivation index (Table 2.3). In other words, the urban centres which belong to the bottom-size classes of the index are mostly large in size. Conforming to this pattern most of the million-plus cities have a low index value. As regards the other class I cities (each with a population size of 100,000 and above), again many of them are better off though a sizeable chunk (97 in absolute terms) among the ones of population size 100,000 to 500,000 have an index value of more than 125. The density plots (probability density function) of all cities and towns (both statutory and census) appear like a log-normal distribution, that is, the highest frequency of urban centres (mode) corresponds to a relatively lower magnitude of the index value (Figure 2A.1 in the appendix).

Table 2.3 Distribution of Index Value by Population Size of Cities and Towns

No. of Towns	Statutory Town 3,716						Census Town 2,563
	Million-plus	500,000–1,000,000	500,000–100,000	50,000–100,000	50,000–10,000	<10,000	
	53	40	370	451	2,230	572	2,563
Total							
Index Range							
0–100	44	27	179	157	361	134	595
100–125	7	9	94	111	352	48	365
125–150	1	1	44	69	350	78	336
150–200	1	3	42	81	577	125	518
200–250	0	0	9	24	380	99	394
250–300	0	0	0	7	152	66	222
>300	0	0	2	2	58	22	133

Source: Based on population census, 2011 (Government of India, 2011).

Statutory towns include all places with a municipality, corporation, cantonment board, or notified town area committee area, and so on. On the other hand, the definition of census towns is based on the following criteria: (*a*) a minimum population of 5,000 (*b*) at least 75 per cent of the male main working population being engaged in non-agricultural pursuits, and (*c*) a density of population of at least 4,00 per square kilometre. The census towns are urban as per the definition of the Registrar General (population census) but not declared as urban centres by the government of India. Among the total census towns of 3,894 only 2,563 appear in Table 2.3 because the rest, as mentioned earlier, are part of the urban agglomerations of the existing cities and six are non-traceable. The statutory cities and towns shown in Table 2.3 include urban agglomerations; not the metropolitan areas only. Table 2.3 verifies that nearly half of the census towns which are not part of the urban agglomerations have a vulnerability index value of more than 150.

There are several states which have cities with very high index values, particularly in some of the low-income states, though West Bengal is an exception in this respect, that is, without being a low-income state it has a number of cities and towns with high index values. In some of the low-income states the level of urbanization is also low but in some other low-income states rural transformation has taken place to a sizeable extent as agriculture is not able to provide sustainable livelihood opportunities, compelling many to take recourse to petty activities in the non-farm sector, which in turn resulted in the emergence of urban centres (Table 2.4).

In the first section we argued that large cities give rise to higher levels of agglomeration economies, resulting in higher levels of productivity. Hence, large cities are expected to have carried out greater investment. Thus population size and deprivation index may move in the opposite direction, indicating an inverse relationship. However, in order to capture the non-linearity that may exist in the real world we have estimated a quadratic function between deprivation index and population size. In other words, both population size and the square of population size have been considered. Since we examine the possibility of a non-linear relationship between population size in the city and the deprivation index, the simple correlation is not reported. Population size is measured in terms of logarithmic transformation of the population magnitude in absolute terms. This is only a transformation on the scale without violating the basic principle of the relationship.

Table 2.4 Number of Statutory Cities/Towns by Deprivation Index Range across States

States and Union Territories	No. of cities	Index Range						
		<100	100–125	125–150	150–200	200–250	250–300	>300
Jammu & Kashmir	111	49	12	17	23	8	2	0
Himachal Pradesh	58	57	1	0	0	0	0	0
Punjab	211	161	37	11	2	0	0	0
Chandigarh	1	1	0	0	0	0	0	0
Uttarakhand	91	64	8	7	11	1	0	0
Haryana	143	77	34	14	15	2	1	0
NCT of Delhi	1	1	0	0	0	0	0	0
Rajasthan	285	58	73	66	76	10	2	0
Uttar Pradesh	800	55	69	90	194	228	128	36
Bihar	173	2	5	9	30	43	48	36
Sikkim	9	7	0	1	1	0	0	0
Arunachal Pradesh	27	8	5	6	8	0	0	0
Nagaland	25	3	1	4	11	6	0	0
Manipur	34	2	1	5	6	10	7	3
Mizoram	23	2	1	9	8	2	1	0
Tripura	42	1	2	6	18	12	3	0
Meghalaya	11	1	2	1	2	5	0	0
Assam	196	16	27	29	51	44	20	9
West Bengal	665	20	27	44	178	175	119	102

Table 2.4 contd.

Table 2.4 contd.

States and Union Territories	No. of cities	Index Range							
		<100	100–125	125–150	150–200	200–250	250–300	>300
Jharkhand	187	4	21	28	62	48	16	8
Orissa	216	10	13	22	58	77	29	7
Chhattisgarh	172	4	3	13	54	63	26	9
Madhya Pradesh	438	29	58	59	151	100	35	6
Gujarat	282	73	58	77	55	15	3	1
Daman & Diu	8	2	1	1	4	0	0	0
Dadra & Nagar Haveli	6	1	1	0	3	0	1	0
Maharashtra	502	176	110	80	110	23	3	0
Andhra Pradesh	269	101	84	62	22	0	0	0
Karnataka	318	119	77	48	56	18	0	0
Goa	63	57	3	2	1	0	0	0
Lakshadweep	6	5	1	0	0	0	0	0
Kerala	63	39	19	5	0	0	0	0
Tamil Nadu	832	288	229	161	135	16	3	0
Puducherry	6	3	3	0	0	0	0	0
Andaman & Nicobar Islands	5	1	0	2	2	0	0	0
Total	6,279	1,497	986	879	1,347	906	447	217

Source: Based on population census, 2011 (Government of India, 2011).

Further, we have included the impact of certain other variables such as per capita income and the overall urbanization of the states to which each of the cities belongs. Besides, the geographical location characteristics are also considered. However, these variables are taken in the form of dummies, that is, we have distributed the states into five categories in terms of income, level of urbanization, and zones. Per capita income is representative of economic growth, which in addition to population size (representing agglomeration aspect) is expected to impinge on deprivation index. Higher economic growth may result in higher investment in infrastructure, provision of basic amenities and remunerations which raise the asset endowment of the population. However, with unequal growth, the asset endowment of a selected few may rise without any increase in the percentage of households/population with a certain type of asset in possession. Higher level of urbanization other than city size reflects on dynamism of the state and the volume of non-agricultural activities carried out. The geography of India being diverse different regions are expected to capture differences in climate, nature of activities, and socio-economic practices which in turn can impact on productivity, earnings, and levels of living though state interventions are supposed to reduce divergences. Hence, it is interesting to test the regional variations in the deprivation index.

The regression of deprivation index on city size and its square shows that larger the city size, lower is the magnitude of index; however, this is after a positive relationship observed between the two at the initial stages. This is understandable as large cities may be attracting large investments. The positive relationship seen between the two initially is possibly because investments and the positive gains in terms of improvement in well-being levels do not take place. However, the explanatory power of the equation is very poor (0.06), implying that the size variable alone is not able to explain a significant variation in the deprivation index. Though with the insertion of state dummies the adjusted R2 improves substantially, the t-ratios corresponding to the coefficients of many of the state dummies are insignificant, indicating the problem of multicollinearity (Table 2.5). It is possible that the adjoining states do not differ significantly from each other when it comes to state averages in the index value and the influence of state specific variables on the index. From this point of view, regrouping of states had to be done and we introduced regional dummies instead of state dummies (see tables in the appendix). There are some overlaps between the geographical location and the growth levels measured in terms of per capita income. For example, some of the geographical spaces comprise mostly the low-income states, and similarly some of the high-income states are also located in the adjoining spaces though there is no one-to-one correspondence, strictly speaking. Hence, we have re-estimated the equations with dummies for geographic regions as well as income levels, separately. Besides, we have regrouped states on the basis of their level of urbanization. The probability density plots of cities/towns (according to the index value) in different geographical regions or income categories are different as can be verified from Figures 2A.2 to 2A.4 in relation to Figure 2A.1 presenting the aggregate picture for all cities and towns (figures are given in the appendix).

As per the regression results, while the inverted U-shaped relationship between size and index remains intact in all the formulations, the dummies are all significant (Table 2.6). Region-wise dummy 4 and dummy 5 correspond to lower indices while 2 and 3 are characterized by higher values relative to the comparison group, which is dummy 1. In terms of per capita state domestic product, the states with very high income levels (category 1) have a lower index value compared to the third category while the second, fourth, and fifth unravel a higher value, not showing a clear-cut relationship between income categories and index values. However, with respect to urbanization there is an inverse relationship: in comparison to the fifth category, which represents the least urbanized states, the other categories have lower magnitudes of the intercept. On the whole, we are able to observe that the relationship between per capita income and the deprivation index is not very distinct. In other words, in the process of growth the cities are not necessarily able to reduce the deprivation index, suggesting the possibility of non-inclusive growth taking place in the country. However, as regards urbanization, its beneficial impact through a positive spill-over effect is evident with declining deprivation index.

Table 2.5 Regression Table with State Dummies

Variable	Equation 1		Equation 2 without state dummy	
	Coefficient	t value	Coefficient	t value
Log Population	30.09311	5.8*	31.96	4.70*
Log Population Square	-2.039416	-8.26*	-2.22	-6.83*
Jammu & Kashmir	-95.85	-1.89		
Himachal Pradesh	-158.75	-3.12*		
Punjab	-129.75	-2.56*		
Chandigarh	-72.4822	-1.03		
Uttarakhand	-128.75	-2.54*		
Haryana	106.17	-2.1*		
Rajasthan	76.59	-1.51		
Uttar Pradesh	-15.33	-0.3		
Bihar	40.89	0.81		
Sikkim	-132.21	-2.49*		

Table 2.5 contd.

Table 2.5 contd.

Variable	Equation 1		Equation 2 without state dummy	
	Coefficient	t value	Coefficient	t value
Arunachal Pradesh	-90.65	-1.77		
Nagaland	-44.46	-0.86		
Manipur	-4.45	-0.09		
Mizoram	-62.85	-1.22		
Tripura	-29.45	-0.58		
Meghalaya	-31.95	-0.61		
Assam	-36.64	-0.72		
West Bengal	6.25	0.12		
Jharkhand	-26.13	-0.52		
Odisha	-16.7854	-0.33		
Chhattisgarh	-6.12	-0.12		
Madhya Pradesh	-35.33	-0.7		
Gujarat	-79.97	-1.58		
Daman & Diu	-87.58	-1.64		
Dadra & Nagar Haveli	-46.12	-0.85		
Maharashtra	-86.68	-1.72		
Andhra Pradesh	-92.3	-1.83		
Karnataka	-89.66	-1.77		
Goa	-145.66	-2.86*		
Lakshadweep	-131.44	-2.42*		
Kerala	-103.55	-2.04*		
Tamil Nadu	-96.31	-1.91		
Puducherry	-99.84	-1.84		
Andaman & Nicobar Islands	-81.01	-1.47		
Constant	114.87	2.15	57.20	1.61
Adj R-squared	0.4932		0.06	
Number of observations	6,279		6,279	

Source: Mitra and Nagar (2018a).

Note: Delhi is the omitted category.

* represents significance at 5 per cent level.

Index = b+b_1 (Log Population) + b_2 (Log Population)^2 + State Dummy + error

OLS estimates with robust standard errors are reported in order to overcome the problem of heteroscedasticity.

Table 2.6 Regression Table with Region/Income/Urbanization Dummies

Variable	Income Level Dummies		Region/Geographic Dummies		Urbanization Level Dummies	
	Coefficient	t value	Coefficient	t value	Coefficient	t value
Log Population	27.59	4.95*	56.33	9.58*	27.93	4.44*
Log Population Square	-1.88	-7.1*	-3.16	-11.29*	-2.003	-6.68*
Dummy 1	-32.72	-5.13*	Omitted		-98.32	-15.25*
Dummy 2	13.44	6.31*	63.36	2.18*	-70.17	-24.51*
Dummy 3	Omitted		21.49	3.4*	-40.52	-14.19*
Dummy 4	80.6	35.32*	-11.43	2.12*	-13.36	-4.81*
Dummy 5	87.05	41.97*	-33.97	2.15*	Omitted	
Constant	19.16	0.66	-93.89	-3.06*	111.8727	3.42
Adj R-squared	0.3756		0.3053		0.2041	
Number of Observations	6,279		6,279		6,279	

Source: Mitra and Nagar (2018a).

Note: For details related to classification and dummies, see appendix tables.

* represents significance at 5 per cent level. The omitted dummy represents the comparison category.

Index = b+b$_1$ (Log Population) + b$_2$ (Log Population)^2 + Region Dummies/Per Capita Dummies/Urbanization Dummies + error

OLS estimates with robust standard errors are reported in order to overcome the problem of heteroscedasticity.

Deprivation Index and Other Characteristics

How the deprivation index stands in relation to the demographic and economic variables is a pertinent question. The deprivation index is estimated based on a limited number of variables whereas the quality of life and well-being needs to be assessed through a number of indicators which can be treated as an outcome of development. Whether large cities are endowed with better demographic, social, and economic development indicators is an important policy question as these cities have attracted a great deal of investment over the decades.

In addition to the deprivation index and city size, the variables considered in our analysis include sex ratio, child–woman ratio, percentage of low caste and tribal population, literacy rate, work participation rate, and the percentage of workforce engaged in non-household manufacturing and services. It may also be noted that some of these variables are taken gender-wise. The expected outcomes (based on *a priori* reasoning) have already been spelt out at the end of the first section while discussing briefly the methodology.

Table 2.7 presents the results from the factor analysis conducted on a wide range of city-specific variables. The list has been augmented by adding the city-specific deprivation index (described in the previous section) and the city size (taken in terms of log transformation). This is done for all urban centres, statutory towns, and census towns separately. These variables mutually reinforce on each other, giving rise to a complex simultaneous equation system. Since such a model is not estimable due to the paucity of information on a number of control variables at the city level, factor analysis is carried out to capture the mutual impact of the variables.

For all urban centres three factors are found to be statistically significant, that is, each with an eigenvalue greater than 1. In none of the factors the city size, however, takes a significant factor loading though the factor loading (in absolute terms) for the deprivation index is relatively high in factor 1 (-0.62). The only variable which is highly significant in explaining the variations in factor 1 is literacy, which in turn is inversely related to the proxy for fertility rate (taken in terms of child–women ratio) and the vulnerability index. The overall gender ratio (female–male) and the sex ratio among the workers both correspond to highly negligible factor loadings. With city size the sex ratio relationship remains positive though one would expect very large cities to have a strong negative association with gender ratio because of single male in-migration. Barring a few such cities, female migration (rural to rural and rural to urban both) in India is on the higher side, mainly for social reasons (such as marriage) while male migration is prompted by employment-related factors and education (Mitra and Murayama, 2008). The male workforce participation rate taken as a broad indicator of dynamism in the job market shows a positive relationship with city size, very mild though. The percentage of workforce employed in non-agriculture and non-household manufacturing also tends to increase with a rise in male workforce participation rate. On the whole, with deprivation index literacy is negatively associated while fertility varies positively. The male work participation rate tends to improve with a decline in the deprivation index and so also non-agricultural employment of both males and females. In relation to city size, deprivation shows a negative association, not very strong though. The incidence of low caste population is not associated strongly with city size in factor 1, refuting the possibility of caste being dissipated in large cities. City size and the incidence of low caste population rather show a negative association in factor 2 which could be an outcome of the weaker section not being able to derive the benefits of agglomeration effects. In fact, in factor 3 the deprivation index and the low caste population tend to vary positively, indicating their vulnerability in comparison to the higher castes.

In factor 2 the most noteworthy point is that the gender ratio in the workforce and the female workforce participation rate take high factor loadings, indicating their strong association. However, this relationship is not positively related to women being engaged in non-agricultural activities. Rather the percentage of women workforce in non-household manufacturing and services sector seems to decline with a rise in the women work participation rate, implying that women tend to work more in activities such as agriculture (and related activities) and household manufacturing. Further, city size is not positively related to women work participation rate or the gender ratio in the workforce, suggesting that the large cities do not necessarily offer more labour market opportunities for women. However, the overall gender ratio (female–male) and the sex ratio among the main workers are positively associated, and in relation to literacy there is a mild positive alliance. As the deprivation index is absolutely insignificant in this factor, we have not tried to examine its association with other variables.

The results pertaining to the census towns by and large conform to these patterns though the absolute value of factor loading corresponding to the deprivation index in factor 1 is only 0.35 (Table 2.7). For statutory towns the findings are, however, different compared to those of the census towns or the combined results for all urban centres. The inverse relation between city size and deprivation index becomes somewhat noteworthy only in factor 3 and the absolute value of the factor loading for the deprivation index reaches a maximum of 0.45 only in factor 2 (not factor 1) as far as the statutory towns are concerned. The most important variables in factor 1 are the female–male ratio of the workforce and the women work participation rate both of which move inversely with fertility rate. Literacy raises the proportion of workforce in non-agricultural activities other than household manufacturing, as seen from factor 2.

Table 2.7 Factor Analysis Result for All Urban Areas, Statutory Towns, and Census Towns

Variable	All Cities (6,279)			Statutory Town (3,716)			Census Town (3,888)*		
	Factor 1	Factor 2	Factor 3	Factor 1	Factor 2	Factor 3	Factor 1	Factor 2	Factor 3
Sex ratio in population	0.0492	0.3729	-0.084	0.2784	0.1333	0.0189	0.2663	0.2528	-0.1019
Percentage male SC/ST population	0.025	0.3154	0.9409	0.1026	0.0346	0.9863	-0.053	-0.026	0.09942
Percentage female SC/ST population	0.0413	0.3054	0.9428	0.1023	0.048	0.9873	-0.052	-0.027	0.9936
Male literacy rate	0.8323	0.1127	0.0368	0.0915	0.9014	0.0722	0.910	-0.06	-0.0446
Female literacy rate	0.8657	0.0907	-0.000	0.0369	0.8883	0.0732	0.9003	-0.026	-1302
Children up to age 6 per 1,000 women	-0.6199	0.4046	0.0781	-0.393	0.5409	0.0406	-0.623	-0.174	-0.077
Percentage main workforce participation: Male	0.398	0.4046	-0.214	0.4803	0.2702	-0.053	0.1869	0.2243	-0.0412
Percentage main workforce participation: Female	0.0138	0.9142	-0.221	0.9462	0.0695	0.1044	-0.014	0.9503	-0.0302
Sex ratio in main workforce	-0.0814	0.9105	-0.159	0.9165	0.0668	0.1703	-0.014	0.9676	-0.0277
Per share of non-agriculture (excluding household manufacturing) activities: Male	0.6984	-0.367	0.0689	-0.2107	0.3522	-0.054	0.2912	-0.105	0.0105

Table 2.7 contd.

Table 2.7 contd.

Variable	All Cities (6,279)			Statutory Town (3,716)			Census Town (3,888)*		
	Factor 1	Factor 2	Factor 3	Factor 1	Factor 2	Factor 3	Factor 1	Factor 2	Factor 3
Per share of non-agriculture (excluding household manufacturing) activities: Female	0.6202	-0.524	0.1506	-0.3827	0.2539	-0.035	0.2898	-0.286	0.0393
Deprivation Index	-0.623	-0.067	0.1317	-0.0815	-0.452	0.1337	-0.347	-0.156	0.0695
Log Population	0.15	-0.126	-0.192	-0.0904	0.0273	-0.182	0.1355	0.0207	-0.1603
Eigenvalue	3.28	2.77	1.98	3.64	3.247	1.24	3.25	2.44	1.91
Percentage Explained	0.35	0.3	0.21	0.37	0.33	0.19	35.52	26.61	20.83

Source: Mitra and Nagar (2018a).

Note: *Urban agglomerations include census towns which are not taken separately; hence the total number of urban centres is not equal to the sum of census towns and statutory towns.

On the whole, among the statutory towns in India, large cities do not seem to have benefitted the population as the decline in deprivation index in relation to size is not striking either from factor 1 or 2. In other words, with an increase in city size agglomeration economies may have gone up, raising the productivity, but all that has not benefitted the residents in reducing their deprivation proportionately. Indirectly it means that productivity growth, increase in investment and earnings involve a great deal of inequality. On the other hand, the census towns which have emerged (*a*) in the periphery of the large cities as satellites and (*b*) in remote areas, in response to the lack of productive employment in agricultural activities and the subsequent shift of the workforce to non-agricultural activities, are able to result in a decline in the deprivation index with a rise in city size. Better outcomes are also evident as demographic cum economic indicators tend to improve with city size.

Conclusion

In this chapter we estimated for Indian cities and towns the deprivation index developed primarily on the basis of dwelling conditions, access to basic amenities, and possession of certain types of assets. In the backdrop of the analytical frame on the relationship between city size and agglomeration economies, with implications on productivity, the nature of association between city size and the deprivation index is assessed. While the relationship between city size and deprivation is of considerable importance, the demographic and economic characteristics in relation to these variables are also analysed. Very large cities are endowed with better living conditions and infrastructural facilities; thus, they dispel lower magnitude of the deprivation index. Our findings also reflect that the size–deprivation relationship is not purely linear; rather, in the initial stages, there is a rising tendency in the index before it actually starts declining with an increase in city size. This does not seem to be in conformity with the inverted U-shaped relationship between size and productivity/growth-specific variable(s) the existing literature brought out because if it were, then an exactly U-shaped curve would have emerged between deprivation and size. Our *a priori* expectation was that despite the possibility of the rising portion of the U-shaped curve not being observable, a negative monotonic relationship between size and deprivation would stand valid. But findings are indicative of an increasing phase before deprivation actually starts declining with city size. At the initial stages it is possible that in-migration and many other dis-amenities are much larger than the investment carried out in cities and the productivity gains and well-being implications associated with it. Only beyond a certain size the agglomeration effects start operating and investment on amenities pick up, which in turn improves the quality of dwelling conditions, living amenities, and the asset base of the households. However, city size alone does not explain much as the prominence of the income and location-specific dummies suggest. In fact, index and city size both are endogenous and could be influenced by two different sets of factors. Growing inequality and the lack of inclusive growth can result in a less-than-proportionate decline in deprivation index in relation to city size in spite of the agglomeration benefits growing with city size. Government policy will have to strengthen the mechanisms of support system so that the decline in deprivation becomes faster in large urban habitations. Splitting the urban centres into two groups we observe a milder (negative) relationship between size and deprivation in the case of the statutory towns (recognized by the government of India as urban centres) whereas the census towns (without an urban local body) rather display it distinctly in a relative sense. The small- and medium-sized statutory towns in India are many and they do not seem to have received any significant investment ever since their emergence (Kundu, 1989). On the other hand, a considerable number of census towns are emerging in the neighbourhood of large and dynamic cities (Mitra and Kumar, 2015). They continue to offer benefits which the large cities conferred and thus the deprivation levels fall as these towns grow in size. In general, a number of urban centres—both statutory and census towns—however need to be strengthened in terms of investment so that the productivity gains and their positive spill-over effects occur to reduce deprivation.

As regards the variables other than the deprivation index, it is observed that with city size fertility declines and literacy improves. Though very large cities are expected to have a lower gender ratio because of single male migration, findings suggest that gender ratio improves with city size. However, with improved gender ratio though one may expect women participation in the job market to rise, there is no significant evidence in favour of women getting opportunities in non-household manufacturing and services. In the case of males the job market prospects seem relatively better in large cities. In general, urbanization does not appear to be inclusive as the percentage of lower castes shows a declining tendency with city size. The opportunities for those who are skilled are growing alongside the agglomeration benefits associated with large cities but the unskilled and semi-skilled do not appear to be benefitting on a large scale, which may be discouraging their pace of migration to large cities. Also, the slum demolition policies adopted on a large scale and the 'greed' to grab land in big cities may have led to lower incidence of disadvantaged classes. A positive association between deprivation index and the incidence of lower castes is a matter of policy concern. Initiating targeted efforts for the disadvantaged social groups may turn out to be beneficial although it is important to bear in mind that caste and deprivation do not necessarily unravel a strong co-movement. The outreach of the Skill India programme can be broadened and developed along the lines of the requirement of the cities. Better infrastructure, amenities, and housing support to the low-income households in large cities need to be augmented so that fall in deprivation and city size move strongly in the years to come.

Appendix

Table 2A.1 Classification of States Based on Per Capita Income (2011)

Income Level	Dummies	State/UT	Per Capita Income (INR)
Very High	1	Delhi, Chandigarh, Puducherry, Goa, Sikkim	>1,00,000
High	2	Haryana, Maharashtra, Andaman & Nicobar, Gujarat, Tamil Nadu	1,00,000–75,000
Medium	3	Uttarakhand, Punjab, Kerala, Himachal Pradesh, Karnataka, Arunachal Pradesh, Andhra Pradesh, Nagaland, Dadra & Nagar Haveli, Lakshadweep	75,000–50,000
Low	4	Meghalaya, Mizoram, West Bengal, Tripura, Rajasthan, Jammu & Kashmir, Chhattisgarh	50,000–40,000
Very Low	5	Daman & Diu, Odisha, Jharkhand, Assam, Madhya Pradesh, Manipur, Uttar Pradesh, Bihar	<40,000

Source: Mitra and Nagar (2018a).

Table 2A.2 Classification of States Based on Location

Region	Dummies	State/UT
North	1	Jammu & Kashmir, Chandigarh, Haryana, Uttarakhand, Punjab, Himachal Pradesh, Delhi, Uttar Pradesh
East	2	West Bengal, Chhattisgarh, Odisha, Jharkhand, Bihar
North East	3	Sikkim, Arunachal Pradesh, Nagaland, Meghalaya, Mizoram, Tripura, Assam, Manipur
West	4	Goa, Maharashtra, Gujarat, Dadra & Nagar Haveli, Lakshadweep, Rajasthan, Daman & Diu
South	5	Puducherry, Andaman & Nicobar Islands, Tamil Nadu, Kerala, Karnataka, Andhra Pradesh

Source: Mitra and Nagar (2018a).

Table 2A.3 Classification of States Based on Level of Urbanization

Urbanization Level	Dummies	State/UT	Percentage Urbanization
Very High	1	Delhi, Chandigarh, Mizoram, Goa, Lakshadweep, Daman & Diu, Puducherry	>50%
High	2	Maharashtra, Gujarat, Dadra & Nagar Haveli, Tamil Nadu, Kerala	50–40%
Medium	3	Haryana, Uttarakhand, Punjab, West Bengal, Andaman & Nicobar, Karnataka, Andhra Pradesh	40–30%
Low	4	Jammu & Kashmir, Uttar Pradesh, Chhattishgarh, Jharkhand, Sikkim, Arunachal Pradesh, Nagaland, Tripura, Manipur, Rajasthan, Madhya Pradesh	30–20%
Very Low	5	Himachal Pradesh, Odisha, Bihar, Meghalaya, Assam	<20%

Source: Mitra and Nagar (2018a).

Figure 2A.1 Deprivation Index: Probability Density Function for All Cities and Towns

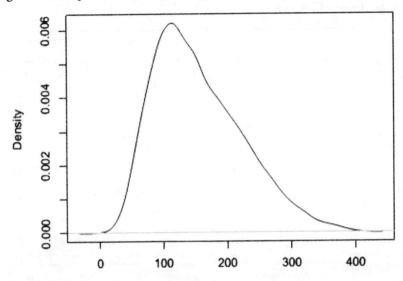

Source: Mitra and Nagar (2018a).

Figure 2A.2 Probability Density Plot of City Deprivation Index (Grouping State/ UT as per Geographical Category)

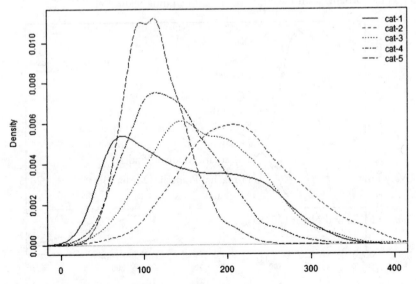

Source: Mitra and Nagar (2018a).

Figure 2A.3 Probability Density Plot of City Deprivation Index (Grouping State/UT as per Income Category)

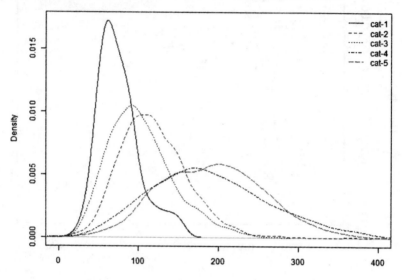

Source: Mitra and Nagar (2018a).

Figure 2A.4 Probability Density Plot of City Deprivation Index (Grouping State/UT as per Urbanization Level)

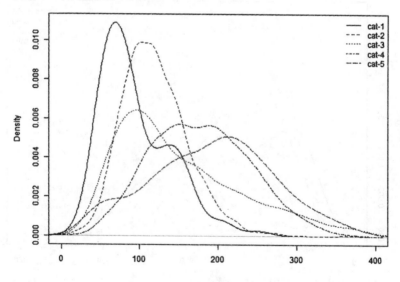

Source: Mitra and Nagar (2018a).

Figure 2A.5 Smart Cities versus Other Cities: Probability Density Plot of City Deprivation Index

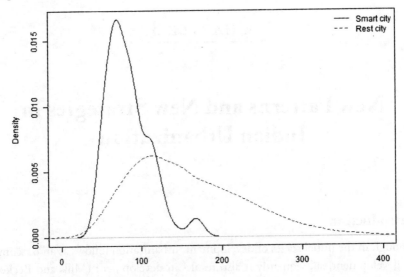

Source: Mitra and Nagar (2018a).

CHAPTER 3

New Patterns and New Strategies in Indian Urbanization

Introduction

Though in the initial stages of development, urbanization follows as an outcome of development, subsequently it also results in development (Mills and Becker, 1986; Fujita and Thisse, 2003). One of the reasons for both being associated with each other is that with urbanization economic opportunities are expected to grow significantly for all sections of the population and thus an inclusive society is likely to emerge. The interactions among different classes at the workplace and in various facets of life may become so intense that the traditional barriers of caste, class, and religion may get dissipated, offering opportunities to those at the lower echelons to experience upward mobility. This is, of course, only a theoretical expectation, the realization of which depends on a variety of preconditions.

The advocates of balanced urbanization often oppose population concentration in a handful of large urban centres (Mills and Mitra, 1997). But it is difficult to ignore the positive outcomes of agglomeration economies associated with population concentration (Mills and Mitra, 1997). As mentioned in the preceding chapters, productivity gains are higher in large urban settlements and thus, there is a tendency for new firms to reap the locational advantages (Mitra, 1999). However, beyond a certain stage these gains tend to get neutralized and subsequently overshadowed by the increasing costs or diseconomies associated with population increase in large cities.

In the Indian context, many mega cities, which once upon a time attracted a lot of investment and accounted for a large component of economic activities, have started indicating signs of decline, possibly because they have attained the saturation limit. Thereafter, whether the next tier cities are ready to take over the lead role, substituting the role that the mega cities once played, is an important question. However, this may not always follow. A usual outcome of this is that as a large city gets saturated, new economic activities gradually come up in the rural hinterland. This is the second best solution for new firms because by being invested in these activities, they are able to avoid the diseconomies that the core city generates and at the same time they may have access (due to locational proximity) to the agglomeration economies that the core city offers. In the backdrop of this perspective we analyse the new trends in Indian urbanization, particularly the small (census) towns which have emerged between 2001 and 2011.

Growth of New Towns

The constituents of urban areas are statutory towns, census towns, and outgrowths. The major distinction between statutory and census towns are as follows: all places with a municipality, corporation, cantonment board, or notified town area committee constitute statutory towns. On the other hand, the census towns are defined on the basis of the following criteria: (*a*) a minimum population of 5,000, (*b*) at least 75 per cent of the male main workers engaged in non-agricultural pursuits, (*c*) a density of population of at least 400 per square kilometre. Even without having an urban local body an area can become a census town if the process of transformation is fast. The results from the 2011 census show a large number of census towns which emerged in the last ten years (2001–11, Table 3.1). A little above 2,500 new towns cropped up during this period whereas only 1,362 census towns had come up in India in sixty years since independence. Nearly double the number emerged in just ten years: what can explain such fast growth?

Can all this be attributed to globalization, reforms, and other policy changes resulting in major shift of activities (even in the rural areas) so as to allow the settlements to wipe out their rural designation and acquire the urban status? If so, do these towns have adequate urban facilities to accommodate the new activities and population growth? These are some of the questions which have to be looked into meticulously before we start rejoicing about the rapid growth of new towns.[1]

We may start the analysis by looking into the locational aspects of these new towns. Are they mostly situated in the neighbourhood of very large cities? If so we

---

[1] Materials have been drawn from an earlier paper of the author (Mitra and Kumar, 2015).

can then explain their emergence and growth in terms of the second best solution, as mentioned above, that the firms seek when a large urban settlement tends to get saturated. If new activities come up in nearby small towns in a big way due to want of space in the large cities, it is natural that the migration of population will also be directed to these towns. On the whole, these towns may be treated as satellite towns growing in response to the spur of economic activities.

Later we examine some of these hypotheses based on several indirect indicators. The simple correlation between the number of statutory towns and census towns is positive as per the 2001 and 2011 censuses (0.43 and 0.44 respectively) and states with more number of statutory towns registered a greater number of increase in the census towns over 2001–11 (0.45). The states which had more number of census towns in 2001 also registered a lager increase in the number of census towns over 2001–11 and this correlation is strong (0.89).

A regional distribution of new census towns from Table 3.1 is indicative of the fact that most of them are concentrated in Kerala, Maharashtra, Tamil Nadu, Uttar Pradesh, and West Bengal (alphabetical order).[2] Of them, Maharashtra, Tamil Nadu, and West Bengal are relatively industrialized, whereas Kerala's growth dynamics is unique with a leading role played by the plantation sector. So it is only Uttar Pradesh which has experienced a significant increase in new towns notwithstanding moderate growth. However, it can partly be attributed to its sheer size – it is one of the states that have a very large number of districts.

Since West Bengal, Maharashtra, Tamil Nadu, Uttar Pradesh, and Kerala are some of the states which recorded a large number of new census towns, using the district level data, we try to verify the association between the number of new census towns in 2011 in a given district and the number of statutory towns in a given district or the number of class I cities in 2001/the population living in the largest class I city in the district (Table 3.2). Some of these variables are correlated though the degree of correlation is not very strong. However, the t-ratio corresponding to the number of statutory towns or class I cities in a given district is statistically significant in West Bengal, Maharashtra and Tamil Nadu. In Uttar Pradesh the number of statutory towns or class I cities is not a significant determinant of the number of census towns but the population in the largest class I city is. On the other hand, in Kerala only the number of statutory towns is statistically significant. More importantly there are several districts which do not have a single class I city and yet they have census towns.

---

[2] West Bengal accounts for 20.74 per cent, Kerala, 14.3 per cent, Tamil Nadu 10.47 per cent, Uttar Pradesh 7.94 per cent, Maharashtra 6.24 per cent, and Andhra Pradesh 5.33 per cent of the new census towns.

Table 3.1 Statutory and Census Towns in 2001 and 2011 across States and Union Territories

	Urbanization (%)			Number of Statutory Towns			Number of Census Towns			
	2001	2011	Increase	2001	2011	Increase	2001	2011	Change	% Distribution
AN	32.63	35.67	3.04	7	9	2	3	5	2	0.08
AP	27.3	33.49	6.19	117	125	8	93	228	135	5.33
ArP	20.75	22.67	1.92		26	26	17	1	-16	-0.63
AS	12.72	14.08	1.36	80	88	8	45	126	81	3.20
BH	10.46	11.3	0.84	125	139	14	5	60	55	2.17
CH	89.78	97.25	7.47	1	1	0	1	1	0	0.00
CT	20.08	23.24	3.16	75	176	101	22	13	-9	-0.36
DN	22.89	46.62	23.73	2	1	-1	0	5	5	0.20
DD	36.26	75.16	38.9	0	2	2	2	6	4	0.16
DL	93.2	97.5	4.3	3	59	56	3	110	107	4.23
GJ	37.36	42.58	5.22	168	195	27	74	153	79	3.12
GO	49.8	62.17	12.37	14	30	16	14	56	42	1.66
HP	9.8	10.04	0.24	56	56	0	1	3	2	0.08
HR	28.92	34.79	5.87	84	79	-5	22	74	52	2.05
JH	22.25	24.05	1.8	44	40	-4	108	188	80	3.16
JK	24.85	27.21	2.36	72	86	14	3	36	33	1.30
KE	25.96	47.72	21.76	60	63	3	99	461	362	14.30
KR	33.99	38.57	4.58	226	220	-6	44	127	83	3.28

Table 3.1 contd.

Table 3.1 contd.

	Urbanization (%)			Number of Statutory Towns			Number of Census Towns			
	2001	2011	Increase	2001	2011	Increase	2001	2011	Change	% Distribution
LK	44.47	78.08	33.61	0	3	3	0	6	6	0.24
MG	19.58	20.08	0.5	10	10	0	6	12	6	0.24
MH	42.43	45.23	2.8	251	256	5	121	279	158	6.24
MN	23.88	30.21	6.33	32	29	-3	5	24	19	0.75
MP	26.67	27.63	0.96	339	366	27	55	113	58	2.29
MZ	49.63	51.51	1.88	22	23	1	0	0	0	0.00
NL	17.74	28.97	11.23	8	19	11	1	7	6	0.24
OR	14.99	16.68	1.69	107	107	0	31	116	85	3.36
PB	33.95	37.49	3.54	139	143	4	18	74	56	2.21
PO	66.57	68.31	1.74	5	6	1	1	4	3	0.12
RJ	23.39	24.89	1.5	184	187	3	38	112	74	2.92
SK	11.1	24.97	13.87	8	8	0	1	1	0	0.00
TN	44.04	48.45	4.41	721	721	0	111	376	265	10.47
TR	17.02	26.18	9.16	13	16	3	10	26	16	0.63
UP	20.78	22.28	1.5	638	648	10	66	267	201	7.94
UT	25.67	30.55	4.88	74	74	0	11	41	30	1.18
WB	27.97	31.89	3.92	123	126	3	255	780	525	20.73
IND	27.82	31.16	3.34	3799	4041	242	1362	3894	2532	100

Source: Population censuses, 2001 and 2011 (Government of India, 2001, 2011).

Table 3.2 Relationship between the Number of Census Towns and Statutory Towns across Districts

Dep. Variable: No. of Census Towns in the District

	West Bengal	West Bengal	Maharashtra	Maharashtra	Tamil Nadu	Tamil Nadu	Uttar Pradesh	Uttar Pradesh	Uttar Pradesh	Kerala
No. of statutory towns in the district 2011	2.44 (1.74)*		1.11 (3.15)**		0.50 (3.89)**		0.20 (1.46)			7.35 (2.57)**
No. of class I cities in the district 2011		3.62 (2.19)**		4.00 (3.90)**		7.41 (2.64)**		2.10 (1.51)		
Population in largest class I city in the district in 2011									3.46e-06 (2.69)**	
Intercept	24.48 (1.91)*	29.37 (3.01)**	-0.18 (-0.06)	2.73 (1.19)	0.61 (0.18)	4.5 (0.94)	1.98 (1.44)	1.83 (1.00)	2.73 (2.84)**	-0.16 (-0.01)
Adj R2	0.10	0.17	0.21	0.35	0.33	0.26	0.03	0.04	0.11	0.30
N	19	19	35	27	32	22	70	52	51	14

Source: Based on population census figures.

Note: ** denotes significance at 5 per cent level and * at 10 per cent level.

On the whole, the number of statutory towns of all sizes is rather positively associated with the number of census towns (though the correlation in only moderate), implying that urbanization as a whole seems to be expanding from the spill-over of the existing urban localities into the rural hinterland. As Bhagat (2011) points out, urbanization increased faster than expected over the decade 2001–11. Also, for the first time since independence, the absolute increase in the urban population was higher than that in the rural population. The non-statutory census towns numbered 1,362 and were home to 21.0 million people in 2001. These numbers increased to 3,892 and 58.6 million, respectively, in 2011. This growth of 37.6 million people amounts to 41 per cent of the total growth of urban population in the decade 2001–11 (Bhagat 2011).

In order to explore further the role of the existing urban centres in reinforcing the transformation process in the rural areas and thus ushering in a change in their locational status (from rural to urban), we have tried to assess the association between the urbanization level in a district and a range of socio-economic and demographic variables pertaining to the rural areas in the same district. This is pursued on the basis of factor analysis.

The variables considered in the factor analysis are the following for the rural areas at the district level – HHSZ: household size; CHILD-WOM: proportion of children to women; WFPR: main work force participation rate; LIT: literacy; SC: percentage of Scheduled Caste population; OTHERACT: percentage of workers engaged in non-household manufacturing and services; CUL: percentage of work force engaged as cultivators; AGLAB: percentage of work force engaged as agricultural labourers; MFGHH: percentage of workers in household industries; F/M: female-male ratio in the population, BPL: percentage of households below the poverty line; AVMPCE: average monthly per capita consumption expenditure; INEQ: inequality in terms of the difference between the minimum and maximum value of the consumption expenditure. In addition to the rural specific variables we have considered URBN which is the percentage of population in the urban areas in the district.

Along with urbanization, rural growth is expected to rise as urbanization is viewed as concomitant to expansion in economic activities. Agglomeration benefits associated with urbanization are likely to result in enhanced productivity growth (see Mitra, 1999) which can also get reflected in rural per capita income and consumption expenditure through the rural-urban inter-sectoral linkages. The increased work participation rate in the rural areas, change in the occupational structure from farm towards non-farm prompted by rural diversification, and reduction in rural poverty are some of the expected outcomes. Based on the village-level data and country-wide NSS data, Himanshu et al. (2013) observed the growing importance, and influence, of the non-farm sector in the rural economy between the early 1980s and late 2000s. Besides, this non-farm diversification, despite being quite a sluggish process, has been pro-poor in terms of distributional incidence. Further, they noted that the non-farm sector is not only increasing incomes and reducing poverty, but is also breaking down barriers to mobility among the poorest segments of rural society. This is again likely to increase urbanization through migration. Himanshu et al. (2011) also noted a close association between urban poverty reduction and rural non-farm growth (and accompanying rural poverty reduction). Through an increase in rural non-farm employment and wages the beneficial effects were realized. Lanjouw and Murgai (2010a, 2010b) brought out a clear-cut link between urban poverty decline and rural poverty decline in India which was not seen from the studies based on data for the pre-reform period. The association between urban development on the one hand and improvement in rural livelihoods on the other was envisaged through the impact of urban development on rural non-farm diversification. So in their conceptualization the causality runs from urbanization to rural poverty decline. One may further hypothesize that the demographic variables such as household size and child–woman ratio also decline with urbanization.

Keeping in view some of these interesting patterns, the analysis in this chapter is pursued at the district level. Most of the variables included in our analysis are for the year 2011 (taken from the population census) and only poverty, inequality, and monthly per capita consumption expenditure are for the year 2011–12 (taken from NSS).

Based on the three significant factors with eigenvalues greater than 1, some of the results are quite interesting (Table 3.3). First of all with urbanization several social, economic, and demographic variables tend to improve. Rural non-household manufacturing and services increase with urbanization (as observed in factor 2 in Table 3.3). In other words, districts with a higher urbanization level are able to witness a rural transformation in terms of changes in activities which are endemic to the shift in the classification of areas from rural to urban. The rural child–woman ratio and household size also decline with urbanization level. On the other hand, rural work participation rises in response to urbanization, suggesting possibilities of spillover of urban based activities to the rural areas which in turn raises demand for rural labour in the rural non-firm sector. Thus, a shift from cultivation going hand in hand with urbanization is discernable (factor 2, Table 3.3).

Table 3.3 Results from Factor Analysis Based on District-Level Data

Variables	Factor 1	Factor 2	Factor 3
RHHSZ	-0.6615	-0.1201	-0.0750
RCHILD-WOM	-0.8758	-0.1914	-0.2291
RWFPR	0.4826	-0.2138	0.1992
RLIT	0.6064	0.2863	0.2864
RSC	0.1626	0.0470	0.0835
ROTHERACT	0.1095	0.7814	0.2365
RMFGHH	-0.0320	0.1394	-0.0442
RCUL	-0.1466	-0.9115	-0.1291
RAGLAB	0.0393	0.0829	-0.1217
RF/M	0.4391	-0.0442	0.0058
RBPL	-0.1700	-0.1488	-0.5527
URBN	0.1797	0.3859	0.2479
RAVMPCE	0.2638	0.2676	0.7903
RINEQ	0.1938	0.1964	0.6557
Eigenvalue	3.92	1.90	1.69
Explained Variation	0.4115	0.1987	0.1775

Number of observations: 608
Source: Author's calculations based on census data, 2011 (Government of India, 2011).
Note: R represents rural areas.

Also growth, inequality, poverty and other development indicators including the urbanization level in the district are related though the factor loadings are much lower in magnitude in factors 1 and 2, implying the absence of a strong association. It is only in factor 3 that the growth–inequality–poverty–urbanization nexus gets sharper. On the whole, districts with higher level of urbanization are associated with reduced rural poverty incidence and higher levels of growth and other development indicators though inequality is likely to rise in the process. Again, such districts with better outcomes are also able to witness higher female–male ratio in the rural population. Hence, based on the district-level data it may be concluded that urbanization delivers better outcomes in terms of not only economic indicators but also social and demographic indicators in the adjacent rural areas, though such processes are on a limited scale.[3] Sharma and Kumari (2012), in fact, argued that rural areas within a distance of 20 kilometres from the urban centres do not require to be addressed separately as far as the poverty reduction strategies are concerned. The investment in urban areas can essentially take care of the issues related to rural development. However, rural areas which are not close to the urban centres need to be tackled exclusively.

All this tends to suggest that the growth of new towns being related to the spillover effect of very large urban centres is valid to some extent. With the exhaustion of further scope for the expansion of the existing large cities the nearby areas tend to get urbanized to some extent and operate as satellite towns conducting activities by and large similar to what the large centres do. However, the correlation is not strong which points to the importance of other factors as well. Though the factor analysis results also present evidence in favour of spillover effects of urbanization, the existence of other forces cannot be ruled out. Towns emerging as a result of the transformation process occurring in the rural areas are indeed an important aspect of urbanization in India. Population growth and diversification of activities in the rural areas are an endemic part of this process. However, there is ample evidence to suggest that a large component of the rural non-farm sector activities is not induced by demand side factors alone. Agricultural stagnation and the lack of scope to enhance productive employment opportunities in the agriculture sector are some of the possible factors responsible for a residual absorption of labour in low productivity non-farm activities. The lack of rural industrialization seems to have aggravated the 'employment problem' in the rural areas. On the whole, these new towns do not seem to have emerged in response to agricultural prosperity. Hence, the contribution of these towns to wealth formation seems to be rather negligible.

Related Problems

But are these census towns well equipped with infrastructure and basic amenities to assure a reasonable quality of life? The extraction of resources in these towns might have taken place in a completely unplanned manner. The residential and infrastructural facilities in these towns are inadequate to keep pace with the new activities that are spilling over as a result of saturation of the large urban centres. The

---

[3] The phenomenon of exclusionary urbanization is quite significant in the Indian context (Kundu, 2009).

new towns do not have enough living space to accommodate the migrant workers who are supposed to move in due to the increasing concentration of activities. As the number of people migrating is usually more than the actual number of job vacancies it would mean that the surplus labour would get residually absorbed in low productivity jobs. Does it not then mean that the problem of slums would be severe sooner or later? Though the very large cities also have had similar problems, there have been several support mechanisms at the same time. Besides, the real earnings in the informal sector have been higher in the large cities than in small towns. The capacity of the small towns to provide for the population is highly limited even after discounting the scale factor that the large cities enjoy. There are problems relating to generation of resources required for sustainable development.

Another way of looking at these towns is to understand the changing land-use pattern in the rural areas adjacent to the large urban centers. If the agricultural land is being increasingly used for non-agricultural purposes as the city limit tends to expand, such new towns come up in the vicinity of the very large cities. If such new towns grow purely in response to the dynamics of agricultural growth and the subsequent demand for trading or other non-agricultural activities, the outcomes are desirable. But the urbanization spill-effect which ushers in a major change in land-use patterns may pose a threat not only in terms of food security but also sustainable livelihood for those who lose their agricultural land. The mismatch between the demand and supply of labour can be serious in these towns keeping in view the employability issue. Of course trade-offs to certain extent between growth and loss of agricultural land are inevitable. But then sufficient safety nets need to be created to meet the deficiencies and new challenges.

The next question is whether these new towns—as a spill-over of very large cities—are the proper substitutes of the second-rank cities which are expected to play the role of engines of growth once the megalopolises or very large cities meet the saturation point. Usually in urban economics literature we have learnt that once the largest cities exhaust the economic opportunities the second-rank cities come up to replace them in terms of investment, growth and employment generation. These cities are certainly much better off in terms of infrastructure compared to the new small towns. But for them to take over the lead role, a proper coordination between the state and those who have a thorough understanding of the growth dynamics of the urban space is essential. It is most unfortunate that in the Indian context no clear-cut initiative for urban investment or planning is taken by examining the growth potential of different cities and towns with an economic-cum-geographic perspective.

New Initiatives: Smart Cities

Keeping in view the inclusiveness of growth it is important to note that urbanization is able to contribute significantly to poverty reduction by creating livelihood opportunities for all, allowing rural migrants to move in and facilitating the transfer of workers from agriculture to non-agricultural activities. The Indian government has initiated certain new programmes which aim at developing certain urban spaces so that new investments can flow in. In the backdrop of this initiative the present chapter aims at examining the smart cities (identified by the government of India) in terms of quality of life based on housing characteristics, access to basic amenities, the level of assets that the households have, and other broad indicators of development.

Even with a low level of urbanization (as mentioned in the next section), Indian cities still remain the major hub of production. Mitra and Mehta (2011) estimated that the cities contribute more than 76 per cent of gross domestic product (GDP), using various approaches. A large strand of urban economic literature has emphasized the role of cities as engine of growth a detailed discussion of which can be found in studies by Becker and Morrison (1999), Montgomery et al. (2013), and Glaeser (2011). Given this background, the present government relies on industry-led growth because compared to services-led growth this approach is expected to be more inclusive. However, the urban space must be developed and it should adhere to international quality standards so that new investment can flow in, resulting in higher levels of employment. The Smart City programme in this context offers a new policy vision though it requires a thorough evaluation.[4]

The Smart City mission was announced in 2015. Under this programme 100 smart cities were to be created with a total investment of INR 48,000 crore ($7.2 billion), and INR 500 crore in each city during the period 2014–2015 to 2019–2020. The present government discontinued JNNURM (Jawaharlal Nehru National Urban Renewal Mission), arguably the first major urban development plan started by UPA-I in 2005, and started AMRUT (Atal Mission for Rejuvenation and Urban Transformation)[5] and HRIDAY (Heritage City Development and Augmentation Yojana)[6] which have similar overall purpose of boosting urban infrastructure. It also increased the coverage of scheme from 67 cities in JNNURM to 500 under AMRUT cities; and HRIDAY covers 12 heritage cities. The 'Smart

---

[4]　For details, see Mitra and Nagar (2018b).
[5]　For details, see http://amrut.gov.in/.
[6]　For details, see https://www.hridayindia.in/.

City mission', a flagship scheme of the Modi government is believed be instrumental to urban progress.

Despite the growing interest of public policy makers, the private sector, urban developers, and other stakeholders in the Smart City project, there is no consensus on what makes a city smart. Different economic, demographic and geographical conditions make it difficult to arrive at a single definition but a central characteristic of the Smart City movement is the pervasive use of ICT technology to improve the efficiency and quality of urban infrastructure.

The US-based Smart Cities Council defines a smart city as one that has digital technology embedded across all city functions. Burte (2014) defined smart city as a system which can 'leverage various computational, networking, self-regulational, and responsive capacities that ICTs can embed into administrative and infrastructural systems (like transport, power and water supply, for instance) and enable more effective, efficient, responsive and resilient management of city amenities'. The core of the smart city idea is the ICT-enabled network infrastructure which involves the use of a wide range of infrastructures including transport, business services, governance, housing, and a range of public and private services amenities (see Graham and Marvin, 2001; Komninos, 2002; Hollands, 2013).

However, only an ICT-based solution will not be able to meet the desired improvement in urban life. Other institutional changes like investment in human capital will also be required to make cities and citizens smart (Neirotti et al. 2014).[7] The importance of other factors is highlighted in Caragliu, Del Bo, and Nijkamp (2011); they used European data to show that the presence of a 'creative class, the quality of and dedicated attention to the urban environment, the level of education, multimodal accessibility, and the use of ICTs for public administration are all positively correlated with urban wealth'.

The Smart Cities initiative of the present government aims at creating cities with basic infrastructure built on a sustainable model. With assured water and electricity supply, sanitation and solid waste management, urban mobility and efficient public transport, IT connectivity, e-governance and citizen participation,

---

[7]   See Neirotti et al. (2014) which provides an excellent literature review of various aspects of smart city notions using the elaboration of a taxonomy of pertinent application domains such as natural resources and energy, transport and mobility, buildings, living, government, and economy and people. See Caragliu, Del Bo, and Nijkamp (2011) for a discussion on the definition of smart city.

and the safety and security of citizens, investment is expected to go up resulting in productivity-induced higher rates of economic growth. One hundred cities and towns[8] have been selected by the Ministry of Urban Development with at least one city from each state. The Smart Cities Council India has been formed which is a part of the US-based Smart Cities Council, operating in 140 countries.

Some common features to identify a smart city and those which appear in the Smart City document (of the urban ministry) are the state-of-art infrastructure, parks, playgrounds and recreational spaces, inclusive housing for all, smart public transport and last mile transport connectivity, and walkable localities using new technological innovation to make governance citizen friendly and cost effective, using IT to bring transparency and accountability, using machine learning and AI to make city transportation, security and other services more efficient.

Under this initiative the government is investing in pan-city infrastructure to improve the quality of urban life and also to develop city amenities through one of the following strategies: (*a*) Retrofitting: implementing the ICT based smart infrastructure solution to already built-in areas of city; (*b*) Redevelopment: replacement of the existing built-up environment and enable co-creation of a new layout with enhanced infrastructure in city; (*c*) Greenfield: Building smart infrastructure in a previously vacant area of city.

In the present chapter we construct the deprivation index corresponding to each of the 100 smart cities and then examine its relationship with respect to other demographic and economic variables. The proposed index is multi-dimensional in nature, which includes a wide range of characteristics (see Mitra and Nagar, 2018b). This enables us to assess the quality of infrastructure existing within the cities. By reflecting on the housing characteristics, access to basic amenities of the households and the asset base of the residents, we are able to develop a broad idea of the quality of urban space both from demand and supply point of view. To what extent the local government is able to provide for and what is the quality of life that the existing residents are able to create for themselves can unfold a broad overview of the urban space which has been selected for further improvement and attract both domestic and foreign investment (Mitra and Nagar, 2018b). The database is drawn primarily from the population census 2011 (Government of India, 2011).

---

[8] In our analysis New Town Kolkata and Bidhannagar are taken as part of Kolkata UA; Navi Mumbai, Thane, Greater Mumbai and Kalyan, Dombivali are part of Mumbai UA; and Gandhi Nagar and Ahmadabad are part of Ahmadabad UA. In total we have 95 smart cities (urban agglomeration).

In the next step we try to assess the relationship between the index and other demographic, social and economic variables, representing the overall development dynamics of the selected cities under the Smart City project. In what ways such relationships are different in smart cities from the remaining urban agglomerations is a key question. This exercise again takes recourse to factor analysis because a regression exercise assumes a cause–effect association whereas this multivariate technique includes a number of variables and multi-directional association among them.

Deprivation Index in Smart Cities

The deprivation index for each of the smart cities is constructed based on the variables mentioned in the previous chapter. Using the factor loadings as weights the index has been formed at the city/town level. Since there are two factors which are statistically significant two sets of indices have been generated and both have been combined using the eigenvalue of each of the significant factors as weight. Factors 1 and 2 are said to be statistically significant because each of the two has an eigenvalue greater than 1. Below we analyse the deprivation index for the smart cities only. Higher the index value, higher is the deprivation. Since the factor loadings do not add up to unity, the index value does not necessarily range between zero and unity.

First of all more than half of the proposed smart cities are very large in size: either million-plus or each with a population of 500,000 and above but less than 1 million (Table 3.4). Another group of 28 cities are in the size class of one to five hundred thousand population. Besides, around five are in the close proximity of some of the larger cities, forming part of the urban agglomerations. Pertaining to the deprivation index value of the smart cities the following results can be discerned: the smart cities to begin with are mostly large in size; hence, their index values are low in magnitude, which conforms to the inverse pattern between size and index as observed in the context of all urban centres (Mitra and Nagar, 2018a). However, what is interesting to note is that even the small towns which belong to this group of proposed smart cities do not have a high index value (see Figure 3.1). Usually the large cities are seen to have benefitted from the past investment and hence, the agglomeration economies are said to have made them large. The small towns in the list of proposed smart cities may have been chosen in such a manner that they have already benefitted from the past investment to some extent. But the worry is why more such urban centres were not selected instead of a few.

Table 3.4 Smart Cities' Deprivation Index and Population Size

Index Range	Smart Cities					
	Million-plus	500,000–1,000,000	500,000–100,000	50,000–100,000	50,000–10,000	<10,000
No. of Cities	37	23	28	2	5	0
0–100	34	16	16	2	4	0
100–125	3	7	6		0	
125–150	0		3		1	
150–200	0		3			
200–250	0					
250–300	0					
>300	0					

Source: Mitra and Nagar (2018a).

The probability density plot of the index in Figure 3.1 indicates that the range of variation for smart cities is much narrower compared to all cities and towns. Second, the average value is much higher than the corresponding figure for all cities and towns. Third, the smart cities by and large follow a normal distribution with short tails on both sides while all cities and towns correspond to log normal kind of a distribution with a very long right hand tail. This implies that among the smart cities an almost equal number have very high and low index values though the difference between these values is not much as mentioned above. Besides, a very large percentage of smart cities concentrate around the average value, unfolding a lower level of inequality across smart cities in terms of the deprivation index. Also, the percentage of smart cities corresponding to their average value is much higher than the percentage of all urban centres concentrating around a modal value. The average value of the index for the smart cities is slightly lower than the modal value of all the urban centres, indicating relatively less deprivation in the smart cities. Besides, among all the urban centres the inequality as seen in terms of index value and the number of cities and towns is highly evident. While a cluster of urban centres can be seen around a lower value of the deprivation index there are other cities and towns with much higher values of the index, and the extreme values tend to vary widely in relation to the modal value.

Table 3.5 Factor Analysis Result for Class I, Million-plus, and Smart Cities

Variable	Class I Cities (466)			Million-Plus (53)			Smart Cities (94)		
	Factor 1	Factor 2	Factor 3	Factor 1	Factor 2	Factor 3	Factor 1	Factor 2	Factor 3
Sex ratio of the population	0.4348	0.2258	-0.0234	0.5669	0.2953	-0.26	0.4276	0.0072	0.1757
Percentage SC/ST population: male	0.0428	0.0407	0.9962	-0.1085	-0.0052	0.9919	0.1583	0.9782	0.0956
Percentage SC/ST population: female	0.0584	0.0458	0.9946	-0.1035	0.0021	0.9909	0.1724	0.9747	0.0965
Male literacy rate	0.1515	0.8619	0.0878	0.895	0.2218	-0.079	0.2413	0.1046	0.8715
Female literacy rate	0.1507	0.8848	0.0333	0.8945	0.2634	-0.155	0.2567	0.1752	0.8551
Children up to age 6 per 1000 women	-0.2892	0.4445	-0.0553	-0.4158	-0.3815	0.1714	-0.3243	0.1709	-0.3118
Percentage main workforce: male	0.3548	0.1593	-0.0007	0.089	0.3077	-0.084	0.192	-0.2125	0.264
Percentage main workforce: female	0.9449	0.119	0.055	0.1804	0.8955	0.0319	0.9147	0.1641	0.2286
Sex ratio of the main workforce	0.9635	0.116	0.0677	0.3207	0.9295	-0.013	0.9131	0.2609	0.2017

Table 3.5 contd.

Table 3.5 contd.

Variable	Class I Cities (466)			Million-Plus (53)			Smart Cities (94)		
	Factor 1	Factor 2	Factor 3	Factor 1	Factor 2	Factor 3	Factor 1	Factor 2	Factor 3
Percentage share of non-agriculture (excluding household manufacturing) activities in total male work force	-0.0208	0.3057	0.0724	0.1707	0.0998	0.0738	0.1612	0.0546	0.3843
Per share of non-agriculture (excluding household manufacturing) activities in total female work force	-0.2661	0.3474	0.0761	0.2693	-0.3083	0.1747	-0.0961	0.1102	0.2429
Deprivation index	-0.1366	-0.2665	0.0743	0.0714	-0.3083	0.1747	-0.1272	0.112	-0.0981
Log population	0.0905	0.0827	-0.1014	0.046	0.0892	-0.177	-0.2111	-0.162	-0.0737
Eigenvalue	4.2161	2.39517	1.9827	4.45	2.17	1.71	4.61599	2.4618	1.668
Percentage explain	0.418	0.237	0.197	0.42	0.2	0.16	0.45	0.24	0.16

Source: Based on population census figures.

Figure 3.1 Smart Cities versus All Cities and Towns: Probability Density Plot of City Deprivation Index

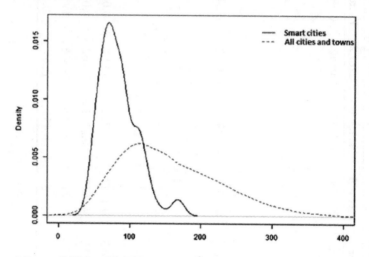

Source: Mitra and Nagar (2018b).

In the next step we have tried to assess the relationship of the deprivation index with other socio-economic and demographic variables. This is done for three sets of cities: all class 1 cities (each with a population of 100,000 and above), million-plus cities, and the smart cities. From the factor analysis results carried out for the smart cities we note a number of counter-intuitive results (Table 3.5: last three columns). First of all in factor 1, the city size and deprivation index are positively associated, not so strongly though. Literacy tends to decline while fertility increases with the city size. Female-to-male ratio among the workers and the female work participation rate correspond to the highest factor loading and both the variables, as per expectation, are positively associated with each other but they are again inversely related to the city size. Further, the male work participation rate which is taken to indicate the dynamism in the job market does not take a significant value in terms of factor loading though in the case of class 1 cities it is somewhat evident.

In the second factor, however, the city size and deprivation index move in the opposite direction. But the percentage of Scheduled Caste and Scheduled Tribe population tend to decline with city size. This result is also discernible in the case of class I cities and million-plus cities but it is distinct only in factor 3 which is statistically less significant in comparison to factor 2. Smart cities are selected to serve a specific purpose, that is, acting as growth centres. Hence, it is of interest to see whether they also tend to follow the principle of inclusive growth.

Since large cities are more productive, resulting in higher growth, the negative association between size and the incidence of lower caste population (representing disadvantaged classes) then, to begin with, suggests that the proposed smart cities are not germane to deliver inclusive growth. It would have been appropriate to take the percentage of slum population instead of the percentage of disadvantaged castes. But information on slum population for each of the smart cities is not available, for which we have been rather compelled to consider the caste data. It has also been observed widely that much of the distress migration comprises of the low caste population in India (Chandrasekhar and Mitra, 2019). Other evidence also suggests that many poor households are not able to migrate to large cities (Mitra and Murayama, 2009). Further, only in factor 3 (for the smart cities) the male and female work participation rates and the percentage of work force engaged in services and non-household manufacturing are somewhat positively associated with each other though in the case of class 1 cities the pattern is decipherable in factor 2 itself. In other words, the proposed smart cities do not unravel a strong employment generating tendency.

Conclusion

This chapter focussed on some of the new trends in Indian urbanization as brought out by the 2011 population census data (Government of India, 2011). A number of new census towns have emerged which are in fact a manifestation of rural areas undergoing a rapid process of transformation. In terms of the definitional criteria these centres have become urban while the urban local bodies still do not exist, implying non-recognition of these areas as 'urban' by the government of India. Based on certain direct and indirect methods one important question which is explored in the chapter is whether such transformation of rural into urban area is a result of ever expanding activities in the large urban areas and then spilling over to the rural hinterland. Evidence is supportive of such a pattern, albeit on a limited scale. With the rise in the urbanization level across districts, the rural specific development indicators are seen to improve. For example, rural poverty tends to decline, and growth, work force participation rate and rural diversification are positively associated with urbanization at the district level. However, these associations are not too strong and thus the other forces leading to rural transformation cannot be ruled out and those forces are not necessarily the positive drivers. The shift from agriculture to rural non-farm activities in several situations unfolds a movement from one class of low productivity activities to another. Thus, there is no marked improvement in development indicators alongside a rise in urbanization. For example, rural poverty tends to decline with urbanization in the district though the association is not very strong. In order to strengthen the positive spillover effects of urbanization on the rural economy a number of policy initiatives need to be pursued. It is pertinent to strengthen the rural-urban ties in terms of infrastructure base, make provisions for skill improvement for the rural population, and create productive jobs in the rural non-farm sector. The growth of rural non-farm sector activities for the productive utilization of the surplus work force in the agriculture sector is of great importance. Initiatives in this direction can result in 'generative' urbanization. Many of the census towns which have been identified in the recent population census need a close intervention. Whether they have the adequate base to accommodate the non-agricultural activities, population increase to take place in the coming years, and the concentration of new activities which may come up subsequently is a pertinent issue.

The Smart City mission is the first holistic urbanization programme of the Indian government with defined priorities and vision plans for each cities. The government may be lacking in giving a single definition of smart city but this also gives each the city freedom to incorporate its own vision of smartness. The decentralized planning differentiated this project from other urban infrastructure development projects like JNNURM where centre and state government released funds only for predetermined infrastructure development projects.

From one point of view the selection of the smart cities seems problematic because some of them are very large and are about to get saturated. Though one may argue that it is an attempt to take advantage of the agglomeration economies already existing in these cities, the diseconomies which may have become substantial given the age of the cities also need to be considered. Rather some of the census towns located in the close vicinity of the large cities could have been considered in large number though a handful of them (five or so) appear in the list of smart cities as they form part of the city urban agglomeration.

The problems of very large cities have to be mitigated before making further investment to reap new benefits. Nevertheless for the first time it seems the government policy very explicitly has recognized the productivity-augmenting effects of urbanization, particularly the economic efficiency of the big cities. Otherwise, the major concern in the past has been for concentration, and the regional policy always argued against it. Though all the class I cities are not included in the list of smart cities the present government has introduced the programme called AMRUT which covers 500 such cities. Hence, urban policy seems to have recognized in a balanced manner what economic theory has been arguing for a long time, and also acknowledged the equity issues.

Our results suggest that the cities under the Smart City project have better quality of urban infrastructure and amenities. Smart cities also show low variation in deprivation index compared to the observed variation in the deprivation index of all class I cities, indicating very similar type or quality of urban life in the selected or proposed smart cities. Since the deprivation index comprises housing characteristics, access to basic amenities, and certain types of assets, they are qualified to reflect the well-being of the residents. In comparison to all urban centres, the proposed list of smart cities is more uniform or homogeneous in terms of available infrastructure and quality of life, irrespective of city size. Our chapter, however, highlights that the proposed smart cities are not highly inclusive. Hence, the success of the project may lead to overall growth but whether it would allow migrants from low-income households to enter such spaces and access new livelihood opportunities is a major area of concern. Since many of the public utilities will be priced in order to ensure quality, it is less likely that the objective of inclusiveness will be served by the proposed smart cities. Making Indian urbanization more inclusive is definitely a major policy challenge for the present government.

CHAPTER 4

Growth, Informal Sector Employment, and Poverty

Introduction

Because of the agglomeration effects and rise in total factor productivity growth, economic growth is expected to be positively associated with urbanization. Also, in the process of urbanization, employment opportunities for all sections of the society including the unskilled and semi-skilled variety of the workforce are expected to grow through several forward and backward linkages between the dynamic sectors and the informal sector. In other words, even the activities that were residual in nature to begin with may acquire productivity gains in the process of urbanization and, thus, offer better levels of living to the workers located in the lower echelons. Since the cost of providing services in urban areas is usually less than that in rural areas (as a result of agglomeration effects), the decline in the incidence of urban poverty is likely to take place at a higher pace with rapid urbanization. Even the rural poor benefit in the process of urbanization through inter-linkage effects.

Growing inequality and increasing poverty are likely to have a direct relationship. Given the level of per capita income if inequality rises, it results in an increase in poverty. However, when both growth and inequality rise simultaneously, the poverty outcome is a bit uncertain. The beneficial effects of growth on poverty tend to get neutralized by the adverse effects of increasing inequality on poverty and thus the net decline in poverty can be quite modest. However, at higher levels of growth when inequality tends to decline, poverty is certain to fall. As economic growth, particularly its compositional change, is expected to bring in rapid urbanization, one may therefore infer that at higher stages of urbanization, the overall poverty is also expected to decline substantially. Since urbanization can offer opportunities to rural migrants to escape poverty—more so because of the agglomeration effects in large human settlements—the relationship between urbanization on the one hand, and rural and urban poverty on the other, can be an inverse one even at the lower levels of urbanization. If rural–urban migration is directed to large cities and much of the economic growth also originates from large cities, the decline in poverty and rise in urbanization can occur simultaneously.

Ferre et al. (2012) provide evidence from eight developing countries in favour of an inverse relationship between poverty and city size. Poverty is both more widespread and deeper in very small and small towns than in large or very large cities and, more importantly, a majority of the urban poor live in medium, small, or very small towns. In other words, the share of small towns in total urban poverty is much more than that of large cities. Also, the authors noted that the greater incidence and severity of consumption poverty in smaller towns is generally compounded by similar greater deprivation in terms of access to basic infrastructure services such as electricity, heating gas, sewerage, and solid waste disposal (also see Lanjouw and Murgai, 2010a, 2010b).

Cali (2008) empirically addressed three important aspects of the urbanization process in India: rural–urban disparities and their relation with economic development; the relation between urbanization and growth; and the convergence hypothesis in cities' growth. The results support the idea of a U-shaped relation between rural–urban disparities in socio-economic indicators and the level of economic development. Though the level of urbanization and that of economic development go hand in hand across Indian states over time, this relation is not strong. Also, the rate of urbanization (change in the proportion of population living in the urban areas) and the rate of economic growth appear to be negatively correlated. Finally, the author noted a tendency towards convergence in growth rates among Indian towns: other things being equal, smaller towns grow faster than large ones. Further, Cali and Menon (2012) pointed out that urbanization has a substantial and systematic poverty-reducing effect in the surrounding rural areas. The authors argue that this effect is causal in nature and is largely attributable to the positive spillovers of urbanization on the rural economy rather than to the movement of the rural poor to the urban areas. As Chatterjee et al. (2016) points out, urbanization and economic growth are seen to be the key drivers of poverty reduction during 2005–12 in India. The factors commonly responsible for the escape from poverty as pointed out by Krishna (2017) include (*a*) diversification of income, (*b*) private sector employment, (*c*) public sector employment, (*d*) government or non-governmental organization (NGO) assistance, and (*e*) irrigation (Mehta et al., 2018). Improving the quality of education in the rural areas is instrumental to capacity-building to escape from poverty, and the realization of the potential of urbanization will require more investments in rural India (Krishna, 2017).

Mahadevia and Sarkar (2012) pointed out that there has been an increase in inequality between the metros and the non-metros. The beneficiaries of economic reforms comprise only the top 20 and 5 per cent of the population in the metros and the non-metros respectively, while the bottom 40 per cent of the population in these cities witnessed a rise in consumption only at a decreasing rate. The McKinsey Global Institute Report (2010) and that of India's High Powered Expert Committee (Report on Indian Urban Infrastructure and Services) (HPEC 2011) vouched for promoting urbanization through metropolization and global linkages of large cities. But in the face of existing inequality, such a recommendation, if implemented, is feared to accentuate the degree of inequality further. Mahadevia and Sarkar (2012) also elucidated in terms of investment the pro-metro bias of the largest urban programme (Jawaharlal Nehru National Urban Renewal Mission, JNNURM).

In a paper by Sharma and Kumari (2012), the authors show a relationship between poverty and weights, which are the combined effects of distance to nearest town and class of towns in India. Higher weights are given to bigger towns and closer rural areas in terms of distance. The authors noted a U-shaped curve, implying that poverty reduces until a certain point and after that it starts increasing. This has a very interesting policy implication: if the government wants to invest in poverty alleviation in villages, the funds should be spent directly within the villages that are more than 20 kilometres away from the nearest town. On the other hand, in the case of poor villages located within 20 kilometres from the towns, government investment should be incurred in the nearby towns, which will indirectly benefit the surrounding rural areas through spillover effects.

In assessing the impact of urbanization on certain key variables, the rest of the chapter is structured as follows. The next section focusses on economic growth, inequality, and poverty in relation to urbanization. The third section deals with migration and informal sector employment while the fourth section delves into sector specific expansions in relation to urbanization and industrialization. Finally, the last section summarizes the major findings. The database of the study is drawn mainly from the population census and National Sample Surveys on migration, unincorporated/unorganized sector enterprises, employment–unemployment and consumption expenditure.

Inclusiveness: Empirical Artefacts

Based on the district-level data, from the regression analysis, rural poverty is seen to decline in relation to growth, though inequality raises poverty (Table 4.1).

Further, male literacy and the work participation rate reduce poverty. The positive relationship between female literacy and rural poverty is indicative of the extensive rural literacy mission aimed at encompassing more women from poor households. Similarly, in the urban areas, poverty declines in response to rise in growth, male work participation rate, and male literacy rate, though inequality raises it. More importantly, urbanization shows a strong beneficial effect on poverty as higher levels of urbanization are associated with lower poverty incidence.

The regression analysis of urbanization suggests that both rural and urban growth contribute to urbanization. The rural male work participation rate and rural male literacy also add to urbanization as the rural male workers and literates are more likely to migrate to cities in search of better jobs after acquiring the requisite work experience and skill. With rural diversification (expansion in non-agricultural activities), the urbanization index also tends to increase, as the rural–urban discontinuum in terms of activities tends to break down. The rural areas start urbanizing and migration also becomes easier as the differences in the nature of activities across space get dissipated. However, in relation to the rural male Scheduled Caste population, urbanization falls as they represent the socially vulnerable lot who are less likely to be able to afford the cost of migration. With respect to women, we reserve our comments because female migration is governed more by social factors such as marriage (Mitra, 2013).

The regression analysis of economic growth in the urban areas again confirms the importance of urbanization. Literacy, increased work opportunities resulting in an enhanced work participation rate, and expansion in activities such as non-household manufacturing and services also contribute to growth. However, economic growth in the rural areas is not significantly influenced by urbanization, though the other factors remain pertinent.

Urban inequality rises in response to both urbanization and urban growth. However, increased work opportunities reduce urban inequality, while the presence of the vulnerable social categories such as the Scheduled Caste population aggravates urban inequality. In the rural context, inequality is not seen to be influenced by urbanization, meaning out-migration does not result in inequality reduction. A greater presence of the Scheduled Caste population does not add to inequality, suggesting no significant differences in the living standards across social categories in the rural areas, while in the urban context, such differences are more pronounced. Again, greater work opportunities and rural diversification are endemic to controlling inequality in the rural areas.

Table 4.1 Regression Results from District-Level Data: Poverty, Urbanization, Growth, and Inequality Functions

				Dep. Variable					
Indep. Variables	RPOV11-12	UPOV11-12	URBN	URBN	UAVMPCE	RAVMPCE	UINEQ	RINEQ	URINEQ
RMWFPR	-0.165 (-1.72)*		0.62 (5.90)**	0.71 (6.97)**					
UMWFPR		-0.23 (-2.05)**							
RFWFPR	0.065 (1.01)		-0.26 (-3.51)**	-0.007 (-0.09)					
UFWFPR		-0.015 (-0.11)							
RWFPR						23.73 (10.65)**		-148.67 (-3.86)**	
UWFPR					15.43 (2.58)**		-189.55 (-3.08)**		4.25 ((0.91)
ROTHERACT				0.37 (7.41)**		16.68 (13.81)**		-55.81 (-2.53)**	
UOTHERACT					20.05 (6.44)**		44.19 (-1.36)		11.77 (4.86)**
RMLIT	-0.464 2(-3.23)**		0.567 (3.49)**	0.44 (2.81)**					
UMLIT		-0.67 (-2.90)**							
RFLIT	0.398 (3.37)**		-0.22 (-1.68)*	-0.31 (-2.38)**					

Table 4.1 contd.

			Dep. Variable						
Indep. Variables	RPOV11-12	UPOV11-12	URBN	URBN	UAVMPCE	RAVMPCE	UINEQ	RINEQ	URINEQ
UFLIT		0.21 (1.31)							
RLIT						9.81 (4.99)**		50.56 (1.61)	
ULIT					21.61 (4.60)**		10.66 (0.22)		-1.88 (-0.51)
RMSC	-1.64 (-1.04)		-8.82 (-4.73)**	-6.80 (-3.77)**					
UMSC		-0.42 (-0.31)							
RFSC	1.38 (0.88)		8.66 (4.64)**	6.78 (3.76)**					
UFSC		0.39 (0.29)							
RSC								-7.60 (-0.30)	
USC							103.44 (2.53)**		
URBN	0.023 (0.66)	-0.086 (-2.51)**			11.34 (8.29)**	1.54 (1.46)	74.29 (4.59)**	-11.85 (-0.72)	-4.22 (-3.38)**
RAVMPCE	-0.026 (-17.74)**		0.006 (3.48)**	0.0008 (0.46)				10.63 (16.84)**	

Table 4.1 contd.

Table 4.1 contd.

				Dep. Variable					
Indep. Variables	RPOV11-12	UPOV11-12	URBN	URBN	UAVMPCE	RAVMPCE	UINEQ	RINEQ	URINEQ
UAVMPCE		-0.014 (-13.48)**	0.004 (3.82)**	0.003 (2.98)**					
RINEQ	0.0005 (5.49)**						7.62 (18.21)**		
UINEQ		0.0005 (5.64)**							0.03 (13.11)**
INTER	84.44 (15.19)*	99.39 (11.39)**	-38.998 (-6.31)**	-37.72 (-6.38)**	-1690.19 (-5.59)**	-235.42 (-2.27)**	-3199.97 (-0.99)	-6709.04 (-4.07)**	-472.08 (-1.99)**
No. of Observations	608	592	592	592	602	608	592	608	592
Adj. R2	0.4927	0.42	0.35	0.40	0.37	0.52	0.49	0.44	0.29

Source: Author's calculations based on NSS and population census data.

Note: While the subscripts RM, RF, UM, and UF represent rural male, rural female, urban male, and urban female respectively, simply R and U refer to rural and urban areas for both the sexes. HHSZ: household size; CHILD-WOM: proportion of children to women; WFPR: main workforce participation rate; LIT: literacy; SC: percentage of Scheduled Caste population; OTHERACT: percentage of workers engaged in non-household manufacturing and services; MFGHH: percentage of workers in household manufacturing; F/M: female–male ratio in the population, BPL: percentage of households below the poverty line; URBN: percentage of population in the urban areas; AVMPCE: average monthly per capita consumption expenditure; INEQ: inequality in terms of the difference between the minimum and maximum value of the consumption expenditure.

The variables are for 2011 or 2011–12 or 2010–11.

** and * denote significance at 5 and 10 per cent levels respectively.

Based on the multivariate analysis (factor analysis), the district-level data for the urban areas confirms a positive association between urbanization, work participation rate, percentage of workforce engaged in non-household manufacturing and services, literacy, and growth and inequality, though the degree of association is a mild one as judged from the moderate factor loadings corresponding to many of these variables (Table 4.2). Further, urban poverty is also seen to be negatively associated with these variables, not strongly though. However, as we move on to the next significant factor (2), this relationship between growth, inequality, poverty, and urbanization turns out to be much sharper. While growth, inequality, and urbanization tend to move in the same direction, poverty declines.

Table 4.2 Results from Factor Analysis (District: Urban)

Variables	Factor 1	Factor 2
UHHSZ	-0.7716	-0.1540
UCHILD-WOM	-0.8534	-0.1684
UWFPR	0.6353	0.1921
ULIT	0.7374	0.2264
USC	0.1201	0.0383
UOTHERACT	0.3282	0.3096
UMFGHH	-0.2011	-0.0983
UF/M	0.3075	0.0014
UBPL	-0.3135	-0.4429
URBN	0.2366	0.4735
UAVMPCE	0.2611	0.8050
UINEQ	0.1276	0.7407
Eigenvalue	3.97	1.18
Explained Variation	0.6374	0.1898

Number of observations: 592
Source: Author's calculations based on NSS and population census data.
Note: U represents urban areas; HHSZ: household size; CHILD-WOM: proportion of children to women; WFPR: main workforce participation rate; LIT: literacy; SC: percentage of Scheduled Caste population; OTHERACT: percentage of workers engaged in non-household manufacturing and services; MFGHH: percentage of workers in household manufacturing; F/M: female–male ratio in the population, BPL: percentage of households below the poverty line; URBN: percentage of population in the urban areas; AVMPCE: average monthly per capita consumption expenditure; INEQ: inequality in terms of the difference between the minimum and maximum value of the consumption expenditure.
The variables are for 2011 or 2011–12 or 2010–11.

Another interesting finding that emerges is that the dependency ratio (child–woman ratio) and the demographic variable (household size) are the two highly significant variables in factor 1 that have a positive association between each other and with poverty as well. On the other hand, they are negatively connected with many of the development indicators. Besides, poverty tends to increase with a

Table 4.3 Results from Factor Analysis (District: Rural)

Variables	Factor 1	Factor 2	Factor 3
RHHSZ	-0.6615	-0.1201	-0.0750
RCHILD-WOM	-0.8758	-0.1914	-0.2291
RWFPR	0.4826	-0.2138	0.1992
RLIT	0.6064	0.2863	0.2864
RSC	0.1626	0.0470	0.0835
ROTHERACT	0.1095	0.7814	0.2365
RMFGHH	-0.0320	0.1394	-0.0442
RCUL	-0.1466	-0.9115	-0.1291
RAGLAB	0.0393	0.0829	-0.1217
RF/M	0.4391	-0.0442	0.0058
RBPL	-0.1700	-0.1488	-0.5527
URBN	0.1797	0.3859	0.2479
RAVMPCE	0.2638	0.2676	0.7903
RINEQ	0.1938	0.1964	0.6557
Eigenvalue	3.92	1.90	1.69
Explained Variation	0.4115	0.1987	0.1775

Number of observations: 608
Source: Author's calculations based on NSS and population census data.
Note: R: rural areas, HHSZ: household size; CHILD-WOM: proportion of children to women; WFPR: main workforce participation rate; LIT: literacy; SC: percentage of Scheduled Caste population; OTHERACT: percentage of workers engaged in non-household manufacturing and services; CUL: percentage of workforce engaged as cultivators; AGLAB: percentage of workforce engaged as agricultural labourers; MFGHH: percentage of workers in household manufacturing; F/M: female–male ratio in the population, BPL: percentage of households below the poverty line; URBN: percentage of population in the urban areas; AVMPCE: average monthly per capita consumption expenditure; INEQ: inequality in terms of the difference between the minimum and maximum value of the consumption expenditure. The variables are for 2011 or 2011–12 or 2010–11.

rise in household-based activities represented by household manufacturing share in the workforce. Interestingly, the female–male ratio appears to be higher in districts with improved outcomes in terms of poverty, growth, urbanization, and work participation rate.

In the rural context, though similar findings are discernible between growth, inequality, poverty, and other development indicators including the urbanization level in the district, the factor loadings are much lower in magnitude in factors 1 and 2, implying the absence of a strong association (Table 4.3). It is only in factor 3 that the growth–inequality–poverty–urbanization nexus becomes sharper. On the whole, districts with a higher level of urbanization are associated with a reduced rural poverty incidence and higher levels of growth and other development indicators, though inequality is likely to rise in the process. Again, such districts with better outcomes are also able to witness a higher female–male ratio in the population. Hence, based on the district-level data, it may be concluded that urbanization not only delivers better outcomes in terms of economic indicators but also social and demographic indicators, though the process of social transformation seems to be taking place at a much slower pace.

Rural-to-Urban Migration and the Urban Informal Sector

In India, much of the urban problems are at times attributed to the rural spillover effects, that is, considerable overlaps among urban slums, informal sector employment, and rural–urban population mobility. In the face of a high natural growth of population, rural–urban migration is believed to aggravate the situation of excess supply of labour in the urban areas. Within the urban informal sector, this tends to reduce the level of earnings and gets manifested in a high incidence of urban poverty. Thus, rural poverty gets transformed into urban poverty—a phenomenon described as 'urbanization of poverty'.[1] But these views seem to be exaggerated. As Mitra (1994) observed, the elasticity of urban poverty with respect to rural poverty, defined as the proportionate rise

---

[1] For details see Harris and Todaro (1970) and Ravallion and Datt (2002). Todaro (1969) treats the informal sector as a transitory phenomenon, but, in reality, it has emerged as a persistent one. Mitra (1994) argued that natural growth of the population maintained the urban supplies of labour at a high level, resulting in informal sector employment and poverty as a persistent phenomenon.

in the incidence of urban poverty due to a proportionate rise in rural poverty, was highly negligible. Though the elasticity was positive, indicating a positive association between rural and urban poverty, many among the urban poor have been actually residing in the urban areas for long and cannot be interpreted as fresh migrants from the rural areas. Hence, urban poverty cannot be interpreted purely as a spillover effect of rural poverty.

In explaining migration the received theory took income differentials as an important determinant of mobilizing people from low-income areas to relatively high-income areas (Harris and Todaro, 1970). In the rural areas, sluggish agricultural growth and limited development of the rural non-farm sector raises the incidence of rural poverty, unemployment and underemployment. Given the fact that most of the high productivity activities are located in the urban areas, the rural–urban income differentials, particularly for the poor and unemployed, are enormous. Thus, many of them are believed to migrate to urban areas in search of jobs. However, this is not empirically true as the cost of migration seems to be very high for the poor (Banerjee, 1986). Singh (2009) noted that the relationship between poverty and migration is not clearly observed as middle- and higher-income groups show higher propensity to migrate. Besides, jobs in the high-productivity activities are limited in number relative to the supply, and often they are not accessible. These patterns are not unknown to the individuals who are in the process of taking a decision to migrate but this does not rule out the possibility that some of the poor may still prefer to move to the urban areas in search of opportunities, even in the informal sector.

A simplistic framework to analyse migration in terms of distress and development-induced movements may not capture the reality in detail (Shah, 2009). Migration for economic motives is an important exit route from poverty irrespective of the initial characteristics of distress influencing mobility. The new perspective, recognizing the complex, multi-patterned and dynamic nature of migration re-emphasizes the positive role of migration, as an integral part of the diversified strategies adopted by the poor (Shah, Pattnaik, and Kumar, 2018; de Haan, 1994; Srivastava, 2011; Deshingkar, 2010; Shah, 2009). As Shah, Pattnaik, and Kumar (2018) point out, migration prevents people from further sliding into poverty and helps some escape poverty (Mohanty et al., 2015; Bhandari and Reddy, 2015; Agrawal and Chandrasekhar, 2015) but at the same time there is a significantly high level of inequality. This may discourage population movement as inequality reduces access to resources including space. Jayaraj (2013) provides an account of family migration which is a relatively under-researched phenomenon in India. While the factors related to both growth theory ('pull') and Third World urbanization ('push') in explaining family migration are important, he argues for evolving a framework that incorporates the complex interplay of social, political, environmental, and development-related factors.

Some of the questions around which Lall et al. (2006) summarized the findings relate to how internal migrants behave at different stages of the migration process, how migrants prepare for migration, how they migrate, what difficulties they face on arriving in urban areas, and what links they maintain with rural areas. While economic opportunities play a key role in labour migration, there are varied motivations pertaining to migration, including not only conditions at the place of origin and destination but also patterns of recruitment and migration networks (de Haan, 2011). The forced nature of migration has been brought out in the context of western India (Breman, 1985). Forced migration refers to displacement of individuals and/or households due to conflicts, destitution and impoverishment, natural or environmental disasters, chemical or nuclear disasters, famine, or development projects. It is a complex, wide-ranging and pervasive phenomenon. Though internal migration from poorer areas signifies a form of safety valve, there are many costs of migration which the data on remittances tends to neglect (de Haan, 2011). Costs of migration include not only the transportation and resettlement costs at the place of destination but also several social costs such as social exclusion, deprivation from familial bonding and the benefits associated with such bonding, and a variety of harassments that the low-income migrants face from the labour contractors, slumlords and city residents (Mitra, 2013). Though there is no city legislation to stop migration legally, these factors tend to discourage the inflow of low-income households to cities.[2]

---

[2] 'The willingness to accept a lower wage in the village reflects the costs of migration as well as the exploitative conditions that labourers face as migrants. The costs of migration include transport costs, uncertain earnings, health hazards, and higher costs of living in urban areas combined with poor living conditions. Migration also results in a breakdown of social life: this is true both in the case of men migrating alone and when entire families migrate. When entire families migrate the situation is even worse: children have to be removed from schools and live in precarious environments. Women and young girls are especially vulnerable to sexual exploitation. Further, urban congestion is a cost of migration that is borne by society at large' (Khera, 2006).

Education and the migration rate show a curvilinear relationship: among urban males, it was relatively high among both the illiterates (17 per cent) and those with an educational level of graduation or above (38 per cent). Migration involves a cost and therefore not all can afford to migrate to urban areas. As Banerjee (1986) argued, the rich do not have the need to migrate and the poor cannot afford to migrate, while the middle-income group has a higher propensity to migrate.

The received theory brought out a great deal of overlap between rural to urban migration and informal sector employment (Todaro, 1969; Udall, 1976). The informal sector was initially envisaged as a group of small and micro enterprises including self-employed workers, that is, enterprises with or without hired workers and with little protection as the labour regulations were not applicable to them (Joshi and Joshi, 1976). In the later years, however, with the vulnerability of the workers being noticed in large units due to a rise in casualization and contractualization, the concept of informal employment came into prevalence. For a detailed review of the literature on the informal sector one may refer to Barnes (2015).

Though in some of the studies the informal sector was taken to be a transitory phenomenon, empirically it was seen to be a persistent phenomenon as the possibilities for workers to graduate to the formal sector were rather dim (Papola, 1981; Banerjee, 1986). Hence, the persistence of the informal sector was taken to understand the dynamics of urban poverty and urban slums (Mitra, 1994). In the cities of many developing countries as Spence, Annez, and Buckley (2009) pointed out, most jobs, including those for new migrants, are in the informal sector of the economy. Further, he urged that little is known about the productivity of the informal sector or the mobility of workers from informal employment to formal jobs. However, the African experience indicates that informal work in the cities is more productive than agricultural labour, even if it is considerably less productive than formal employment, and second, the opportunity to shift to a formal job from informal employment is rather meagre (Spence, Annez, and Buckley, 2009).

Turning to the data on migration, the quality of migrants in terms of education seems to be inferior compared to the non-migrants. As Table 4.4 indicates, the percentage of illiterates is higher among migrants. Similarly, the share of those with a primary and secondary level of education is smaller among migrants compared to non-migrants.

Table 4.4 Composition of Education Level of Usual Principal Status Workers (15
Years and Above) in Urban Areas by Migration Status (2007–8)

Educational Level	Migrants	Non-migrants
Not literate (0)	18.1	14.5
Below primary (1–4)	7.0	7.6
Primary (5)	10.8	13.1
Middle (8)	16.4	19.4
Secondary (10)	14.3	15.8
Higher secondary (12)	12.5	12.1
Graduate+ (15 and above)	20.9	17.6
Total	100	100

Source: Calculated from unit level data of NSS of 64th round (2007–8).
Note: UPS workers: workers who have worked for a major part of the year.

The most prominent reason for female migration in both rural and urban areas
was *marriage*, while the reason for migration among males was dominated by
employment-related factors (nearly 56 per cent in urban areas). A higher percentage
of persons reported to have been engaged in *economic activities* after migration
compared to the pre-migration status: for males, the percentage of workers increased
from 46 per cent before migration to 70 per cent after migration in urban areas.
Srivastava (2011) noted that in 2007–8, excluding seasonal migrants, around 31
per cent of the workforce could be classified as migrants.

In the case of urban males, the percentage of regular wage/salaried employees has
shown a major increase—from 18 per cent before migration to 39 per cent after
migration. However, there has been an increase in the share of self-employment
as well after migration (from 17 per cent to 22 per cent), though the relative size
of casual labour declined after migration (from 11 per cent before migration to 8
per cent) at the all-India level.

Is this shift in the occupation of migrants related to the urbanization level?
From the regression based on state-level data, we noted that the higher the level
of urbanization, the greater the decline in the unemployment rate after migration
in comparison with the unemployment rate prevailing prior to migration. Also,
based on the cross-sectional data, the rise in overall labour force participation

and the relative size of regular wage employment after migration show a positive relationship with urbanization, though neither of them is found to be statistically significant (Table 4.5). Only the changes in self-employment and urbanization level are positively connected.

The factor analysis has been carried out on a large number of variables including the informal sector employment which has been estimated as employment in small enterprises reported by the NSSO (2009–10). The results suggest that higher rural literacy tends to raise the migration rate, moderately though (Table 4.6). The percentage of Scheduled (SCs) in rural areas also has a positive impact on the migration rate, supporting the view that the disadvantaged sections migrate to escape their vulnerability (factor 1). The most interesting part is that migration reduces both rural and urban poverty as seen from both factor 1 and factor 4. This is, however, not a very strong pattern emerging from the cross-sectional data.

Higher urbanization and work participation rate in both rural and urban areas are positively associated with migration (factor 2), suggesting that those in the labour market are more likely to migrate and after migration they are likely to continue in the labour market. Such patterns are more prevalent in states which are more urbanized than the others.

Table 4.5 Urbanization and Change in Labour Market Characteristics: Regression Analysis

Exp. Var.	Dep. Var. Change in LF	Dep. Var. Change in Self-emp.	Dep. Var. Change in Casual Emp.	Dep. Var. Change in Reg. Wage Emp.	Dep. Var. Change in Unemp.
URBN	0.45	0.82	-0.29	0.23	-1.37
	(1.06)	(1.95)*	(-0.89)	(0.29)	(-1.96)*
CONSTANT	-106.47	10.03	0.0325	168.32	-60.14
	(-5.74)**	(0.54)	(0.001)	(4.95)**	(-1.94)*
Adj R2	0.004	0.07	-0.001	-02	0.07
No. of Obs.	36	36	36	36	36

Source: Author's calculation based on NSS and population census data.
Note: LF is labour force (2007–8) and URBN is urbanization (2011).

Table 4.6 Factor Analysis: Migration, Urban Informal Sector, and Other Rural and Urban Labour Market Characteristics

Variables	Factor 1	Factor 2	Factor 3	Factor 4
MIG	-0.1138	0.1812	0.2294	0.1403
UINF	-0.1574	-0.0995	0.6029	-0.0252
MIG EMP MALE	0.1105	0.1661	-0.1277	0.0488
RHHSZ	0.6576	-0.4285	-0.1047	-0.1598
RCHILDWOM	0.8675	-0.2058	-0.1431	-0.1511
RWFPR	-0.1262	0.6799	-.0787	-0.1019
RLIT	-0.5362	0.0718	-0.0909	0.5245
RSC	-0.1469	-0.0411	0.9067	-0.0705
ROTHERACT	-0.1406	0.0425	-0.1517	0.8636
UHHSZ	0.4938	-0.7729	-0.0294	-0.0745
UCHILDWOM	0.8359	0.0413	-0.1793	0.0322
UWFPR	-0.0001	0.9216	-0.0934	0.1698
ULIT	-0.4368	0.2878	-0.2512	0.2123
USC	-0.0547	-0.0303	0.9247	-0.0724
UOTHERACT	-0.1567	0.1456	-01291	0.4363
RPOV	0.1190	0.1737	-0.1193	-0.2127
UPOV	0.2697	-0.1800	-0.0965	-0.2519
URBN	-0.0244	0.1433	0.0027	0.8671
Eigenvalue	5.43	2.97	2.18	1.60
% Explained	0.3563	0.1951	0.1432	0.1045

N=35.

Source: Author's calculation based on NSS and population census data.

Note: R and U subscripts stand for rural and urban areas respectively, MIG: migration rate (2007–8), MIG EMP MALE: migration rate for employment among males (2007–8), UINF: the share of informal sector employment in urban non-agricultural activities (2009-10), CHILDWOM: child-woman ratio (2011), LIT: literacy rate (2011), SC: percentage of Scheduled Caste population (2011), HHSZ: household size (2011), WFPR is work participation rate (2011), OTHERACT: percentage of workforce in other activities (2011), POV is poverty (2011–12) and URBN: percentage urbanization (2011).

Migration, urban informal sector employment, and the incidence of SC population (representing lower social categories in terms of caste) in the urban and rural areas are all positively connected with each other, suggesting that the socially backward groups are more likely to migrate and land up in the urban informal sector. However, this pattern is accompanied by a decline in the incidence of poverty in both rural and urban areas, though in nominal terms only (factor 3).

In factor 4, urbanization takes the highest factor loading and is associated positively with the percentage of the rural and urban workforce engaged in non-household manufacturing and services. Also, urbanization is negatively related to rural and urban poverty.

The relationship between urbanization and informal sector employment is not distinct: the factor loadings of both urbanization and urban informal sector employment do not turn out to be high or moderate simultaneously in any of the four significant factors. In factor 3 or factor 4, only one of the two is closer to unity, while the other is negligible. From this, we may conclude that informal sector employment and urbanization do not show any significant relationship.

Keeping in view the literature suggesting interlinks between rural-to-urban migration, informal sector employment, and poverty, we estimated the following three equations: rural-to-urban migration function, urban informal sector employment function, and urban poverty function. We conceptualized a simultaneous equation system, that is, rural-to-urban migration impacts urban informal sector employment which, in turn, influences the rural-to-urban migration rate. Further, informal sector employment and rural to urban migration both exert effects on urban poverty. Though the Hariss-Todaro model (1970) upholds that it is the formal sector which motivates rural to urban migration, studies have shown the importance of the urban informal sector in providing sources of livelihood to rural migrants. Even when they do not have the expectation of getting absorbed in the formal sector, migration still takes place precisely because urban informal sector earnings are higher than what the rural economy is able to offer. Further, some of the informal sector jobs enable an above-poverty-line level of living. Therefore, it is worth examining the nature of relationship between urban informal sector employment and poverty. Given that both the phenomena—overlaps between informal sector employment and poverty and informal sector enabling some to escape poverty—are prevalent, the relationship may not turn out to be statistically significant.

The findings confirm simultaneity between informal sector employment and the migration rate, both being dependent on each other (Table 4.7).

Table 4.7 Results of the Three-Equation Model (OLS Estimates)

Exp. Var.	Dep. Var. MIG	Dep. Var. INF	Dep. Var. UPOV
INF	0.38 (2.45)**		0.0065 (0.93)
RPOV	-1.29 (-0.84)		0.59 (6.86)**
UOTHERACT	4.27 (0.95)	-9.24 (-2.66)**	
RLIT	-0.73 (-0.25)		
MIG EMP MALE	0.30 (1.41)		
RHHSZ	-95.55 (-2.19)**		
RPOPF/M	-578.66 (-1.72)*		
MIG		0.32 (2.17)**	
USC		8.30 (2.74)**	0.004 (0.03)
URBN		1.26 (1.41)	
UHHSZ		61.46 (1.60)	
UCHILD-WOM		-1095.24 (-1.85)*	
ULIT			-0.45 (-2.69)**
PCNETSDP			-0.0004 (-0.78)
ROTHERACT			0.08 (1.36)
INTERCEPT	655.31 (1.02)	1143.57 (2.90)**	30.04 (2.10)**
Adj. R2	0.33	0.42	0.76
N	35	35	31

Source: Author's calculation based on NSS and population census data.

Note: PCNETSDP is per capita net state domestic product (2010–11) and for other variables see Table 4.6. The OLS estimates provide consistent estimates; hence there is no need to provide system estimates.

Migration for employment among males tends to raise the overall migration rate in urban areas, though it is not significant at the 10 per cent level. Large rural households and a higher female–male ratio are associated with reduced rates of migration since a higher level of dependency, captured in terms of a large household size, and higher poverty levels in female-headed households reduce the ability and propensity to migrate.

Other than the migration rate, a higher incidence of SC population is associated with higher informal sector employment. Both urbanization and household size raise the incidence of informal sector employment, though the variables are not statistically significant at the 10 per cent level. Expansion in non-household manufacturing and services activities leads to a decline in the share of informal sector employment, implying that household manufacturing, livestock and other primary activities constitute a higher incidence of the informal sector. Interestingly, a higher child–woman ratio and informal sector employment are negatively connected though usually women from large households and children from low-income households are believed to be engaged in the informal sector due to the flexibility the sector offers. However, this result needs to be interpreted carefully. Given the household size, if the child–woman ratio rises, it is indicative of greater domestic responsibility for women, which deprives them even from working in the informal sector.

Finally, there is a strong association between rural and urban poverty: the role of migration cannot be ruled out, though migration may be contributing to a reduction in poverty in both rural and urban areas as seen from the factor analysis. In addition, urban literacy contributes to reduction in poverty significantly. Though the incidence of informal sector employment has a tendency to raise poverty, the coefficient is not statistically significant. Similarly, an enhanced share of non-household manufacturing and services in rural areas is expected to reduce urban poverty, though it is not significant even at the 10 per cent level.

On the whole, based only on the significant results, we conclude that migration and urban informal sector employment are closely connected. Migrants do not necessarily move in search of jobs within the formal sector only; even the possibility to work in the informal sector induces population mobility across space. Further, rural and urban poverty are connected through migration and other state-specific characteristics, though migration and an increased urbanization level tend to reduce both rural and urban poverty.

The inter-linkages among the formal and informal sectors exist but they are not necessarily favourable to the informal sector workers always (see Mitra, 1994; Shaw, 1990). Through sub-contracting from the formal to the informal sector, inter-sectoral input linkages and recycling of waste products generated by the formal sector, the informal sector workers earn their livelihood but often they are not in a position to dictate the terms of transactions, and hence the trickle-down effects of growth are limited. At times the informal sector workers are seen to work within this sector for almost their entire working life without being able to graduate to the formal sector though within the informal sector they have experienced upward mobility (Mitra, 2003).

Papola (1981) argued that the size of the informal sector is large in situations of both limited industrial spread and rapid industrialization. In the former case it is mainly a manifestation of residual absorption of labour whereas in the latter, a complementary relationship exists between the industrial and informal sectors. Also, in this situation the informal sector is described to be no more of a low productivity one by virtue of its close linkage with the industrial sector and income percolating from this sector to the rest.

Based on the city-level data, Mitra (1994) observed that the partial elasticity coefficients of informal sector employment with respect to different components of the formal sector employment including the organized industry were extremely low in magnitude though positive in sign. And this would explain why in relative terms there is a negative relationship between organized/formal industry and informal sector employment. The inverse relation between industrialization and informal sector is indicative of the lack of strong inter-linkages and the absence of possibilities of complementary relationship between the sectors (Mitra, 2001). However, based on the NSSO's estimate of informal sector, the effect of industry and urbanization both on the former is found to be statistically insignificant (Table 4.7). In other words, states which are highly industrialized and urbanized and states which are not so, both show a large size of the informal sector in the rural as well as urban areas. This is in conformity with the view which Papola (1981) suggested: the large size of the informal sector in states with low level of industrialization is mostly of residual type whereas the same in industrialized states reveals complementary relationship between industry and informal sector, that is, the possibilities of sub-contracting result in a large size of the informal sector in the industrialized states. If wages in some of the informal sector activities have shown an increasing pattern in the recent past, the linkage effect as perceived by Papola (1981) can be a possible explanation.

Clustering within the Informal Sector[3]

As we turn to the unorganized manufacturing, trade, and services based on the National Sample Survey (NSS, 2010–11) data, two components are perceptible: own account manufacturing enterprises (OAEs) and the establishments. First of all the distribution of the unorganized sector across states is not even. The OAEs in the rural areas are mostly concentrated in Andhra Pradesh (AP), Karnataka (KAR), Madhya Pradesh (MP), Maharashtra (MH), Odisha (ODS), Uttar Pradesh (UP) and West Bengal (WB) (each with a more than 5 per cent share) and among them AP, UP, and WB alone constitute almost 45 per cent of the units in the whole of rural India (Table 4.8). As regards the establishments again AP, Kerala (KER), Tamil Nadu (TN), UP, and WB constitute more than 50 per cent of the units in the rural areas (Table 4.8).

In the urban areas also AP, Gujarat (GUJ), Madhya Pradesh (MP), Maharashtra (MH), TN, UP, and WB comprise more than 70 per cent of the OAEs and similarly in terms of establishments many of them are concentrated in AP, Delhi (DEL), GUJ, MH, TN, UP, and WB. This pattern tends to suggest that states with higher urbanization levels, per capita income and also rapid industrialization and modernization levels tend to encourage the growth of the unorganized manufacturing units though there are certain exceptions such as MP, ODS, and UP: handicrafts, cottage industries, and other home based activities at times provide a major source of livelihood in not-so-dynamic areas. The question now is whether a similar pattern prevails in the trade and services components as well.

In the case of trade sector again a similar pattern is evident. Rural OAEs are concentrated in the states of AP, MH, OD, UP, and WB and the rural establishments are mostly located in AP, Assam (ASM), KER, MH, TN, UP, and WB. AP, GUJ, KAR, MP, MH, TN, UP, and WB comprise nearly 70 per cent of the urban OAEs and the urban establishments are located largely in AP, DEL, GUJ, KAR, MH, TN, UP, and WB.

In the case of services rural OAEs are seen largely in AP, BH (Bihar), MH, OD, TN, UP, WB, and the rural establishments are found in AP, BH, KER, MH, OD, Rajasthan (RAJ), TN, UP, and WB. The urban OAEs are located in a significant manner in AP, GUJ, MAH, TN, UP, WB and a large proportion of the urban establishments are situated at AP, DEL, GUJ, KAR, MH, TN, UP, and WB. Since the services sector constitutes several residual type activities the low-income states such as BH, ODS, RAJ, and UP appear in the list. The coefficient of variation is not much different across manufacturing, trade, and services or within an activity across OAEs and establishments.

---

[3]	For details, see Mitra and Pandey (2016).

Table 4.8 Percentage Distribution of Manufacturing, Trade, and Services Enterprises: 2010–11

States/UTs	Rural Manufacturing		Urban Manufacturing		Rural Trade		Urban Trade		Rural Services		Urban Services	
	OAE	EST	OAE	EST	OAE	EST	OAE	EST	OAE	EST	OAE	EST
Andhra Pradesh	9.69	11.56	9.15	7.61	7.97	8.86	7.3	7.74	14.94	7.49	10.42	7.65
Arunachal Pradesh	0.01	0.02	0	0.02	0.09	0.13	0.07	0.08	0.01	0.03	0.01	0.04
Assam	1.57	4.76	0.27	0.8	3.93	6.64	0.99	2.11	2.89	3.7	0.69	0.95
Bihar	3.84	2.53	0.97	1.15	7.12	2.47	2.48	1.56	7.16	5.68	2.02	1.92
Chhattisgarh	1.2	0.94	0.69	0.5	1.73	1.39	0.92	2.02	1.12	1.4	0.92	1.22
Delhi	0.03	0.27	1.23	7.41	0.11	0.32	3.87	8.82	0.06	0.32	3.11	7.57
Goa	0.02	0.18	0.05	0.13	0.09	0.24	0.08	0.21	0.1	0.28	0.09	0.26
Gujarat	2.5	4.14	17.92	11.06	3.41	4.13	8.54	6.03	2.89	2.95	8.39	6
Haryana	0.74	1.36	1.42	1.86	1.75	3.65	2.54	2.73	1.48	2.17	2.78	2.03
Himachal Pradesh	0.78	0.85	0.14	0.23	0.69	0.95	0.3	0.33	1.1	2.24	0.26	0.4
Jammu & Kashmir	1.34	1.8	1.33	0.68	1.06	1.88	1.06	0.89	0.69	2.92	0.57	0.85
Jharkhand	3.05	1.84	0.56	0.51	3.14	2.29	1.45	1.05	2.47	3.79	1.35	1.34
Karnataka	5.49	3.57	4.52	4.7	4.03	2.87	5.01	7.15	4.58	3.48	4.67	8.12
Kerala	2.88	7.31	2.17	2.94	2.81	12.67	1.68	3.84	4.53	7.32	2.83	3.86
Madhya Pradesh	5.66	2.75	5.67	2.21	4.52	3.83	5.52	3.58	2.97	3.81	4.45	3.75
Maharashtra	6.43	4.28	9.35	14.5	5.94	6.19	12.41	11.34	6.57	6.25	12.91	13.3
Manipur	0.3	0.09	0.22	0.05	0.3	0.1	0.31	0.03	0.15	0.08	0.14	0.11
Meghalaya	0.15	0.42	0.02	0.04	0.29	0.38	0.07	0.11	0.21	1.28	0.04	0.14

Table 4.8 contd.

Table 4.8 contd.

States/UTs	Rural Manufacturing		Urban Manufacturing		Rural Trade		Urban Trade		Rural Services		Urban Services	
	OAE	EST	OAE	EST	OAE	EST	OAE	EST	OAE	EST	OAE	EST
Mizoram	0.02	0.02	0.02	0.04	0.04	0.01	0.07	0.05	0.02	0.04	0.04	0.07
Nagaland	0.06	0.06	0.02	0.01	0.07	0.08	0.05	0.04	0.04	0.12	0.03	0.03
Odisha	5.53	4.42	1	0.79	8.48	3.38	2.16	1.69	5.56	6.05	1.96	1.78
Punjab	1.46	2.89	2.81	4.27	1.66	3.36	3.61	3.86	1.96	3.35	3.11	2.47
Rajasthan	3.16	2.67	4.61	3.81	3.83	3.59	3.82	3.26	3.51	5.79	3.87	3.2
Sikkim	0.01	0	0	0.01	0.07	0.02	0.08	0.04	0.07	0.15	0.03	0.04
Tamil Nadu	6.28	11	13.74	13.54	3.82	7.82	7.69	10.28	5.33	7.27	10.02	11.32
Tripura	0.6	0.73	0.11	0.1	1.69	2.48	0.24	0.07	0.99	1.6	0.21	0.09
Uttaranchal	0.61	1.46	0.27	0.78	0.93	1.43	0.75	0.77	1.06	2.33	0.57	1.15
Uttar Pradesh	14.62	11.55	13.33	10.36	18.6	6.53	16.64	9.29	13.78	11.72	13.32	12.17
West Bengal	21.92	16.29	8.12	9.56	11.72	12	9.85	10.71	13.66	6.1	10.62	7.64
Andaman & N. Islands	0.02	0.03	0.01	0.03	0.03	0.05	0.02	0.04	0.03	0.04	0.03	0.04
Chandigarh	0.01	0.03	0.07	0.04	0.02	0.06	0.26	0.08	0.02	0.03	0.28	0.15
Dadra & N. Haveli	0.01	0.05	0.01	0.01	0.01	0.06	0.01	0.03	0.02	0.1	0.01	0.02
Daman & Diu	0	0.04	0.02	0.01	0.01	0.11	0.02	0.01	0.01	0.05	0.01	0.02
Lakshadweep	0	0	0	0	0	0	0	0	0	0.01	0	0
Puducherry	0.02	0.06	0.17	0.23	0.03	0.03	0.13	0.13	0.03	0.07	0.27	0.27

Table 4.8 contd.

Table 4.8 contd.

States/UTs	Rural Manufacturing		Urban Manufacturing		Rural Trade		Urban Trade		Rural Services		Urban Services	
	OAE	EST	OAE	EST	OAE	EST	OAE	EST	OAE	EST	OAE	EST
All-India	100	100	100	100	100	100	100	100	100	100	100	100
Coeff. Of Variation	162.64	141.35	162.61	149.22	140.04	119.85	141	127.65	142.57	103.52	141.24	135.14

Source: NSS (2010–11) Survey on Unincorporated Non-agricultural Enterprises (excluding Construction).

Note: OAE: Own account enterprise, EST: Establishment.

Table 4.9 Results from Factor Analysis of Data on Percentage Distribution of Enterprises across States: 2010–11

Variables	Factor 1	Factor 2
Rural Manufacturing OAE	0.3991	0.7786
Rural Manufacturing EST	0.4275	0.6070
Urban Manufacturing OAE	0.7859	0.3061
Urban Manufacturing EST	0.9199	0.2260
Rural Trade OAE	0.3499	0.8863
Rural Trade EST	0.3545	0.4093
Urban Trade OAE	0.7924	0.5582
Urban Trade EST	0.8569	0.3328
Rural Services OAE	0.3862	0.7900
Rural Services EST	0.4081	0.6386
Urban Services OAE	0.8061	0.4845
Urban Services EST	0.8831	0.3529
Eigenvalue	9.65	1.10

Source: Author's calculations based on NSS (2010–11) Survey on Unincorporated Non-agricultural Enterprises (excluding Construction).

The correlation matrix again confirms a strong relationship among most of the variables. However, the factor analysis conducted among the percentage distribution of units in various categories across states shows two important factors: (*a*) the urban specific ones are the most dominant ones (urban OAEs manufacturing, urban establishment manufacturing, urban OAEs trade, urban establishment trade, urban OAE services, urban establishment services); (*b*) the next factor is constituted by the rural specific ones (rural OAE manufacturing, rural establishment manufacturing, rural OAEs trade, rural OAEs services, rural establishment services). In other words, the urban specific variables explain most of the variations and are highly interconnected (Table 4.9).

Usually some of the earlier literature suggested that informal trade and services are of the residual type (Udall, 1976), though informal manufacturing may be connected with the large-scale industrialization. However, with a few exceptions we noted from the empirical analysis that unorganized manufacturing, trade, and services all show a strong association inter-spatially. Besides, their concentration in relatively advanced states tend to suggest that the dynamics of growth influence all the three activities positively. Higher per capita income, urbanization, and industrialization can impact small manufacturing and trade simultaneously as both the activities are complementary to each other. Though analytically services may not be connected to manufacturing or trade in that sense, higher incomes generate demand for new services which are provided by the informal segment (see Rakshit, 2007).

Conclusion

Rural poverty is seen to decline in relation to growth, though inequality raises poverty. Further, male literacy and the work participation rate reduce poverty. Similarly, in the urban areas, poverty declines in response to rise in growth, male work participation rate, and male literacy rate, though inequality raises it. More importantly, urbanization shows a strong beneficial effect on poverty as higher levels of urbanization are associated with a lower poverty incidence.

Both rural and urban growth contributes to urbanization. Rural male work participation rate and rural male literacy also add to urbanization as the rural male workers and literates are more likely to migrate to cities in search of better jobs after acquiring work experience and skill. With rural diversification (expansion in non-agricultural activities), the urbanization level also tends to increase as the rural–urban discontinuum in terms of activities tends to break down. The rural areas start urbanizing and migration also becomes easier as the differences in the nature of activities across space get dissipated.

Migration and urban informal sector employment are closely connected. Migrants do not necessarily move in search of jobs within the formal sector only; even the possibility of finding work in the informal sector induces population mobility across space. Further, rural and urban poverty are connected through migration and other state specific characteristics, though migration and increased urbanization levels tend to reduce both rural and urban poverty. Unorganized manufacturing, trade, and services all show a strong association inter-spatially. Besides, their concentration in relatively advanced states suggests that the dynamics of growth influences all the three activities positively. While some of these positive changes are discernible, urban areas will have to be made more inclusive through interventions in order to reduce poverty significantly and improve the overall well-being.

On the whole, urbanization due to limited demand for labour is not able to absorb the rural surplus labour productively. States with both higher and lower levels of urbanization seem to be having poor quality employment, which explains why there is no relationship between the level of urbanization and the incidence of the informal sector. Further, from the supply point of view, the labour migrating to urban areas has poor employable skills. Third, there are costs associated with migration which discourage the flow of population from rural to urban areas. So the major policy challenge is how to raise the level of urbanization and make it of better quality so that the enhanced level of urbanization can be taken as a positive indicator of development. The agglomeration benefits can be utilized in the direction of poverty reduction, which would indeed be cost effective. Expansion in labour intensive and productive activities is a prerequisite. Besides, the productivity growth that takes place in large cities can partly be utilized for providing social and infrastructure support and training facilities to low-income households. The land market, which is under severe speculation, has reduced the accessibility of low-income migrants to city space. In terms of housing and neighbourhood characteristics, employment and earnings, and accessibility to public services, there is glaring evidence on a segregation process alongside the growth process. Therefore, the policy focus needs to be developed to make the overall urbanization process generative so that it results in better labour market outcomes and becomes inclusive by creating a more conducive environment for the rural migrants, rather than treating rural-to-urban population movement as a negative epithet.

CHAPTER 5

Upward Mobility of the Disadvantaged Sections

Perspective

In what way human behaviour intermingles with changing economic activities and results in better sources of livelihood for making the urbanization process inclusive is a pertinent issue. The disadvantaged section can be conceptualized in a number of ways. The most convenient way of capturing it is to focus on those who suffer from housing poverty. In what way the slum households located at the lowest rungs of urban space do or do not benefit in the process of urbanization can then be analysed with profundity.

Focussing on the survival strategies of the slums we note that migrants, particularly from the rural areas, access information on the urban labour market through various informal channels, and hope to experience upward income mobility by migrating to the urban areas.[1] However, one missing area of research relates to the segmented nature of the urban labour market due to specialization of activities in different areas (zones) within a city. Segmentation along the lines of caste, skill, and education has of course drawn adequate attention of the scholars, but the physical segmentation of the labour market is an issue that has received relatively less attention. By physical segmentation we mean inaccessibility of certain kinds of jobs by certain group of individuals, primarily because of the distance factor within a city: high-income jobs may be available in a particular locality, but their physical distance from the place where one specific group of migrants resides in the city could be so enormous that such jobs may remain inaccessible to them. Even inexpensive (intra-city) transport for commutation need not eliminate these

[1]   Materials have been drawn from Mitra (2008, 2010a, 2010b, 2013).

labour market barriers, especially in developing countries. Hence, occupational choice is greatly determined by the narrow spectrum of jobs available within the geographic area where the migrants reside, rather than by what they are capable of pursuing. Contact-based migration tends to provide jobs in neighbourhoods close to their residence: the early settlers help their relatives, friends, members of the same caste groups and co-villagers to migrate to the city by providing information on job and space to settle down, which is often in the same gamut of space and activities that they themselves have access to. As a result, occupational choice is more or less supply-driven, though from the macro point of view—keeping the entire city in the perspective—the equilibrium choice of occupation would be the outcome of both demand and supply side factors. This is also in sharp contrast to the popular interpretation of informal sector employment, namely the supply (of labour) 'push' phenomenon. This perception gets further substantiated by the fact that intra-city differences (across space) in terms of development, infrastructure, and activities are too significant to be ignored.

The work of Banerjee and Bucci (1994) based on labour market in Delhi evidenced rural-based search for urban jobs. It confirmed that about one half of the rural migrants moved after fixing a job or after receiving assurances of employment from those with whom they had contact in the urban areas. This proportion was almost the same in both formal and informal sector entrants, indicating that informal sector jobs also act as pull factors for migration, rather than offering only a stop-gap arrangement as the probabilistic models would hold. On the whole, the contact factor plays a crucial role in obtaining the desired employment within a short time span.

Further, we argue here that migrants in low-income households prefer to reside near the workplace and that the role of contact is not confined to merely information on jobs. It often provides shelter in the initial stages and helps in settling down. The co-villagers, relatives, kith, and friends have a strong tendency to live in the vicinity of the early settlers primarily because the jobs obtained through contacts are quite similar to those of the contact persons, particularly in the case of manual and unskilled jobs as also observed by Banerjee (1986).

The urge to reside near the workplace is determined by a large number of factors, some of which could be traced to the very nature of activities the migrants perform. The self-employed workers in petty manufacturing and repairing activities often have their enterprises within the household premises (see Sethuraman, 1976). Similarly the self-employed and wage labourers in trading activities are required to use their workplace for residential purposes as well, from the security point of view. Sometimes their encroachment on public land poses the threat of demolition, and their constant vigilance of the unit of operation may be essential. At other times they are engaged by their employers outside the working hours to check burglary. This enables them to reduce their expenditure on rent thus reducing their cost of living in the city. Besides, community latrine and provision of drinking water in the market place attract many of them to reside close to the workplace.

Another reason to stay in the vicinity can be identified in terms of multi-jobs that the members of the low-income migrant households usually take up. Women, who combine their household activities with jobs outside home (for example, domestic maids) are engaged in similar kind of jobs but in a large number of households, and prefer to have the place of work and place of residence close to each other. Even if the total income earned from all jobs is less than the income which could have been earned from the job available at a distant place, the former would be preferred as long as the cost of commuting and the opportunity cost of the time spent on commuting are large enough to reduce the potential earnings as compared to the actual earnings. Perhaps this could be a reason why Banerjee (1986) observed in Delhi that even a majority of informal-wage sector entrants, who are believed to be the vulnerable lot, did not continue their search after joining the first job.

The reason to reside in the neighbourhood of their relatives and friends or co-villagers deduces its roots from—other than economic factors—sociological and political factors also. With wide regional diversities in the cultural background of the migrants, in the face of their difficulties to adapt themselves to an urban cosmopolitan culture of the upper-income groups, and their urge to keep alive and enjoy in the city, their cultural identity induces them to reside in close proximity to each other. In India, the multilingual and multi-ethnic identities of its citizens make such phenomenon even more important. Thus, the more heterogeneous culturally and ethnically an area/country is, the more likely it is that migrants would seek to settle in and around the areas of their brethren. Besides, as mentioned earlier, activities of the contact persons (early entrants) and the late entrants being mostly similar, sharing of family or individual endowment in their pursuit of economic goals becomes almost inevitable. Efforts to delay demolition programmes planned by the city administrators, and attainment of quasi-permanent residential rights in the city are realized only through collective efforts which help secure the political patronage in exchange of their promise to operate as vote banks.

After mentioning the importance of contact in securing jobs and the urge to reside in groups formed on the basis of caste–kinship–co-villager bonds, and the preference of the low-income migrant households to be located near the workplace, we now turn to the development of various nodes (centres) within the city, each characterized by specialized activities. As the literature on agglomeration (particularly the localization) economies suggests, firms conducting similar activities tend to locate close to each other so as to reap the economies of scale (Henderson, 1988). Extending this argument—usually made at the inter-city level to explain the differences in activities that cities specialize in—to the intra-city level, the heterogeneity across space even within a specific city can be noted. In other words, not all areas would conduct all activities—each would be responsible for the growth of a predominant activity depending upon the availability of resources required for its generation. Thus different centres within a city would have specialized activities, though from the overall city point of view all activities would appear to exist within its territory, thus creating the myth of a vast labour market. Empirically also, the heterogeneity of the city structure across space has been documented: the study by Dupont and Mitra (1995) divided the city of Delhi into several small units—census charges—and observed wide inter-spatial variations of socio-economic characteristics and activities. Further, they also found an incidental matching of these socio-economic variables with geographic zones of the city: while certain attributes were more conspicuously present in certain zones, others were absent in other zones.

The literature on social capital and livelihood issues is quite rich. As we begin with a discussion of some of the studies it not only helps us formulate the hypothesis in a meaningful way but also allows us to understand the links intensely. The notion of social capital as suggested by Putnam (1993) has been used extensively to account for a wide variety of outcomes (Dasgupta and Serageldin, 2000). The two key elements of social capital include the resource endowments of one's associates and the social relationship itself through which associates' resources can be accessed (Portes, 1998 and Ioannides and Datcher Loury, 2004). Though job search through informal channels such as friends and relatives is generally said to be productive (Ioannides and Datcher Loury, 2004), there are, however, reservations against Putnam's (1993) work (Dasgupta and Serageldin, 2000).

Irrespective of their nature,[2] the informal contacts, as some of the studies noted, are indeed important for accessing means of livelihood, particularly among the low-income households. Elliott (1999) noted that workers from high-poverty

---

[2]   The channels of information-flow and support mechanisms at times are given exogenously in the sense that the contacts that the job seekers have with close relatives, members of the same caste groups, and friends are an outcome of long-term interactions and familial ties carried over generations. However, in due course some of the contacts are developed gradually and they are endogenous from the individual point of view. Channels operating through previous/present employers/colleagues are possibly some examples of such endogenously determined contacts.

neighbourhoods were substantially more likely to use informal job search methods than those from low-poverty neighbourhoods. Through the informal networks mutual benefits are ensured (Stark, 1995; Mitra, 2004). The job search theory, as Mortensen (1986) writes, portrays the decision maker's acquisition and use of information to take rational action in an environment that is ever changing and uncertain. The 'social capital' theory supplies this link between the decision maker's willingness to pursue rational action and the information required to do so.

The other dimension of social network relates to its variations across activities. Even within the set of informal networks differences across activities can be located: depending upon the kind of network that one has, his/her occupational choice gets determined accordingly. Networks which operate through purely familial ties are less likely to provide skilled jobs (Ioannides and Datcher Loury, 2004). Those employed in own account enterprises operating in sales and trading activities help their relatives and friends access similar kinds of activities as the requirement in terms of skill and financial capital and other barriers to entry in these occupations are nominal. On the other hand, as job aspirants look beyond the familial ties and access private contractors for example, wage employment in manufacturing and commercial services becomes accessible. Similarly, neighbours and co-villagers may provide more diversified information on the job market than the close relatives.

We may now turn to the other class of literature in this area, which highlights the negative aspect of networks. First, the existence of networks—given the specialization of activities in different parts of the city leading to heterogeneity in the city's economic structure—leads to market information asymmetry resulting in physical segmentation of the labour market (Mitra, 2004). Further, excess supply of labour in certain activities reduces the possibility of upward movement in incomes. Also, in the long run, the scope of experiencing upward income mobility remains quite modest as the contact persons and the new migrants both pursue their jobs in similar activities and in the same neighbourhoods. The surplus resources, which could be utilized for productive channels, are often spent on social commitments, which may be directed towards reducing each other's uncertainties relating to housing, income, consumption, and health. But the lack of direct investment on productivity-enhancing projects and human capital formation restricts the scope for upward mobility to a much larger extent than what the indirect gains may usher in. Also, the social ties do not often release them from the close cohorts they have formed and do not allow them to diversify their job search across space. Hence, the trade-offs between social inter-mingling and economic gains may turn out to be substantive: Elliott (1999) noted that for less-educated workers the use of informal contacts results in significantly lower wages.

The paper by Kono (2006) demonstrates that hiring workers through employee referrals reduces the new applicants' payoffs while a diversification of networks can raise their payoffs. In the market with information asymmetry the 'lemon effect' that is, the decrease in the market equilibrium wage induced by the increase in network density (Montgomery, 1991), is caused by network extension or pursuance of similar networks while network diversification raises referral wages through the bargaining effect (Kono, 2006). Empirically, Munshi and Rosenzweig (2006) noted that male 'working-class-lower-caste-networks' in Bombay continue to channel boys into local language schools that lead to the traditional occupation although returns to non-traditional white-collar occupations rose substantially in the nineties. On the whole, benefits of the network come with social obligations (Luke and Munshi, 2006) and thus it may result in sluggish or no upward mobility of both the contact persons and the new entrants. Munshi (2003) observed that there is an externality associated with the individual's migration decision: Mexican migrants in the US face a strong pressure to remain in low-skill jobs that have traditionally been chosen to maintain the stability of the network. In other words, stability of the network has implications in terms of low levels of education and low-skill occupations.

On the whole, the debate in the area of social capital and urban job market accessibility relates on the one hand to the importance of networks in seeking livelihood and on the other, the negative role of social capital in experiencing upward mobility. In the context of migration the most pertinent issue revolves around the possible economic gains associated with population mobility.[3] From an empirical standpoint the present chapter therefore proposes to examine two specific questions. First, how important the informal networks are in accessing jobs; second, whether the informal networks tend to restrict upward mobility in the long run. A related question also is whether migrants tend to improve their well-being at the place of destination.

Social Capital and Occupations

Based on a fairly detailed listing of activities/occupations, the workers in our survey of slum households in Delhi (2004–5) have been broadly categorized into eight occupation classes. The distribution of slum workers shows that a very large

---

[3] In explaining migration across space, income differentials are taken as motivating factors in moving people from low-income areas to relatively high-income ones (Harris and Todaro, 1970). Lall, Selod and Shalizi (2006) synthesize the current state of knowledge concerning internal migration in developing countries.

percentage of them are engaged in sales and trade (nearly 30 per cent). Next to that is manufacturing, accounting for nearly 20 per cent of the workers. The male–female differences in terms of occupational distribution are quite evident particularly in relation to activities such as personal services, transport, construction, and tailoring. While personal services and tailoring are quite dominant activities in the case of female workers (accounting for nearly 45 per cent) and employ male workers marginally, transport and construction each employ 10 per cent of the total male workers with a negligible presence of female workers. The detailed description of activities indicates that most of them are engaged in the informal sector or employed informally in the formal sector.[4]

Since slums receive population primarily through migration it may be useful to cite a few major characteristics relating to the migrants. Nearly 85 per cent of the slum population in the sample migrated from the rural areas of the adjoining states though they have been residing in the city for more than 10 years. Many of them possess poor levels of human capital including education, skill, and training. Another 10 per cent of the sample moved to the city in the last ten years and the rest were found to be natives. However, those who have been staying in the city for more than ten years cannot be interpreted as fresh migrants. Hence we redefine 'migrants' as those who moved into the city in last ten years or less and the category 'others' includes non-migrants and migrants of more than 10 years duration. The headcount measure of consumption poverty turns out to be 57.08 and 61.85 per cent among migrants up to 10 years duration and 'others' respectively. Given these poor living standards it is quite important to assess how social networks help them cope with uncertainties.

Since the incidence of all-duration migration is high in the sample, it may be interesting to identify some of the factors which cause and influence population mobility.[5] The empirical results suggest that those in larger households are less likely to be migrants (0 to 10 years duration) possibly because of the high cost of migration associated with large households' mobility. With a rise in the age, the

---

4 The informal sector is characterized by small size, lack of union, low capital–labour ratio and the inapplicability of government regulation. Informally employed in the formal sector means contract labour hired through other agencies, that is, dispatched labour and casual daily wage labour working in the formal sector.

5 However, due to the lack of information at the place of migration this kind of an exercise could not be carried out with precision. On the other hand, we have attempted a binomial logit model distinguishing between the migrants up to 10 years duration (represented by 1) and the non-migrants including the very long duration migrants who have been residing in the city for more than 10 years (represented by 0). This exercise is pursued at the individual level.

probability of being a migrant increases though after a certain threshold level it declines, implying that very old persons are rather more likely to be natives or very long duration migrants than being fresh migrants. In other words, the propensity to migrate is high in relatively younger age brackets, and this declines with age. Among occupational categories, personal services (manufacturing) tend to have more (less) migrant workers than natives while other activities seem to have an almost equal incidence of both types of workers. Households with property at the place of origin (rural areas) are less likely to move to the city permanently whereas for those without property it is possibly easier to take a decision to migrate on the long-term basis. On the other hand, the very long duration migrants are more likely to have political contacts than the relatively short duration migrants. Those with lower and higher levels of education seem to have the same propensity to migrate as that of the illiterates. On the whole, the relatively young people with or without education, without property at the place of origin and job market experience show a higher propensity to migrate to the city from their rural residence. This in turn leads to a residual absorption of labour in low-productivity activities with relatively less entry barriers. Subsequently, by accessing political contacts they fall into the trap of perpetual misery. How informal networks help them cope with uncertainties particularly in an anonymous urban atmosphere is indeed an interesting issue to which we turn below.

The occupational choice model estimated by Mitra (2008) to capture the effect of social capital perceives networks in terms of contacts with (*a*) relatives, (*b*) co-villagers and neighbours, (*c*) members of the same caste group, (*d*) friends, (*e*) colleagues at or employer of the present or previous job, (*f*) religious organizations, NGOs, and private contractors, and (*g*) slum or community leader.[6] Along with network dummies, educational categories,[7] household size, caste groups

---

[6] (NTW1), (NTW2), (NTW3), (NTW4), (NTW5), (NTW6), and (NTW7) respectively.

Though part of NTW6 (those who accessed jobs through government employment exchanges) does not fall into the domain of social capital, their number is minuscule and, hence these cases have been clubbed with the rest.

The effect of the networks mentioned above is examined in the occupational choice model keeping self-initiative (that is, those who pursued job search independently) as the comparison category.

[7] Dummies (EDUi = 1, 2.3): with illiterates as the reference category, EDU1 represents those who are literate and those who have studied up to a maximum of class 9, EDU2 encompasses those who have studied above class 9 and completed secondary education but not graduation, and EDU3 represents graduates or those who have acquired a higher level of education including technical and non-technical, professional, and vocational courses.

differentiating among Scheduled Caste/Tribe, backward castes, and the rest as the comparison group, migration of different durations, gender differences, access to political contact, and the availability of property at the place of origin and age as a proxy for experience in the job market are included as explanatory variables. Age-square is also considered to verify if accessibility to a particular job declines after a certain age.

Empirical results suggest that many of the network dummies are significant, and the differences in networks operating across occupations are also evident. For example, in trade and sales relatives, co-villagers and neighbours, members of the same caste group, and friends; in personal services relatives and co-villagers; in manufacturing and commercial services relatives, co-villagers, friends, colleagues at or employer of the present or previous job, religious organizations, NGOs, and private contractors are important determinants. Similarly in transport NTW1, NTW2, and NTW4, in tailoring NTW1, NTW2, NTW3 and NTW4 and in construction NTW1, NTW4 and NTW6 are statistically significant. It is evident that the informal channels of information flow are dominant over the formal channels. The NTW6 is seen to be important only in the case of manufacturing, commercial services and construction mainly because the role of private contractors in recruiting labour and supplying to other organizations has become a distinct phenomenon after the economic reforms initiated in 1991.

The fact that informal networks play a crucial role in accessing jobs and that they vary across occupations, suggests that even within the informal sector not all activities are available to all the job seekers. Depending upon the nature of contact they land up in different activities though the impact of other variables like work experience, household size and gender is important as well. The caste factor does not turn out to be significant, possibly indicating its less relevance in the urban setup, particularly in the context of informal sector or informal employment, to which neither the reservation policy nor the caste-specific discriminating factor applies. The education dummies are significant in some of the activities like sales and trade, manufacturing, commercial services, and tailoring whereas in activities like construction and personal services they are least important. On the whole, the relevance of networks tends to strengthen the premise of excess supplies of labour in certain activities. Various types of informal channels of information flow that operate in the society pertaining to the urban labour market determine the ultimate selection of occupation. In other words, depending upon the nature of contact that one is able to cultivate, the job accessibility is determined, though in such a situation the activity pursued by the contact person is most likely to be the entry point of the newcomer as well (Mitra, 2004).

The prevalence of low-income jobs across activities without much variability is a strong possibility as the occupational differences captured through dummies do not turn out to be significant in explaining the variations in individual income.[8] With age, income increases but beyond a threshold level it shows signs of decline. Relative to the non-migrants the migrants tend to have lower levels of income, possibly because the natives are able to access the relatively high-income jobs first. The gender differentials in terms of earnings are also evident indicating lower earnings for women workers. From policy point of view what is noteworthy is that with higher levels of education incomes tend to increase.[9]

Mobility

Usually mobility is studied in terms of occupation and also income though the latter is widely preferred.[10] It can cover a period ranging from one or two years to much longer periods involving intergenerational change (Narayan and Petesch, 2012). Fox and Miller (1965) studied the intergenerational mobility across countries in terms of an occupational shift from manual to non-manual or vice versa in relation to the determinants such as GDP per capita, education, urbanization, political stability, and achievement motivation. McAllister (1995) talked about three forms of occupational mobility of the migrants: intergenerational mobility, career mobility and migratory mobility. Several studies noted that an overwhelmingly large proportion of migrants settled for low-status jobs in the early years upon arrival, and later the job status improved significantly conforming to a U-shaped curve (Bagahna, 1991; Melendez 1994; Nguyen, 2005; Raijman and Semyonov, 1995). A shift from an occupation which bears more manual work to an occupation with less manual work can be treated as upward mobility though it is not necessarily a shift in terms of 'class' as defined on the basis of hierarchy at work (Weber, 1968).[11]

Fields (2000)[12] describes five basic approaches to conceiving income mobility: time dependence measures the extent of change in one's current position determined by the past position; positional movement gauges changes to an individual's

---

[8] Average incomes of course showed differences across activities.
[9] However, those who are just literates or studied up to class 9 earn as low as the illiterates.
[10] See Mitra (2010a, 2010b) for details.
[11] Social class concept is grounded in the presumption that the social location of individuals is determined primarily by their employment status and job characteristics (Grusky and Kanbur, 2006).
[12] As summarized by Narayan and Petesch (2012).

position in the income distribution; share movement captures changes in the share of income; symmetric income movement identifies the magnitude but not the direction of movements, and directional income movement weighs the fraction of upward and downward movers and the change in the average amount of the gainers and losers. Baulch and Hoddinott (2000) present studies using household longitudinal data ranging from 18 months to 18 years to examine poverty dynamics and economic mobility. In studying such movements, households which move in and out of poverty over time can be identified and so also their vulnerability changes in relation to changes in their endowments and the returns to those assets.

Among the various determinants of mobility transport, network is an important one. It is not evenly spread out in all parts of the city to facilitate labour mobility. It rather has a strong bias in favour of the well-off (Dayal et al., 2012). Nor are the transport costs too low to facilitate mobility of the low-income households between their workplace and residence. Hence, many slum dwellers have a strong preference to reside near the workplace. Thus, there is enough reason to presume segmentation along the lines of job availability, accessibility to job market information, and ability to participate in the jobs within a given city. Particularly for the well-off, geography does not matter; however, for the low-income households it is indeed a significant factor which may restrict upward mobility.

The size and distribution of the local middle class is a significant determinant of upward mobility of the poor. It is observed that all else being equal, upward mobility is higher in metropolitan areas where poor families are more dispersed among mixed-income neighbourhoods (Leonhardt, 2013 referring to the work of Chetty et al., 2013). The middle-income households are not only role models for the low-income households but also are charitable in providing guidance to the latter. This argument can be further stretched to suggest that even within a metropolitan region slum clusters adjacent to the middle-income households may show a greater drive in improving their economic conditions compared to the ones which are located at the outskirts.

In the context of the urban slums dominated by the low-income households, upward mobility cannot be visualized unless one is able to take a long time horizon of at least a decade or so.[13] Those who are already in the relatively high-income strata are less likely to undergo further increase within a short time frame. Similarly, those with higher levels of education are likely to have been placed in

---

[13] See Rosenzweig (2003) suggesting that household-level panel surveys that cover time periods of a decade or more have the potential for studying economic mobility.

jobs of desirable status, and thus for them upward mobility actually can be sluggish within a limited time range. With an increase in educational levels, wages also increase and the probability of acquiring formal sector employment again rises (Gong and Soest, 2002; Gong et al., 2004). However, if the incidence of illiteracy was already low in the base year, further increase in the income of the educated ones is less probable to occur. Chetty et al. (2013) also noted in the context of USA that the children from smaller towns showed a strong association with upward mobility in later life. Following some of these views we argue that the poorest would rather have a greater expectation and a stronger drive to experience increased mobility in a region that is characterized by strong forces of dynamism and growth. They have moved to such cities compromising on living conditions in their rural place of origin or in small towns to which they could have migrated, primarily with the motivation that agglomeration effects would result in better outcomes for a given level of initial endowment. However, while assessing the standard literature on upward mobility we need to be careful enough to allow for significant deviations that may possibly arise across countries pertaining to social, cultural and familial practices.

Econometric Analysis of Upward Mobility[14]

In order to identify the determinants and the possibilities of upward mobility among the low-income households we have used a binomial logit model applied to the data on slum households from our primary survey (2006–7) in four cities: Jaipur, Ludhiana, Mathura, and Ujjain. The variables included in the model to identify those which raise (or reduce) the probability of experiencing upward mobility are household size, gender (taken in the form of a dummy with 0 for males and 1 for females), age of the worker as a proxy for job market experience, levels of education of the workers taken in terms of three dummies with illiteracy as the comparison category (EDU1 takes a value of 1 for those who studied up to primary level and 0 otherwise; EDU2, 1 for those who studied above primary level but up to secondary and 0 otherwise; EDU3, 1 for those who studied above secondary and 0 otherwise), migration status taken in terms of four dummies with non-migrants as the comparison category (MIGD1 takes a value of 1 for those who migrated in last 5 years, MIGD2, 1 for those who migrated in last 5 to 10

---

[14]   See Mitra (2010a, 2010b) for details.

years, MIGD3, 1 for those who migrated in last 10 to 15 years and MIGD4, 1 for those who migrated more than 15 years ago), occupation categories based on dummies, and finally the types of networks that the workers used in accessing the job market information. Nine dummies (OCCPi = 1 ... 9) have been used for the nine occupation categories taking other workers (or unspecified workers) as the comparison group. The nine occupations include semi-professionals, sales and trade, personal services, manufacturing, commercial service and security workers, transport, tailoring, construction, and labour. Four network dummies (NETi= 1 ... 4) have been used, taking those who depended on self-initiative as the comparison category. NET1 takes a value of 1 for those who used the connections with family members to access the job market information. NET2 refers to those who accessed jobs through general relatives (other than family members or close relatives). NET3 represents friends, neighbours, members of the same caste group and co-villagers, and so on, and NET4 corresponds to formal institutions such as employment exchanges or any welfare organization run by NGOs, employers of the previous or current jobs, and so on. Recalling the hypothesis, our major objective is to examine if the traditional or informal networks tend to reduce the probability of upward mobility though they offer survival strategies.

Empirical results suggest that networks operating through close relatives neither enhance nor reduce the probability of upward mobility (Table 5.1). On the other hand, networks which include general relatives (other than close relatives) reduce the probability of upward mobility in Jaipur. In Mathura also it shows a similar effect though not significant at 10 per cent level. In the other two cities the networks of general relatives turn out to be highly insignificant. Networks, which represent friends, neighbours, members of the same caste group, co-villagers, and so on, reduce the probability of upward mobility in Jaipur. Though a similar effect is evident in Ludhiana and Ujjain also, it is not significant at 10 per cent level. On the other hand, NET4, representing formal institutions, raises the probability of upward mobility in all the three cities except Jaipur. Strictly speaking, though it is statistically significant only in Ujjain, the effect is not completely negligible in Ludhiana and Mathura. On the whole, these findings tend to suggest that informal networks do not have any positive effect on upward mobility while formal networks do reveal such a tendency. This is despite the fact that the informal networks are indeed inevitable in providing an access to the urban job market in the initial stages.

Table 5.1 Network and Upward Income Mobility: Binomial Logit Model (Maximum Likelihood Estimates)

Explanatory Variables	Jaipur	Ludhiana	Mathura	Ujjain
Age of Worker	0.018	0.022	0.019	0.032
	(2.79)**	(2.30)**	(2.22)**	(4.01)**
Household Size	-0.010	0.530	-0.059	0.023
	(-0.48)	(1.15)	(-1.40)	(0.52)
Gender Dummy	-0.068	-1.167	-0.047	-0.493
	(-.0.32)	(-2.29)**	(-0.11)	(-1.70)*
Primary Education	0.104	-0.479	-0.933	-0.112
	(0.57)	(-1.56)	(-2.39)**	(-0.42)
Secondary Education	0.003	-0.336	-0.160	-0.299
	(0.02)	(-1.35)	(-0.59)	(-1.02)
Above Secondary	0.261	-0.233	-0.407	0.257
	(0.84)	(-0.65)	(-1.21)	(0.65)
Migration in last 5 Years	-0.412	-0.384	-1.014	-0.051
	(-1.30)	(-1.02)	(-2.41)**	(-0.13)
Migration: >5 to 10 Years	0.212	-0.230	-0.353	-0.439
	(0.70)	(-0.61)	(-0.90)	(-0.93)
Migration: >10 to 15 Years	0.322	0.345	0.058	-0.235
	(1.01)	(1.03)	(0.14)	(-0.46)
Migration: >15 Years	0.314	0.147	0.064	-0.336
	(1.56)	(0.54)	(0.21)	(-1.05)
NET1 (Family Members)	0.061	-0.160	-0.064	-0.426
	(0.31)	(-0.47)	(-0.21)	(-0.83)
NET2 (General Relatives)	-0.645	0.193	-1.343	0.314
	(-2.78)**	(0.43)	(-1.3)	(0.54)
NET3 (Friends, Neighbours, etc.,	-0.372	-0.424	0.408	-0.605
	(-1.84)*	(-1.29)	(0.98)	(-1.53)
NET4 (Formal Institutions)	-0.298	2.35	0.589	1.528
	(-0.46)	(1.47)	(1.29)	(2.95)**
OCCP1 (Semi-Professionals)	-.0708	-0.540	0.341	0.143
	(-1.50)	(-1.10)	(0.58)	(0.19)
OCCP2 (Sales and Trade)	-0.158	-0.336	0.560	-0.012
	(-0.38)	(-0.85)	(1.06)	(-0.02)
OCCP3 (Personal Services)	-0.577	-0.265	-0.193	-1.379
	(-1.29)	(-0.47)	(-0.29)	(-1.51)

Table 5.1 contd.

Table 5.1 contd.

Explanatory Variables	Jaipur	Ludhiana	Mathura	Ujjain
OCCP4 (Manufacturing)	-0.170	-0.572	-0.149	-0.311
	(-0.37)	(-1.32)	(-0.24)	(-0.41)
OCCP5 (Commercial	-0.743	-0.932	1.279	0.454
Services)	(-0.79)	(-1.31)	(1.66)*	(0.55)
OCCP6 (Transport)	-0.218	-0.790	0.349	-0.039
	(-0.49)	(-0.16)	(0.59)	(-0.05)
OCCP7 (Tailoring)	-0.753	-0.614	-0.195	-0.568
	(-1.60)	(-1.29)	(-0.21)	(-0.54)
OCCP8 (Construction)	-0.436	-0.729	1.004	0.263
	(-1.00)	(-1.12)	(1.65)*	(0.33)
OCCP9 (Labour)	-0.503	0.529	-0.695	-0.339
	(-0.91)	(1.06)	(-1.12)	(-0.48)
Constant	0.077	-1.951	-1.874	-2.715
	(0.16)	(-3.35)**	(-2.68)**	(-3.10)**
Chi-Sq	40.85	52.05	48.72	53.78
No. of observations	903	796	722	887

Source: Based on author's survey data (2006–7).

Note: ** and * represent significance at 5 and 10 per cent levels, respectively. Given the large sets of observations in each of the four cities we have considered significance at 10 per cent level also instead of judging it at 5 per cent level only. The chi-square values are significant at 1 per cent level.

Among the other variables, the age of the worker is an important determinant of upward mobility. Household size (though not significant at 10 per cent level) shows a negative effect in Mathura. Education does not show any positive effect on upward mobility. Migrants who moved to the city in last five years were less likely to improve their income compared to other long duration migrants and non-migrants. The very long duration migrants (more than 15 years) show a higher probability of experiencing upward income mobility only in Jaipur though it is hardly significant at 10 per cent level.

On the whole, from the slum survey (2006–7) in four other cities the traditional networks are seen to reduce the pace of mobility. With city size upward mobility varies positively implying that large cities offer better opportunities (Mitra, 2010a, 2010b). Even the well-being levels in the slums tend to improve with city size (Mitra, 2010a, 2010b), supporting the positive effect of agglomeration economies on living standards and other measures of well-being.

Mobility Envisaged from Inter-temporal Surveys[15]

Keeping in view some of the correlates of mobility suggested in the literature as cited above, this study tries and explains the income mobility overtime (surveys in Delhi conducted in 2007–8 and 2012; Mitra and Tsujita, 2014). We are not in a position to study the inter-generational mobility in this chapter—we cover only the mobility (or its absence) of individuals who have been working earlier and now, with a time gap of around five years. Though a duration of five years is too short a period in this context, Delhi being a high growth centre and also the national capital, this time frame is adequate to decipher mobility, if any. In order to identify the importance of some of the variables such as education, geographical differences, and past income in determining the upward mobility we have estimated a binomial probit model.

The sample is confined to those who worked in both the survey years. The possibility of collinearity between education and past income cannot be ruled out. Besides, the time difference is only of five years which may not bring in any substantial increase in the income of those who were already better-off, relatively speaking. Rather, those without education or in the lower-income brackets are likely to have put in efforts to maximize their income. A number of other variables have been controlled for. They include ethnic background, age, gender, migration status etc. With age the possibility of mobility declines as at higher age brackets workers are less likely to change jobs or job status. And in the informal sector in which these workers are mostly employed the concept of income increments does not apply. The labour market again holds less prospects for women workers as far as the upward mobility is concerned. Women's job search is severely constrained by the domestic activities they are required to pursue. Besides, their inability to remain outside home for long hours or travel long distances reduces their bargaining strength considerably. Even with similar levels of human capital women receive less pay compared to the males (Mitra, 2005).

Mobility has been considered mainly in terms of workers' income-increase though the set of explanatory variables includes both past income and consumption alternately. The results from the probit model are presented in Table 5.2 addressing the issue of upward mobility directly. Binomial probit model taking 1 for upward mobility and 0 for none has been estimated in terms of certain explanatory variables which are included keeping in view the reasoning presented in the preceding sections: gender dummy (Male, representing 1 for males and 0 for females),

[15] For details, see Mitra and Tsujita (2014) and Mitra and Tsujita (2016).

age (Age), caste-cum-religion dummies (Scheduled Castes and Tribes: SC/ST, Other Backward Classes excluding Muslim: OBC, and Muslims irrespective of caste: MUS, with non-Muslim general castes as the reference category), dummy making a distinction between the natives (those born in Delhi) and the migrants (BORNDEL), dummy representing whether the worker's household encountered any crisis between the two survey years (CRISIS), past average income, that is., income in the base year (PASTINC), household's saving amount in the base year (SAV), education dummies (representing one for those who acquired education below primary level: BPRIM, primary: PRIM, middle: MID, secondary: SEC, higher secondary: HSEC and graduates: GRAD, with those who have never attended school as the reference category), dummy if the worker used any formal network in accessing the current job but not the past job(s) (FNET), dummy if the worker changed his/her job or occupation (CHJOB), dummy if the worker accessed a public sector job in 2012 (PUBSEC), dummy representing clusters located in south Delhi[16] (SOUTHDEL) since this part of the city is more developed than the rest in terms of various socio-economic indicators (Dupont and Mitra, 1995), dummy indicating if the worker got married between the two survey years (MAR), dummy if the worker had fallen ill for more than seven consecutive days during the previous one year of the first survey (ILL), and the household size in the base year (HHSZ).

From Table 5.2 we may observe that several of these variables/dummies turn out to be significant. In equation 1, males show a higher probability of experiencing upward mobility compared to the females. Among the caste-cum-religion dummies OBCs seem to have a higher probability while the other categories do not have higher probability than that of the reference category. The education dummies suggest that those with higher secondary qualification were more likely to undergo a rise in income. Accessing a public sector job (largely manual work such as sweeper, gardener, and some on) resulted in income increase due to pay hike in recent years. Households in clusters located in south Delhi were more probable to experience upward mobility. What is a bit surprising is that the income in the base year takes a negative coefficient and is statistically significant. But this can be rationalized by arguing that those who already were in higher-income slabs had realized their expected income, whereas those with lower incomes had the scope and motivation to maximize it further. The negative sign of the past

---

[16] South Delhi dummy is constructed to represent a region and not just a district. South Delhi region comprises the four districts of south Delhi, New Delhi, south west Delhi, and central Delhi.

income is acceptable particularly if we keep in view the sign of the coefficient of saving included in the model which is positive and significant. Those who could generate savings could improve their incomes possibly by making investment in the occupation they were engaged in or by being able to undertake greater risks in their job which helped them realize income mobility. Given the positive impact of saving on income mobility the negative effect of the past income on the same does not appear implausible. Though poor health conditions (measured in terms of whether the person fell ill) did not turn out to be significant, the occurrence of any kind of crisis/exigency seems to have a negative impact on mobility. The individual health effect is possibly captured by the crisis at the household level.

The most startling result is in relation to the dummy which makes a distinction between the natives and migrants. The literature usually argues that the natives are better-off compared with the migrants because they have better access to the job market information. Also, the natives do not seem to have the immediate problems related to housing and other amenities as their parents are likely to have worked out at least a quasi-stable solution. Moreover, they are expected to be aware of the education and health facilities available for the low-income households in the cities and may have utilized them as per their need. Higher productivity and higher earnings are usually, therefore, some of the positive pay-offs that are associated with the natives vis-à-vis the migrants. However, the negative coefficient of the native dummy or the positive coefficient of the dummy representing those born outside Delhi in an alternative specification is indicative of a lower probability of mobility for the natives, possibly urging that there is a need to revisit the thinking prevailing in the migration literature. As Stark (1995) pointed out, the migration decision is often taken rationally by the entire household: the most potential one is sent to the urban areas from the rural areas who could earn in the urban labour market and send remittances regularly facilitating the household consumption, repayment of loans, investment in agricultural land, and so on. This is in fact an effective strategy against exigency adopted by the households not having adequate sources of livelihood within the rural areas. Also, as Banerjee (1986) pointed out, the rural migrants are well informed about the urban job market and are able to pursue an effective job search process through their contact persons. Hence, it could be rather faulty to assume that the migrants are worse-off in the urban labour market. Our findings support this strand of argument.

Table 5.2 Estimations of Upward Mobility in Delhi Slums

Dependent variable= upward mobility	Equation (1) Probit		Equation (2) Probit		Equation (3) Tobit	Equation (4) Tobit
	Coefficient	Marginal effect	Coefficient	Marginal effect	Coefficient	Coefficient
MALE	0.4563 * (0.2487)	0.1777 * (0.0979)	-0.1583 (0.2038)	-0.0591 (0.0743)	178.3749 (153.2933)	-171.5945 (150.1854)
AGE	-0.0135 (0.0086)	-0.0051 (0.0032)	-0.0248*** (0.0076)	-0.0094 *** (0.0029)	0.3087 (5.5856)	-8.1628 (5.7106)
SC/ST	0.2239 (0.2117)	0.0833 (0.0778)	0.1801 (0.2083)	0.0679 (0.0777)	121.4410 (165.6923)	119.6656 (171.1046)
OBC	0.3974 * (0.2265)	0.1433 * (0.0773)	0.3769* (0.2190)	0.1380 * (0.0764)	184.5160 (170.9081)	181.1510 (176.5281)
MUSLIM	0.2525 (0.2356)	0.0925 (0.0838)	0.2365 (0.2295)	0.0879 (0.0829)	252.8617 (179.4190)	256.1866 (185.6341)
BORNDEL	-0.3623 ** (0.1765)	-0.1386 ** (0.0683)	-0.3515 ** (0.1692)	-0.1356 * (0.0656)	-304.5989 ** (128.8099)	-309.0930 ** (133.4038)
CRISIS	-0.2772 * (0.1666)	-0.1066 * (0.0648)	-0.1393 (0.1693)	-0.0536 (0.0657)	-222.3867 (128.8099)	-124.0062 (131.2722)
PASTINC	-0.0007 *** (0.0001)	-0.0003 *** (0.0001)			-0.3986 *** (0.0599)	
MPCE			-0.0005 * (0.0003)	-0.0002 * (0.0001)		-0.1072 (0.2066)
SAV	0.0003 * (0.0002)	0.0001 * (0.0001)	0.0000 (0.0001)	0.0000 (0.0001)	0.1293 (0.1002)	-0.7950 (0.1001)

Table 5.2 contd.

Table 5.2 contd.

Dependent variable= upward mobility	Equation (1) Probit		Equation (2) Probit		Equation (3) Tobit	Equation (4) Tobit
	Coefficient	Marginal effect	Coefficient	Marginal effect	Coefficient	Coefficient
BPRIM	-0.3974* (0.2087)	-0.1544* (0.0822)	-0.2826 (0.2075)	-0.1099 (0.0819)	-7.0771 (151.9918)	23.1497 (158.9638)
PRIM	-0.2654 (0.1937)	-0.1019 (0.0753)	-0.3261* (0.1828)	-0.1265* (0.0716)	27.0322 (138.9869)	-22.9886 (144.6981)
MID	-0.3018 (0.2299)	-0.1170 (0.0908)	-0.4283* (0.2257)	-0.1678* (0.0892)	12.3880 (172.2866)	-83.6753 (178.6491)
SEC	-0.0063 (0.2963)	-0.0024 (0.1118)	-0.4182 (0.2967)	-0.1643 (0.1175)	190.8879 (233.2054)	-98.2997 (242.0439)
HSEC	5.4354*** -1.1876	0.3828*** -0.0264	0.0800 -0.7409	0.0301 -0.2742	4000.2120*** -638.4862	2191.7420*** -580.7890
GRAD	-0.1510 (1.2994)	-0.0581 (0.5091)	-0.6055 (0.7202)	-0.2379 (0.2754)	66.2029 (542.8117)	-522.7511 (592.6732)
FNET	0.2065 (0.2673)	0.0752 (0.0938)	0.1079 (0.2325)	0.0405 (0.0858)	37.1275 (174.6510)	-59.5867 (181.3107)
CHJOB	-0.0503 (0.1631)	-0.0190 (0.0619)	-0.0450 (0.1569)	-0.0172 (0.0601)	46.8769 (117.1940)	70.0197 (121.4879)
PUBSEC	2.4421** (1.1621)	0.3759*** (0.0286)	0.7930 (0.6522)	0.2452* (0.1450)	2579.3930*** (463.9793)	1654.8960*** (464.9282)

Table 5.2 contd.

Table 5.2 contd.

Dependent variable= upward mobility	Equation (1) Probit		Equation (2) Probit		Equation (3) Tobit	Equation (4) Tobit
	Coefficient	Marginal effect	Coefficient	Marginal effect	Coefficient	Coefficient
SOUTHDEL	0.3857 ***	0.1426 ***	0.2106	0.0795	175.1443 *	116.1963
	(0.1499)	(0.0541)	(0.1398)	(0.0522)	(105.2487)	(108.1999)
MAR	0.0124	0.0047	0.0800	0.0301	397.0266	455.2701 *
	(0.3447)	(0.1293)	(0.3489)	(0.1294)	(248.2244)	(187.2931)
ILL	-0.0012	-0.0004	0.0256	0.0097	-14.1480 *	-0.5117
	(0.2589)	(0.0975)	(0.2285)	(0.0863)	(179.6418)	(187.2931)
HHSZ	-0.0003	-0.0001	-0.0250	-0.0095	57.7359	53.9119
	(0.0423)	(0.0159)	(0.0407)	(0.0155)	(29.4849)	(31.6852)
Constant	1.5726 ***		1.7611 ***		129.7357	231.8381
	(0.5065)		(0.4731)		(322.0884)	(353.7059)
Pseudo R2		0.1948		0.0592	0.0219	0.0058
No. of observations		399		399	399	399
Left-censored observations					154	154
Uncensored observations					234	245

Source: Surveys in Delhi conducted in 2007–8 and 2012; Mitra and Tsujita (2014).

Note: Figures in parentheses are standard errors. To calculate marginal effects, the mean value was used for the continuous variable and a value of zero was used for the dummy variables. ***, **, and * represents statistical significance at 1 per cent, 5 per cent, and 10 per cent, respectively.

We have tried to make a distinction among the migrants of different origin (the results are not shown for brevity). Those who were born in places other than Bihar and Uttar Pradesh performed better, indicating that not all migrants hold the same potentiality to improve their earnings. Since the place of destination is the same for all the slum-dwellers, opportunities and hindrances are supposed to impact them equally. Hence, the differences in the outcome variable may be attributed to ethnic/cultural background that the migrants represent. Possibly the job search methods, the networking styles, the initiatives to undertake investment, and the responses to facilities available which have not been captured through our survey very rigorously vary along the lines of cultural background.

In an alternative specification (equation 2), the past income has been replaced by the past monthly per capita consumption expenditure (MPCE). Though the age of the worker was not found to influence mobility in the earlier specification, now it turns out to be significant with a negative coefficient. Since in the low-income households job search begins relatively early, the age factor could have taken a positive coefficient. However, the negative coefficient is suggestive of the lack of better job opportunities for the older workers. In contrast to the standard labour demand model for the educated workers where age is taken as a proxy for experience that raises the income, in the informal sector the younger workers are better-off in terms of employability than the older ones. Several strenuous activities pursued manually require younger workers who are physically strong rather than work experience which is believed to create greater mental capabilities. This could explain why the low-income households prefer to join the labour market early instead of spending time on education. It is not only a loss in terms of present income but also reduces the probability of securing a better-paying job through experience.

In equation 2, the coefficient of past MPCE again turns out to be negative after controlling for saving. Some of the educational dummies, representing primary and middle-level schooling show a positive and significant effect on mobility which possibly because of multicollinearity between education and past income did not turn out to be significant in the earlier specification except in the dummy for higher secondary education. In terms of marginal effect, in fact, this variable showed the largest impact on mobility (0.38) in equation 1. Accessing public sector job is also seen to have an almost equally strong effect (0.37) in equation 1. These findings have strong policy implications. Interventions in terms of educational support for the slum children can be an effective way of enabling them to experience mobility in the long run. On the other hand, keeping in view the downsizing of the public sector, the government needs to contemplate upon the possibility of introducing a national level employment guarantee programme in the urban areas which can be treated at par with the ongoing public work called Mahatma Gandhi National Rural Employment Guarantee Act

(MGNREGA).[17] Males in the labour market are better-off compared to the females as the gender dummy gives a marginal effect of almost 0.18 in equation 1. In other words, the probability of mobility goes up by 0.18 if the worker happens to be a male. This suggests for the necessity of probable moves towards job creation, specifically for females.

The district dummies do not turn out to be significant (the results are not shown for brevity). However, the south Delhi region dummy is positively associated with mobility, showing a marginal effect of almost 0.14 (equation 1). Our qualitative observations also confirm that some of the clusters in south Delhi are not only better-off in terms of housing structures and availability of basic amenities but also in their awareness about education, health, and the job market.

Geography seems to have a significant effect in the context of mobility. Some of the households are able to perform better in certain areas compared to their counterparts in certain other areas. Across different types of urban settlements these patterns are very much prevalent: large cities are characterized by better indicators relative to their small counterparts (Mitra, 2010a, 2010b). Now, we are able to observe that even within a given city behavioural differences and outcome variables tend to vary considerably across space, which can provide greater insight to developing policy strategies relating to city planning and slum rehabilitation. We pursue this point in the next section as we focus on the well-being index constructed for each of the slum households located in different parts of the city.

Well-being Index for Households: Average across Clusters and Districts (Zones) and Inter-temporal Changes

Usually, the consumption poverty is taken to reflect on living standards. However, an enormous amount of literature has appeared in the past to indicate that sufficient overlaps do not exist between various aspects of well-being. Several households above the monetary poverty line can still be poor in terms of housing or access to health and education. It may be, therefore, useful to construct an index which can encompass a large number of indicators (see Mitra and Tsujita, 2008).

Since these variables are heterogeneous, it is not easy to combine all of them into a well-being index. For this, the factor analysis more specifically, the maximum likelihood factor analysis, was conducted. In this process, some variables were discarded in order to avoid the Heywood cases. Only select variables were thus combined to generate a composite index of well-being.

---

[17] MGNREGA aims to improve the livelihoods of the adult rural population by providing unskilled manual work for 100 days per household per year.

Table 5.3 Average of Well-being Index across Districts, and Inter-temporal Changes

District	No. of observations	2007–8		2012	
		Sample mean	Coefficient of variation (within district variation)	Sample mean	Coefficient of variation (within district variation)
Central	3	705.77	42.90	922.67	4.56
East	14	708.58	41.01	674.55	72.99
New	10	1,100.55	58.83	762.21	59.38
North	11	986.81	36.89	732.36	67.85
North-east	23	722.42	36.57	704.87	39.30
North-west	71	952.90	84.96	636.25	56.80
South	86	849.16	44.50	713.94	73.36
South-west	41	914.76	68.28	761.19	93.62
West	20	793.05	39.39	605.89	53.12
Total	279	875.57	63.35	695.34	53.12

Source: Surveys in Delhi conducted in 2007–8 and 2012; Mitra and Tsujita (2014).

Note: Coefficient of variation across district is 16.24 per cent in 2007/08 and 12.64 per cent in 2012, respectively.

The following variables are combined through a factorial analysis to form the well-being index at the household level: household size, proportion of household members employed, average per capita monthly income in constant (2001) prices, MPCE, average education level of the household members aged 15 and above (in terms of years), proportion of household members not debilitated by sickness for more than 7 consecutive days during previous 12 months, and the proportion of male members in the household.

The well-being index across districts is shown in Table 5.3. Though the district-specific average values are not significantly different from each other as seen from the coefficient of variation of the mean values, within some of the districts large variations exist across clusters. This means that within a given district some of the clusters are much better off compared to the others. In other words the districts are large areal units; socio-economic variations exist even within a given district. Some of the slum clusters are possibly closer to the neighbourhood of the middle-class households. Some clusters because of their locational advantages are able to access better services for their residents while others cannot. What is quite prominent from our analysis is that such better-off clusters and worse-off clusters are present across many districts. Besides, there is a decline in 2012 in the mean value of the well-being index in most of the districts; across-district-variations have declined too. However, within-district-variations continue to be high and have rather increased over time in at least five of the districts, indicating the rising distance between the good performers and the bad performers.

The transition matrix constructed on the basis of the well-being index size classes in the base and the terminal years shows a significant deterioration over time (Table 5.4). Several households slid down in 2012. This comes as a great surprise because at the national level the country witnessed a significant decline in the incidence of poverty during 2004/05 to 2009/10. Delhi being one of the high-growth regions in the country, the beneficial effects of growth should have been sizeable. This deterioration in the overall well-being happened despite a decline in the incidence of consumption poverty seen at the national level. First of all in our survey the consumption poverty did not decline significantly. Moreover, the index of well-being encompasses not only income and consumption aspects but also other indicators. The deterioration in those indicators in spite of a rise in income for many workers is reflected in the adverse changes in the well-being index. We also need to consider the fact that poverty does not refer to a fixed set of households: as Krishna (2012: 187) argues 'people are falling into poverty in the developing world even as other people escape poverty'.

Table 5.4 Cross-tabulation of Well-being Index in 2007–8 and 2012

Well-being index in 2007/08	Well-being index in 2012						
	less than 0.5Z	0.5Z to 0.75Z	0.75Z to Z	Z to 1.25Z	1.25Z to 1.5Z	More than 1.5 Z	Total
less than 0.5Z	10	9	4	3	1	0	27
	37.04	33.33	14.81	11.11	3.70	0.00	100.00
	43.48	9.89	5.26	8.33	5.88	0.00	9.68
0.5Z to 0.75Z	9	41	20	4	2	4	80
	11.25	51.25	25.00	5.00	2.50	5.00	100.00
	39.13	45.05	26.32	11.11	11.76	11.11	28.67
0.75Z to Z	2	29	28	14	5	5	83
	2.41	34.94	33.73	16.87	6.02	6.02	100.00
	8.70	31.87	36.84	38.89	29.41	13.89	29.75
Z to 1.25Z	2	7	7	8	3	5	32
	6.25	21.88	21.88	25.00	9.38	15.63	100.00
	8.70	7.69	9.21	22.22	17.65	13.89	11.47
1.25Z to 1.5Z	0	2	9	3	2	6	22
	0.00	9.09	40.91	13.64	9.09	27.27	100.00
	0.00	2.20	11.84	8.33	11.76	16.67	7.89
More than 1.5Z	0	3	8	4	4	16	35
	0.00	8.57	22.86	11.43	11.43	45.71	100.00
	0.00	3.30	10.53	11.11	23.53	44.44	12.54
Total	23	91	76	36	17	36	279
	8.24	32.62	27.24	12.90	6.09	12.90	100.00
	100.00	100.00	100.00	100.00	100.00	100.00	100.00

Source: Surveys in Delhi conducted in 2007/08 and 2012; Mitra and Tsujita (2014).

Note: Z stands for mean value of well-being index. The two figures below each number of households refer to frequency by percentage in

Conclusion

Based on slum study in Delhi (2004–5), the importance of network in accessing jobs is evident though the extent of upward mobility was not facilitated by the traditional network. From the slum survey (2006–7) in four other cities the traditional networks are again seen to reduce the pace of mobility. With city size the extent of upward mobility varies positively implying that large cities offer better opportunities. Even the well-being levels in slums tend to improve with city size in the sense that a smaller percentage of slum households is located in the bottom size classes of well-being index in the large and dynamic cities compared to the small and stagnant ones. From all this it may be inferred that urbanization has a positive impact on upward mobility in comparison to the rural areas, though such movement may not be observed across the entire urban space. Large cities—though the cases of downward mobility also exist there—offer avenues to migrants and natives both for combining their efforts with possibilities which result in income enhancement. In fact, the study based on household level longitudinal data (2007–8 and 2012) collected from Delhi slums with a focus on income mobility covers a wide range of factors such as past income, saving, and education level of the workers which impinge on mobility in a dynamic city. The broad patterns are not indicative of significant mobility across all occupations though within a given wide category of economic activity movements are discernible.

Since education is a strong determinant of rise in income it can provide important policy directives. Accessing a public sector job is also positively associated with income mobility. Perhaps it is time to contemplate the possibility of introducing a national level employment guarantee programme in the urban areas which can be treated at par with the ongoing MGNREGA. The findings tend to confirm gender and a somewhat caste bias in upward mobility. Males in the labour market are better-off compared to the females. This suggests that there should be probable moves towards job creation, specifically for females.

Geography does play an important role providing validation to some of the hypotheses on locational advantages. These findings can provide inputs to city planning and developing cost effective slum relocation policies. The relationship between the base year and the terminal year income is negative implying that those who already were in higher income slabs had realized their expected income whereas those with lower incomes had the scope and motivation to enhance it further. Saving shows a positive and significant effect on mobility from which policy lessons can be drawn in terms of asset creation and provisions for productive investment for developing long-term strategies towards poverty reduction. The occurrence of any kind of crisis/exigency seems to have a negative impact on mobility, reinforcing the importance of health support measures for the low-income households. That migrants show a higher probability of experiencing upward mobility compared to the natives confirms the positive gains associated with rural to urban migration, and thus opposes the creation of barriers that hinder the entry of rural job seekers to the cities.

The findings also bring out the importance of cultural factors as migrants of certain specific origins are more likely than others to experience an income rise. The lack of better job opportunities for the older workers makes a case for strengthening the support system in favour of the elderly. The negative relationship between age and upward mobility explains why the low-income households prefer to join the labour market early instead of spending time on education, which is not only a loss in terms of present income but also reduces the probability of securing a better paying job. If this perception has to change, quality education with provision for skill formation has to be introduced.

CHAPTER 6

Erosion of the Caste Factor?

Introduction

Though in his book Kuznets (1966) had considered fifteen characteristics to define modern economic growth he later compressed them into the now famous six characteristics, falling into three main groups: (1) aggregate growth (*a*. high rates of increase in per capita product, accompanied by substantial rats of population growth and *b*. high rates of increase in output per unit of all inputs), (2) structural transformation (*c*. a high degree of structural transformation, encompassing a shift from agriculture to industry and services and *d*. changes in the structure of society and its ideology, including urbanization and secularization), and (3) international spread (*e*. opening up of international communications and *f*. a growing gap between developed and underdeveloped nations). Quite clearly he envisaged social changes alongside economic transformations. More specifically, urbanization and modernization of thoughts and ideology are seen as concomitant phenomena. The functioning of the rural labour market may be largely caste-based, but that is expected to get faint in the urban job market (Mitra, 2006). In other words, urbanization follows and results in commercialization, which in turn is likely to erode the influence of the caste factor in the job market although the job seekers may access information pertaining to the urban labour market on the basis of caste and kinship bonds (Banerjee, 1986; Desai, 1984; Mitra, 2003). From this point of view it becomes pertinent to assess if the caste factor which remained deep-rooted in the Indian social system for centuries started subsiding after the economic growth and development started off in the post-Independence era. In this chapter we try to examine if within the universe of the low-income households (slums) the caste factor matters or all social categories are equally vulnerable.

Many argued that the disadvantaged (social) classes usually get uprooted from the rural areas and strive hard in an alien urban situation to access livelihood sources (Singh and D'Souza, 1980). However, in an anonymous urban space the caste factor is usually expected to get blurred and, hence, caste-based occupations which might have been pursued in the rural setup prior to migration may change significantly, implying availability of jobs in the urban labour market being independent of caste. Similarly non-availability of jobs may also cut across castes. In such a situation what individuals from different caste background pursue is an important line of research. Do they then return to their caste-based activities in the urban setup in an attempt to earn a livelihood, or the residual (supply-push) absorption of labour becomes a complete random phenomenon, suggesting equal probability of locating individuals of every caste background in a given set of activities? From another angle, even within the informal sector some of the activities may require certain specific type of skill or experience and, thus, the concentration of certain castes in certain activities need not be interpreted always as a phenomenon of social discrimination.

The literature on caste and occupations is vast and varied (Kannappan, 1985). While one class of studies tends to suggest the erosion of the caste base in the process of development both in the rural and urban areas, the other line of research exemplifies the dominance of the caste factor in every sphere. Thus, human capital formation, sources of livelihood and well-being may be expected to move along the caste lines. It is often argued that in India the underemployed and poor mostly belong to the lower castes—Scheduled Castes (SCs) and Scheduled Tribes (STs). Social seclusion is said to have led to economic deprivation. Hence, the essence of the government policy in an attempt to reduce poverty and rehabilitate the poor rested on the reservation policy since Independence. Social integration was to be achieved through availability of education and employment opportunities to the lower castes. However, even after pursuing the reservation policy for more than five decades the percentage of population below and marginally above the poverty line is not negligible (Thorat, 1993). It may not be unrealistic to assume that the poor belong to higher castes also, and that economic progression cannot be attained purely on the basis of caste.

Mitra (1988) examined the issue of castes in city-slums and noted that the disadvantaged castes had migrated to the cities from the rural areas either recently or decades back through caste, kinship, and village networks. However, the existence of other castes in slums due to the shortage of housing, that is, the phenomenon of downward social mobility, certainly cannot be overlooked. Some of the findings from other studies note that despite the dissociation between caste and traditional occupations, large sections of 'lower' and artisan castes are concentrated in unskilled or low paid semi-skilled occupations in the informal sectors (Breman, 1990, 1993; Jeffrey, 2001; Kumar, 2008). Available evidence suggests that although urban and industrial occupations and professions have attracted members of diverse castes, here too certain castes tend to be concentrated in specific occupations. Deshpande (2003) calculated the poverty–caste relationship on the basis of the National Sample Survey Organisation (NSSO) consumption data, which reinforces the strong relationship between low-caste status and poverty.

Using the slum survey data (2006–7) in four cities we wish to examine in this chapter whether certain caste groups are more prone to migrate and whether the well-being levels of different social categories differ significantly. Does caste still plays an important role in determining people's choices among occupations, levels of education, place of residence, and income, and does caste continue to reproduce inequality?

Propensity to Migrate

In this section, based on our primary survey of slum households, we have tried to explain in a logit framework what induces or discourages the probability to migrate to the urban slums.[1] After controlling for relevant variables we try to assess if caste still matters within the broad context of slums, which are largely occupied by the low-income households. The dependent variable is a dummy capturing migrants (those who moved into the city over a period of less than ten years) and non-migrants, characterized in terms of 1 and 0 respectively (Table 6.1). The findings confirm that regular wage employment raises the probability to migrate compared to self-employment or casual wage employment. Individuals in the General category and the OBCs show a higher propensity to migrate in comparison to the SCs and the STs. The socially disadvantaged categories are possibly not able to mitigate the cost of dislocation and access better economic opportunities. Relative to Ujjain (comparison category) Mathura does not show a different propensity to migrate. In this sense the stagnant cities tend to share a similar migration pattern. On the other hand, Ludhiana unravels a higher propensity to migrate which is as per expectation for the dynamic and industrial cities. Jaipur on the other hand, shows a lower migration propensity, in spite of being a million-plus city. Space constraint and overcrowding in this city which is a state capital must have held less prospects for migrants, discouraging them to move in.

[1]   See Chandrasekhar and Mitra (2019).

What is most startling is that the illiterates and those with primary, middle, and secondary level of education are more likely to migrate than the graduates or those with a higher level of education. Those with less education are more vulnerable in a rural setup and thus in search of jobs they are more likely to migrate. With age the probability to migrate increases. Further, women are more likely to migrate compared to the males possibly because of marriage and other social reasons.

Table 6.1 Probability to Migrate (Binomial Logit) with Marginal Effects

Dep Var: MIG	Coeff.	z-ratio	dy/dx	z-ratio
EMP1	0.228	1.58	0.010	1.47
EMP2	0.489	3.17**	0.024	2.69
SOC1	1.058	1.78*	0.054	1.47
SOC2	1.318	2.23**	0.068	1.79
SOC3	0.885	1.49	0.044	1.24
CITY1	-1.286	-7.39**	-0.044	-9.3
CITY2	0.445	3.58**	0.021	3.17
CITY3	0.152	1.24	0.007	1.2
EDU1	0.846	4.71**	0.044	3.87
EDU2	0.513	3.07**	0.024	2.76
EDU3	0.900	5.27**	0.050	4.13
EDU4	0.737	3.63**	0.041	2.83
NET1	-0.015	-0.07	-0.001	-0.07
NET2	0.178	0.51	0.008	0.47
Hhsize	-0.002	-0.1	0.000	-0.1
Age	0.092	2.43	0.004	2.43
Gender	-0.904	-8.77**	-0.040	-8.29
Constant	-4.319	-6.96		

Number of observations = 8996; chi2(17)= 347.3
Source: Based on the Slum Survey (2006–7) carried out by Institute of Economic Growth, Delhi under the UNDP–GOI project on urban poverty.
Note: ** and * denote significance at 5 and 10 per cent levels respectively.
EMP1 = Casual; EMP2 = Regular; SOC1 = General; SOC2 = OBCs; SOC3 = SCs; CITY1 = Jaipur; CITY2 = Ludhaina; CITY3 = Mathura; MIG1 = less than 1 year; MIG2 = 1–4 Year; MIG3=5–9 Year; EDU1 = Illiterate; EDU2 = Primary; EDU3 = Middle; EDU4 = Secondary; (ref cate graduation and above); NET1=Networks through family members; NET2=Network through relatives; Hhsz = Household Size; Age= Age of the principal earner; Gender = Gender Dummy (female = 0 and male = 1)

Well-being and Caste[2]

The concentration of various castes in particular professions and occupations is well documented in sociological studies. Navlakha's (1989) study highlights the concentration of upper and middle castes in modern professions such as engineering, medicine, banking, and journalism. Jayaram (1977) shows a continuing high concentration of upper and dominant castes in higher education, including engineering and medical colleges. Holmstrom's studies (1976, 1985) in Bangalore and Bombay show that the upper and middle castes dominate the supervisory and skilled worker category whereas the unskilled workers are drawn from the 'lower' castes. He finds that in the unorganized sector, caste is particularly critical for underprivileged workers because they lack resources other than those offered by their caste linkages.

On the whole, there is no dearth of argument suggesting that the underemployed and poor belong mostly to the lower castes. Social seclusion is said to have led to economic deprivation. Hence, the essence of the government policy—in an attempt to reduce poverty and rehabilitate the poor—rested on the reservation policy in use since Independence. Social integration was to be achieved through availability of education and employment opportunities to the lower castes.[3] However, even after pursuing the reservation policy for more than five decades the percentage of population below and marginally above the poverty line is not negligible. Perhaps this would tend to suggest that poor can belong to higher castes also, and that improvement in economic well-being cannot be attained purely on the basis of caste.

There may lie a point of justification in holding the framework of social and economic dualism because in the rural context, as Srinivas (1969: 268) pointed out, 'the ban on contact between castes and the solidarity of a sub-caste, express themselves in the spatial segregation of castes'. Extrapolating the similar situation to the urban context—though one would expect the impact of caste factor to get diluted in the process of urbanization—spatial segregation of residence, education and skill formation, and sector of employment all may be in relationship, each deducing its root from the manifestation of caste, 'the prototype of rigid social inequality' (Beteille, 1969: 263).

---

[2] For details, see Kumar, Kumar, and Mitra (2009).
[3] The Mandal Commission (1990) reinforced these issues by including OBCs as beneficiaries.

The nature of employment gauged in terms of daily wage, regular wage, and self-employment is structurally different across social groups (Table 6.2). For example, a relatively higher percentage of ST and SC workers are engaged as regular wage employees compared to other social categories. However, at the same time a higher percentage of SC workers along with Muslim (OBC and General both) workers are engaged in daily wage employment. The percentage of General Hindu workers in self-employment is the highest among all if we ignore the category of 'others'.

Inter-city variations are substantive. In Jaipur nearly half of the General Muslims, OBC Muslims, and OBC Hindus are engaged in daily wage employment. On the other hand General Hindus and SCs and STs are relatively better off as a comparatively higher percentage of workers from these social categories are employed in regular wage jobs. However, the General and OBC Hindus are proportionately more present in self-employment also.

Ludhiana being an industrial city, the percentage of daily wage employment is lowest in most of the social categories. General Hindus, OBC Hindus and SCs are more prominently engaged in regular wage employment than the rest. However, an equally high percentage of General Hindus are also located as self-employed workers. Nearly half of the Muslims (both General and OBCs) are also employed in this category of employment.

Nearly half of the SC workers are employed in daily wage jobs in Mathura. However at the same time nearly 40 per cent of the Hindu workers (General and OBCs) and around 50 and more than 40 per cent of the General Muslim and OBC Muslim workers respectively are also engaged in self-employment. Ujjain being a purely religious city with a relatively scarce possibility of getting absorbed in high-income jobs a very high percentage of the workers across all social categories are by and large employed in daily wage jobs. Only the percentage of General Hindus is less than 50 in this category of employment while nearly 33 per cent from this social group are located in a relatively better category of employment, that is, regular wage employment. On the whole, evidence across all the four cities seems to be quite mixed and therefore we need to examine many other variables before concluding that lower social categories match the lower economic categories.

Table 6.2 Distribution of Workers across Social Groups and Nature of Employment (%)

All Cities Combined	Daily Wage	Regular Wage/Sala-ried	Self-Employment
General Hindu/Sikh	26.7	38.7	34.6
General Muslim	44.4	28.0	27.6
Other Backward Classes–Hindu/Sikh	37.3	32.4	30.3
Other Backward Classes–Muslim	47.4	23.4	29.2
Scheduled Castes	44.4	37.0	18.6
Scheduled Tribes	31.5	46.6	21.9
Others	25.0	25.0	50.0
All	38.7	33.9	27.4
Jaipur			
General Hindu/Sikh	30.6	39.2	30.2
General Muslim	53.8	26.9	19.2
Other Backward Classes–Hindu/Sikh	45.1	22.0	32.9
Other Backward Classes–Muslim	46.3	30.6	23.1
Scheduled Castes	37.5	42.8	19.7
Scheduled Tribes	22.4	51.0	26.5
Others	0.0	0.0	0.0
All	41.0	34.7	24.3
Ludhiana			
General Hindu/Sikh	17.2	42.5	40.3
General Muslim	17.8	31.1	51.1
Other Backward Classes–Hindu/Sikh	20.9	47.6	31.4
Other Backward Classes–Muslim	29.0	25.8	45.2

Table 6.2 contd.

Table 6.2 contd.

All Cities Combined	Daily Wage	Regular Wage/Sala- ried	Self- Employment
Scheduled Castes	24.5	55.0	20.4
Scheduled Tribes	0.0	33.3	66.7
Others	0.0	33.3	66.7
All	20.8	46.5	32.8
Mathura			
General Hindu/Sikh	26.5	36.1	37.4
General Muslim	18.2	31.8	50.0
Other Backward Classes–Hindu/ Sikh	25.6	34.0	40.4
Other Backward Classes– Muslim	42.2	15.0	42.9
Scheduled Castes	44.5	38.4	17.1
Scheduled Tribes	41.7	50.0	8.3
Others	50.0	0.0	50.0
All	32.7	32.0	35.3
Ujjain			
General Hindu/Sikh	43.5	33.1	23.4
General Muslim	72.7	22.7	4.5
Other Backward Classes–Hindu/ Sikh	53.3	24.7	22.0
Other Backward Classes– Muslim	63.9	17.5	18.6
Scheduled Castes	59.7	22.8	17.5
Scheduled Tribes	77.8	22.2	0.0
Others	20.0	20.0	60.0
All	56.4	24.1	19.5

Source: Slum Survey (2006–7) carried out by Institute of Economic Growth, Delhi under the UNDP–GOI project on urban poverty.
Note: Each row adds up to 100 per cent.

The occupational structure varies considerably across caste groups (Table 6.3). For example, around 13 and 34 per cent of the General Hindus are engaged as semi-professionals and sales and trade workers respectively whereas among the General Muslims the comparative figures are only 4.2 and 21.2 per cent, respectively. Certain occupations are caste-centric, for example, a very large chunk of the SC workers (around one-fourth) are engaged in one of the most vulnerable categories of occupation (daily wage labour). Similarly among the OBC Hindus around 15.6 per cent are located in this category of occupation. Though the ST population is quite nominal in the sample a very significant percentage of them are seen to be employed as semi-professionals and trade and sales workers. Along the line of religion, Muslim workers, both General and OBCs, correspond to a higher percentage figure in tailoring. Based on some of these patterns it would be of great interest to examine if these differences are related to differences in educational levels and access to social capital of workers across different social groups.

The educational levels however vary substantially across caste groups (Table 6.4). The incidence of illiteracy is higher among the SCs compared to the General or OBC Hindus. Again OBC Hindus and OBC Muslims correspond to a higher incidence of illiteracy than the General Hindus and General Muslims, respectively. At the secondary and higher levels of education the differences between the General and OBCs are evident both among the Hindus and Muslims, indicating that the OBCs are somewhat worse off compared to the General category. However, the incidence of illiteracy and the percentage of population with low levels of education are sizeable among the higher social categories too.

Whether the educational differences translate themselves into income differences is an important question. The income structure at the top level (INR 50,000 to 100,000 per month) does not seem to be much different between Hindus and Muslims though OBCs are worse off compared to the General category among both the communities. On the other hand, the percentage of SCs in the higher-income category (5,000 and above) is slightly smaller than that of the OBCs. Though low levels of education and low-level incomes are present among both higher and social categories across both the religions, the incidence of low incomes and low levels of education is a bit higher among the lower social categories. Besides, a religion-based distinction can also be deciphered—Muslims seem to be worse off compared to the Hindus (Table 6.5).

Table 6.3 Occupational Structure of the Workers (%)

All Cities Combined	General Hindu/ Sikh	General Muslim	OBC Hindu/ Sikh	OBC Muslim	SC	ST	Others
Semi-professional	13.3	4.2	7.9	4.8	7.0	23.3	0.0
Sales and Trade	34.4	21.1	27.3	28.4	18.1	28.8	66.7
Personal Services	4.1	2.4	5.6	3.3	15.1	5.5	0.0
Manufacturing and Repair	11.7	23.5	16.2	18.5	13.1	9.6	11.1
Commercial and Security	4.8	1.4	2.7	1.5	2.6	1.4	0.0
Transport	8.0	10.4	5.6	12.9	5.3	6.8	11.1
Tailoring	6.1	16.3	6.6	9.1	3.6	4.1	0.0
Construction	4.6	12.5	7.8	8.3	7.2	6.8	0.0
Labour	7.9	5.2	15.6	9.3	23.8	12.3	11.1
Others	5.3	3.1	4.7	3.9	4.2	1.4	0.0
Total	100.0	100.0	100.0	100.0	100.0	100.0	100.0

Source: Slum Survey (2006–7) carried out by Institute of Economic Growth, Delhi under the UNDP–GOI project on urban poverty.

Table 6.4 Level of Education: All Cities Combined (%)

Education	General Hindu/ Sikh	General Muslim	OBC Hindu/ Sikh	OBC Muslim	SC	ST	Others
Illiterates	21.3	35.1	25.6	39.5	31.7	17.9	18.2
Non-formal	2.3	5.2	1.5	7.2	2.1	1.9	0.0
Primary	22.0	30.1	31.0	31.2	28.3	19.8	27.3
Middle	21.9	16.8	21.4	13.9	21.5	31.9	9.1
Secondary	16.2	7.2	10.9	5.4	10.2	17.9	31.8
Higher Secondary	6.7	2.9	4.7	1.5	3.0	4.8	13.6
Graduate and Others	9.6	2.7	5.0	1.3	3.2	5.8	0.0
Total	100.0	100.0	100.0	100.0	100.0	100.0	100.0

Source: Slum Survey (2006–7) carried out by Institute of Economic Growth, Delhi under the UNDP–GOI project on urban poverty.

On the whole, educational, occupational, and income disadvantages are somewhat more pronounced among the socially disadvantaged classes though it will be equally erroneous to suggest that those in higher social categories are all well off. All this would tend to indicate that while caste-based reservation policy may help the socially disadvantaged classes reap benefits, it will leave out a large percentage of the economically weaker section of the population who belong to higher social categories, residing particularly in deprived areas, which can be slums as in the present context or can be any other geographical location in a broader sense. However, before drawing any substantive conclusion in this regard we need to pursue a more rigorous analysis using the unit level data as attempted in Table 6.5.

Table 6.5 Distribution of Workers across Monthly Income Categories (in INR)

All City	Less than 500	501– 1,500	1,501– 3,000	5,001– 10,000	Above 10,000	Total
General Hindu/Sikh	5.2	19.8	43.6	29.7	1.7	100
General Muslim	5.6	14.6	51.3	25.1	3.4	100
Other Backward Classes– Hindu/Sikh	6.6	28.5	44.7	19.9	0.3	100
Other Backward Classes– Muslim	7.3	23.9	47.6	19.9	1.3	100
Scheduled Castes	7.0	29.6	45.2	17.1	1.2	100
Scheduled Tribes	1.4	21.1	35.2	35.2	7.0	100
Others	12.5	12.5	12.5	62.5	0.0	100
Total	6.3	24.8	45.2	22.3	1.4	100

Source: Slum Survey (2006–7) carried out by Institute of Economic Growth, Delhi under the UNDP–GOI project on urban poverty.

Turning to the occupational choice model we made a distinction among migrants from General category, migrants who are OBCs, migrants belonging to SCs, non-migrants from the General category, non-migrants who are OBCs and non-migrants belonging to SCs, with the migrants from general category taken as the comparison group. We have controlled for several other variables such as education, age, household size, gender, networks, and house asset in the place of origin. In most of the occupations it is evident that migrant SCs and the non-migrants across different social categories have a lower probability of joining the relatively better jobs, indicating that migrants from the General category and OBCs are better off (Chandrasekhar and Mitra, 2019).

In order to assess the overall well-being of the households across various social classes we need to construct a well-being (or deprivation) index at the household level for which various dimensions of poverty rather than only income or consumption poverty need to be considered. However, the other aspects which we could include are only those that are quantifiable.

The following variables have been combined to construct the household-specific well-being index: household size, child–woman ratio, per capita consumption expenditure,[4] proportion of persons in the household who reported illness, percentage of household members who acquired at least primary level education, percentage of members in the age group 15 to 59, which is a proxy for adult potential earners, percentage of working individuals, age of the household head/principal earner taken as a proxy for experience in the job market, health expenditure per capita, and per capita household income. Variables such as household size, child–woman ratio, and the percentage of ill members in the household are likely to reduce the well-being of the household. Health expenditure per capita on an *a priori* basis may raise the well-being of the household if it tends to enhance productivity. On the other, it may reduce well-being if it is incurred at the expense of consumption of essential items. On the other hand, other variables would be expected to enhance the well-being. Since these variables are heterogeneous, it is difficult to combine them to indicate an overall living standard of the households. Factor analysis has been conducted, and using factor loadings as weights from the rotated matrix (using varimax rotation technique in order to obtain statistically independent factors), variables have been combined to generate a composite index of well-being.

---

[4] It excludes health expenditure.

Across various social groups we have considered the percentage distribution of households as per the size classes formed on the basis of the well-being index (Table 6.6). Based on the combined figures for all four cities the percentage of General Hindus in the bottom two size classes is somewhat lower than the corresponding figures of other social groups. In the top two size classes the percentage figures are again a bit higher in the case of General Hindus and Muslims compared to the OBC Hindus or Muslims or SCs, suggesting that those belonging to the General category are slightly better off. Though Ludhiana and Mathura are more or less in conformity with this pattern, the percentage of SCs in Jaipur in top two size classes is around 8 per cent which is higher than the corresponding figure among General Hindus or Muslims. In Ujjain, the top two size classes are mostly empty for all categories except for SCs. The percentage figures of households in the bottom two size classes are indeed higher than those in other cities (except among SCs in Mathura) implying that in general the well-being levels are worse off in Ujjain. However, based on the percentage figure of bottom two size classes, SCs in Ujjain do not seem to be worse off in comparison to Muslims or OBC Hindus. In Ludhiana and Ujjain the General Muslims and in Mathura the OBC Muslims are the least well off. This may tend to indicate a religion-based distinction which is more prominent than a caste-based one. Based on the combined data for all four cities, STs seem to be better off than the rest. However given the limited number of observations on STs in the sample, any conclusion in this regard has to be drawn carefully.

However, these patterns are aggregative in nature. We may therefore like to pursue further experiments. One important line of enquiry could be relating to the factors which explain the overall well-being. Since well-being is measured in terms of a number of variables we need to be careful in selecting the determinants so that they do not include some of the constituents of the well-being index. The right-hand-side variables include nature of employment, caste categories, duration of migration categories (the long-duration migrants of more than 20 years and the natives constitute the comparison category), nature of construction of the huts, and the number of rooms per household, ownership pattern, access to sanitation and water, and ability to remit. As there are mainly three types of employment—daily wage, regular wage and self-employment—two dummies representing the first two categories have been included. In relation to the social groups STs and 'others' have been taken as the comparison category.

Table 6.6 Percentage Distribution of Households across Size Classes Formed on the Basis of Well-being Index

All Cities Combined	General Hindu/Sikh	General Muslim	Other Backward Classes–Hindu/Sikh	Other Backward Classes–Muslim	Scheduled Castes	Scheduled Tribes	Others
Up to 200	4.9	0.8	6.6	9.4	5.8	8.3	0.0
201–400	37.2	42.4	46.4	43.7	46.5	12.8	6.7
401–600	29.3	28.7	27.8	30.9	29.7	37.6	40.0
601–1,000	21.2	20.3	16.4	14.9	13.5	22.7	36.7
1,001–1,500	4.6	6.7	1.8	0.5	3.2	16.9	0.0
Above 1,500	2.8	1.0	1.0	0.5	1.3	1.7	16.7
Total	100	100	100	100	100	100	100

Jaipur	General Hindu/Sikh	General Muslim	Other Backward Classes–Hindu/Sikh	Other Backward Classes–Muslim	Scheduled Castes	Scheduled Tribes	Others
Up to 200	3.6	0.0	0.0	0.0	1.8	1.7	0.0
201–400	29.6	37.9	28.5	29.6	21.3	9.2	0.0
401–600	35.4	35.7	41.0	44.7	41.3	38.2	0.0
601–1,000	24.5	20.8	25.5	23.9	27.7	24.9	0.0
1,001–1,500	3.1	4.9	2.1	0.9	4.7	23.7	0.0
Above 1,500	3.9	0.7	2.9	0.9	3.1	2.3	0.0
Total	100	100	100	100	100	100	0.0

Table 6.6 contd.

Table 6.6 contd.

Ludhiana	General Hindu/Sikh	General Muslim	Other Backward Classes–Hindu/Sikh	Other Backward Classes–Muslim	Scheduled Castes	Scheduled Tribes	Others
Up to 200	4.0	0.0	2.1	5.8	5.8	60.0	0.0
201–400	28.2	48.2	32.2	35.0	36.5	0.0	0.0
401–600	32.4	8.8	32.4	25.2	34.5	40.0	100.0
601–1,000	24.3	21.1	26.7	30.1	15.5	0.0	0.0
1,001–1,500	7.7	17.5	4.3	1.9	6.7	0.0	0.0
Above 1,500	3.4	4.4	2.3	1.9	1.0	0.0	0.0
Total	100	100	100	100	100	100	100.0

Mathura	General Hindu/Sikh	General Muslim	Other Backward Classes–Hindu/Sikh	Other Backward Classes–Muslim	Scheduled Castes	Scheduled Tribes	Others
Up to 200	6.2	5.3	8.7	20.5	5.0	0.0	0.0
201–400	49.5	38.2	51.5	60.1	61.0	34.3	0.0
401–600	20.4	22.9	25.3	18.0	20.2	31.4	44.4
601–1,000	17.6	24.4	12.1	1.5	10.4	34.3	0.0
1,001–1,500	4.0	9.2	1.8	0.0	3.0	0.0	0.0
Above 1,500	2.2	0.0	0.6	0.0	0.5	0.0	55.6
Total	100	100	100	100	100	100	100

Table 6.6 contd.

Table 6.6 contd.

Ujjain	General Hindu/Sikh	General Muslim	Other Backward Classes–Hindu/Sikh	Other Backward Classes–Muslim	Scheduled Castes	Scheduled Tribes	Others
Up to 200	6.9	0.0	9.6	16.6	8.2	45.8	0.0
201–400	45.8	79.7	56.7	57.4	57.4	12.5	11.8
401–600	32.7	13.0	23.0	17.0	26.1	41.7	23.5
601–1,000	14.7	7.2	10.7	9.0	7.0	0.0	64.7
1,001–1,500	0.0	0.0	0.0	0.0	0.3	0.0	0.0
Above 1,500	0.0	0.0	0.0	0.0	1.0	0.0	0.0
Total	100	100	100	100	100	100	100

Source: Slum Survey (2006–7) carried out by Institute of Economic Growth, Delhi under the UNDP–GOI project on urban poverty.

Table 6.7 Binomial Logit Model (Maximum Likelihood Estimates)

Explanatory Variables	Jaipur		Ludhiana		Mathura		Ujjain		All Cities Combined	
	Coeff	M.Eff	Coeff	M.Eff	Coeff	M.Eff	Coeff	M.Eff	Coeff	M.Eff
Gender	-0.45	-0.09	-0.52	-0.12	-0.07	-0.02	-0.10	-0.02	-0.33	-0.08
	(-0.92)	(-0.84)	(-1.27)	(-1.2)	(-0.2)	(-0.2)	(-0.35)	(-0.36)	(-1.87)*	(-1.86)*
Daily Wage	0.11	0.02	0.25	0.05	-0.31	-0.07	-0.10	-0.02	-0.08	-0.02
	(0.45)	(0.45)	(0.85)	(0.88)	(-1.18)	(-1.2)	(-0.42)	(-0.42)	(-0.67)	(-0.67)
Regular Wage	0.83	0.13	0.54	0.11	0.82	0.20	0.50	0.12	0.63	0.15
	(2.69)**	(3.04)**	(2.08)**	(2.18)**	(3.31)**	(3.37)**	(1.84)*	(1.81)*	(5.04)**	(5.25)**
General Hindu/Sikh	-0.96	-0.19	1.06	0.21	-0.59	-0.14	0.09	0.02	-0.77	-0.19
	(-1.67)*	(-1.53)	(0.78)	(0.84)	(-0.74)	(-0.77)	(0.1)	(0.1)	(-2.24)**	(-2.28)**
General Muslim	-1.33	-0.28	0.83	0.14	-0.05	-0.01	-1.11	-0.21	-0.73	-0.18
	(-2.23)**	(-2.03)**	(0.58)	(0.72)	(-0.05)	(-0.05)	(-0.95)	(-1.27)	(-1.93)*	(-1.97)**
Other Backward Classes–Hindu/Sikh	-0.60	-0.12	1.01	0.19	-0.68	-0.16	-0.34	-0.08	-1.07	-0.26
	(-0.92)	(-0.84)	(0.74)	(0.88)	(-0.87)	(-0.91)	(-0.37)	(-0.38)	(-3.08)**	(-3.23)**
Other Backward Classes–Muslim	-1.21	-0.25	1.54	0.22	-1.44	-0.30	-0.81	-0.17	-1.16	-0.28
	(-2.07)**	(-1.89)*	(1.06)	(1.78)*	(-1.75)*	(-2.18)**	(-0.82)	(-0.95)	(-3.26)**	(-3.54)**
Scheduled Castes	-0.65	-0.13	0.80	0.16	-0.93	-0.21	-0.08	-0.02	-0.99	-0.24
	(-1.11)	(-1.03)	(0.59)	(0.64)	(-1.17)	(-1.29)	(-0.09)	(-0.09)	(-2.9)**	(-3.00)**

Table 6.7 contd.

Table 6.7 contd.

Explanatory Variables	Jaipur		Ludhiana		Mathura		Ujjain		All Cities Combined	
	Coeff	M.Eff	Coeff	M.Eff	Coeff	M.Eff	Coeff	M.Eff	Coeff	M.Eff
Duration of Migration < 1 yr			0.42 (0.35)	0.08 (0.39)	-0.23 (-0.28)	-0.05 (-0.29)	0.89 (1.09)	0.22 (1.11)	-0.20 (-0.41)	-0.05 (-0.41)
Duration of Migration 1-3 yr	-1.13 (-1.23)	-0.25 (-1.08)	0.36 (0.65)	0.07 (0.7)	0.55 (1.46)	0.14 (1.46)	-0.03 (-0.06)	-0.01 (-0.06)	-0.18 (-0.85)	-0.05 (-0.85)
Duration of Migration 4-5 yr	0.86 (0.78)	0.12 (1.06)	1.09 (1.39)	0.18 (1.95)*	0.14 (0.32)	0.04 (0.32)	0.43 (0.87)	0.10 (0.85)	-0.02 (-0.06)	0.00 (-0.06)
Duration of Migration 6-10 yr	0.15 (0.32)	0.03 (0.33)	-0.05 (-0.13)	-0.01 (-0.13)	-0.06 (-0.18)	-0.01 (-0.18)	-0.04 (-0.1)	-0.01 (-0.1)	-0.25 (-1.48)	-0.06 (-1.47)
Duration of Migration 10-20 yr	-0.26 (-0.82)	-0.05 (-0.78)	-0.71 (-2.66)**	-0.16 (-2.57)**	0.28 (0.97)	0.07 (0.97)	0.53 (2.04)**	0.13 (2.02)**	-0.12 (-0.93)	-0.03 (-0.92)
Sending Remittance	0.87 (1.68)*	0.12 (2.17)**	0.68 (2.25)**	0.13 (2.48)**	0.97 (2.41)**	0.24 (2.56)**	-1.55 (-1.29)	-0.26 (-2.13)**	0.91 (4.85)**	0.20 (5.62)**
Ownership of House	-0.50 (-1.43)	-0.09 (-1.44)	-0.36 (-1.13)	-0.07 (-1.13)	-0.14 (-0.46)	-0.03 (-0.46)	0.40 (1.66)*	0.09 (1.67)*	-0.01 (-0.06)	0.00 (-0.06)
No. of Rooms	-0.02 (-0.19)	0.00 (-0.19)	0.22 (2.28)**	0.05 (2.3)**	0.02 (0.24)	0.00 (0.24)	0.38 (3.79)**	0.09 (3.79)**	0.09 (2.42)**	0.02 (2.42)**

Table 6.7 contd.

Table 6.7 contd.

Explanatory Variables	Jaipur		Ludhiana		Mathura		Ujjain		All Cities Combined	
	Coeff	M.Eff	Coeff	M.Eff	Coeff	M.Eff	Coeff	M.Eff	Coeff	M.Eff
Concrete Roof	-0.87 (-2.98)**	-0.16 (-2.92)**	-0.08 (-0.19)	-0.02 (-0.19)	-0.20 (-0.96)	-0.05 (-0.97)	-0.64 (-2.65)**	-0.15 (-2.61)**	-0.36 (-3.31)**	-0.09 (-3.31)**
Brick Wall	-0.01 (-0.02)	0.00 (-0.02)	-0.30 (-0.71)	-0.07 (-0.69)	0.17 (0.21)	0.04 (0.21)	0.08 (0.2)	0.02 (0.19)	-0.11 (-0.55)	-0.03 (-0.55)
Municipality Water	0.75 (2.38)	0.12 (2.73)**	0.02 (0.05)	0.00 (0.05)	-0.32 (-1.27)	-0.08 (-1.29)	-0.81 (-1.17)	-0.17 (-1.4)	0.06 (0.45)	0.01 (0.45)
Individual Latrine	-0.27 (-0.81)	-0.05 (-0.78)	-0.40 (-0.84)	-0.09 (-0.8)	-0.21 (-0.68)	-0.05 (-0.69)			0.05 (0.29)	0.01 (0.29)
Piped Water	-0.25 (-0.93)	-0.04 (-0.92)	-0.31 (-0.63)	-0.07 (-0.6)	-0.68 (-2.55)**	-0.17 (-2.57)**	-0.53 (-2.28)**	-0.13 (-2.27)**	-0.73 (-6.52)**	-0.18 (-6.57)**
Constant	3.19 (3.46)**		-0.04 (-0.03)		1.12 (1.16)		-1.14 (-1.06)		1.36 (3.17)	
Chi-Sq	54.14		56.53		67.36		75.96		239.66	
No. of Observations	500		500		500		500		2000	

Source: Slum Survey (2006–7) carried out by Institute of Economic Growth, Delhi under the UNDP–GOI project on urban poverty.
Note: Coeff. and M. Eff represent coefficients and marginal effects respectively. ** and * represent significance at 5 and 10 per cent levels respectively.

The analysis is carried out in a binomial logit framework with households which registered a well-being index of less than 400 are assigned 0 and those lying above the threshold limit are designated as 1. The estimation is carried out for the samples drawn from the four cities separately and also for the pooled sample. Results presented in Table 6.7 tend to suggest that households in which heads are engaged in regular wage employment correspond to higher levels of well-being while those in daily wage employment are statistically not different from those in self-employment. In individual cities gender dummy does not appear to be significant though in the pooled sample it is significant at 10 per cent level with a negative sign, implying that women-headed households have lower well-being index though in terms of marginal effect the probability of having higher levels of well-being drops marginally (-0.08) as one moves from male-headed to female-headed households.

In relation to the caste categories we may again refer to the marginal effects. Relative to the STs and 'others' most of the categories seem to have a lower probability of experiencing a higher well-being index. However, the extent of fall in the case of OBC Hindus, OBC Muslims, and SCs measured in terms of marginal effect is higher than that for General Hindus or Muslims. However, these results hold only when we pool the data from all the four cities. Otherwise, based on individual cities this pattern is not uniformly evident. For example, only OBC Muslims in Ludhiana and Mathura have a different impact on well-being while the rest of the categories are statistically insignificant. However, in Ludhiana they tend to have a higher well-being while in Mathura the marginal effect corresponding to OBC Muslims is -0.30. In Ujjain none of the caste dummies is significant, implying that the variations in well-being across categories are not substantive. In Jaipur both General and OBC Muslims tend to have a lower well-being index than the rest. On the whole, based on the individual city data it is not possible to conclude that lower castes such as OBCs and SCs show lower well-being though based on the pooled data such a tendency is evident.

The duration of migration does not play a significant role in enhancing the well-being level of the households as seen from the pooled data. However, households which are able to remit and are residing in greater space (measured in terms of the number of rooms) are able to acquire higher levels of well-being. The only surprising result is in relation to the access to piped water and the concrete roof, which have negative coefficients. The access to piped water does not mean individual access; it could be the accessibility of the cluster as a whole. Similarly, the households with concrete roof do not seem to be better off in terms of the well-being index. On the whole, while some of the physical characteristics of the shelter and the well-being levels of the households move in the positive direction, some other do not show any such pattern. This would imply that even in better dwelling structures one may locate households with lower well-being index in terms of income, consumption, education, health and certain social and demographic variables. Land tenure can improve the quality of shelter but that does not ensure improvement in well-being. Similarly accessibility to piped water can be a function of the residents' association with political parties and such political contacts are of mutual help only when well-being levels are poor (Edelman and Mitra, 2006).[5]

Conclusion

The results are not very distinct: while some of the outcomes are better for higher castes some others are almost similar with minor variations across different social categories. But these findings refer to the slum pockets only and not the entire urban space, though certain extrapolations can be made in this regard. If within the set of homogeneous dwelling the higher castes are slightly better off, for the urban areas as a whole with greater heterogeneity, much higher social inequality may be found going hand in hand with economic inequality. In other words, the erosion of the caste factor may not have actually taken place in the course of urbanization, as expected.

Though in the formal sector the reservation policy is in vogue and in many other activities the caste factor may not be considered by the employers, the differences in the outcome variables may still exist because of the marked divergence in the endowments. The diversity in education and skill levels, for example, across social categories translates them into occupational and income variations. On the other hand, our micro-level evidence also unravels the presence of higher castes at the lower echelons of the economic ladder. Hence, the poverty issues cannot be resolved simply in terms of caste-based reservation policy; rather such interventions may inflict violence and caste wars. There can be situations where poverty and well-being issues will have to be tackled through purely economic measures.

While urbanization has not dissipated the influence of caste factor and has not empowered the weaker social categories, the larger concerns of urbanization and inclusiveness are still relevant in the sense that the poor in general—irrespective of their caste background—may not have benefitted significantly in the process of urban headway. These ramifications can be better understood when various measures of well-being are encompassed, going beyond the measure of consumption or income poverty.

---

[5]   The clusters act as political vote banks and in return they are assured of legal tenure and accessibility to basic amenities.

CHAPTER 7

Changes in a Cultural Variable

Perspective

Urbanization envisaged as a process of transformation of ideas and ideologies is expected to counter social backwardness. Poor cultural practices and strong gender biases are expected to get eroded with modernization following as a concomitant of urbanization. This chapter proposes to focus on how the women workforce participation rate (WFPR), which is considered to be a variable influenced more by cultural factors than economic changes, responds to the shifts in the levels of urbanization. Further, Odisha being one of the backward states in India is expected to be within the realms of gendered division of labour, and hence, as a matter of illustration, this state is considered for an in-depth analysis though the district-level data across India are also included. In this context whether urbanization is able to mitigate the influence of social backwardness is a critical question. Which types of rural transformations are in progress and whether they allow women to participate in the labour market more explicitly is a pertinent question. Similarly, in the urban context, whether economic growth is ushering in opportunities for women to participate in remunerative activities is a key issue. Overall, the chapter looks at urbanization, economic growth, and poverty on the one hand and the changing role of women in this dynamic context on the other.

Among various supply and demand side factors, which impinge on women WFPR, economic growth and urbanization are said to be strong determinants (see Mathur, 1994; Agarwal, 1985; Durand, 1975; Sinha, 1965). Initially, growth is found to have a negative impact on WFPR but at higher levels of growth WFPR tends to increase, thus giving rise to a U-shaped relationship. Cagatay and Ozler

(1995) also suggest the possibility of a U-shaped relationship between the long-term development and women's share in the labour force. Even the historical records of developed countries indicate such a relationship between economic development and women's labour force participation rate (LFPR) (Goldin, 1994).[1]

With urbanization and industrialization, female-dominated home-based production is expected to decline as it would be largely replaced by male-dominated factory production (Boserup, 1970). This falling part of the U-shape curve corroborates Boserup's analysis of women's contribution to home-based production. However, with further economic development, women's LFPR is expected to increase as enhanced urbanization and industrialization, more education for women, commodification of domestic labour, and falling fertility rates help women workers participate in the labour market more explicitly (Oppenheimer, 1970; Boserup, 1970). Also, as per the neoclassical approach, with economic growth, gender inequalities in terms of access to employment opportunities, work conditions, nature of work, and earnings tend to decline (Forsythe, Korzeniewicz, and Durrant, 2000). This implies an increase in women's work participation rate since discouraged dropouts tend to decline; with improved and equal status in the job market women get encouraged to participate in the labour market (Mitra, 2005).

Some of the recent evidences also suggest that even higher human development index (HDI), let alone growth, does not necessarily ensure gender equality in terms of the gender development index (GDI). In the Asia-Pacific context, Japan and Korea have the highest HDI–GDI gap while Thailand and China whose HDI and GDI are both lower in absolute terms than Japan and Korea, demonstrate lower gender gaps (Murayama, 2005). Gender norms and systems vary widely across cultures but they shape people's lives and interactions in all societies (Hayase, 2005). In general, as women's educational level improves, gender inequality declines (United Nations, 2001a, 2001b). In other words, with improved levels of education, labour market participation of women in high-income jobs is expected to rise (Murayama, 2005; Pradhan, Singh, and Mitra, 2015); though in India many educated women remain outside the labour market, implying that the education level of women non-workers is higher than that of women workers. Keeping in view a long-term perspective, the Gender Kuznets Curve and the U-shaped relationship between women's work participation rate and development are mutually consistent.

---

[1] Goldin (1994) found this association for women aged 45 to 59 years for cross-sections of countries using GDP per capita as an index of development.

A variety of factors have been considered as determinants of female LFPR. These include opportunities for informal employment which tend to decline with development (Bharadwaj, 1989), technological and structural change, spouse's income (Sen, 1981),[2] the conflict between housework (including childcare) and earning opportunities in the labour market, and so on. Among various socio-economic factors, fertility, cross-regional cultural norms, attitude towards manual work, the relative incidence of low-caste and tribal population, size of the agricultural sector, cultivation techniques, crop patterns, poverty, and technology are some of the determinants of female work participation rate (see Agarwal, 1988). Also, there can be a positive association between work participation rate and the percentage of workers engaged in the tertiary sector as activities in this sector provide greater employment opportunities for women and teenage workers. However, low-productivity activities are mostly concentrated in the tertiary sector, and hence, as the share of the tertiary sector in total employment increases, dropouts from the labour market are expected to be high, thus reducing the work participation rate (Nord, 1989).

In the backdrop of this framework we analyse women's work participation rate in Odisha using the district-level data. In the second section we compare the work participation rate, urbanization level, and per capita income in Odisha in relation to other states and the all-India average. The third section presents the results of the factor analysis carried out on the basis of district-level data from Odisha on a number of variables including work participation rate, poverty, consumption expenditure per capita, inequality, urbanization level, incidence of low-caste population, literacy, employment structure, and other demographic variables. The fourth section examines the relationship between female work participation rate and labour productivity using the data for various Indian states. Finally, the last section summarizes the major findings.

Growth, Urbanization, and WFPR[3]

Economic growth in India in the post-crisis period (between 2009–10 and 2011–12) was around 6 per cent per annum while in Odisha it was barely 3.6 per cent per annum. Even some of the states such as Bihar, Jharkhand, Madhya Pradesh, and Rajasthan at comparable levels of income experienced much faster rates of

---

[2] Sen (1981) in the case of Indian agriculture showed that women withdraw from the labour market as male income increases.

[3] For details, see Mitra (2019).

growth (Table 7.1). In terms of urbanization again Jharkhand, Madhya Pradesh, and Rajasthan are at a much higher level as compared to Odisha. However, when it comes to female work participation rate (worker–population ratio), Odisha is at par with the all-India average in the rural areas and slightly higher in the urban areas. States such as Assam, Bihar, Jharkhand, and Uttar Pradesh are well below the Odisha figures and interestingly the urban-specific estimates for Odisha are quite close to those of the high-income states of Maharashtra and well above the figures corresponding to Delhi and Gujarat. Women work participation issue is the most complex one and it has been thoroughly researched, highlighting the importance of economic, social, demographic, and cultural factors. Besides, there are issues related to backward supply curve, that is, women withdrawing from the labour market at higher levels of income. Hence, it is unlikely that a linear relationship in terms of income or urbanization can be perceived as far as women work participation rate is concerned. The received theory on urbanization and women LFPR, however, suggests that urbanization not only brings in economic transformation, creating productive opportunities, but also social changes which motivate women to enhance their skill levels and participate in the job market. Of course, the social dimension of transformation can be sluggish, particularly in the context of the developing or less-developed regions. Hence, there could be situations in which economic opportunities may outpace the social backwardness, but the latter suppresses the women labour market participation.

Nevertheless, in the context of Odisha two important features seem to be prominent. First, the presence of the tribal-dominated districts raised the average figure corresponding to the rural areas since among the tribal population women contribute substantially to livelihood creation. Also, in general, Odisha being a poor state, women in the rural areas are forced to participate in the labour market. With the struggle faced by the poor households to access livelihood opportunities, these households cannot afford to have a high dependency ratio, as observed from the theoretical literature (Mitra, 2005). Second, Odisha at a comparably low level of urbanization shows a sizeably higher work participation rate. It may again be an outcome of a higher incidence of tribal population who migrated to some of the cities and towns. Besides, a high incidence of poverty compels most of the adult members of the households to explore earning possibilities. Often, women take recourse to multiple sources of livelihood given the responsibility of the domestic chores which do not allow them to accept regular jobs. The present chapter attempts to explore the effect of urbanization on both rural and urban work participation of women in order to capture some of the intricate issues.

Table 7.1 Per Capita NSDP, Urbanization, and Female WFPR

States/Union Territories	NSDP per capita 2009–10	NSDP per capita 2011–12	Rate of Growth % p.a.	URBAN (%) 2011	FWFPR: NSS (R) 2011–12	FWFPR: NSS (U) 2011–12
Andaman & Nicobar Islands	61,411	68,356	5.36	35.67	26.1	20.0
Andhra Pradesh	35,677	38,556	3.88	33.49	44.5	17.0
Arunachal Pradesh	33,893	35,527	2.35	22.67	27.8	12.7
Assam	20,406	21,741	3.17	14.08	12.2	9.0
Bihar	10,635	13,149	10.61	11.30	5.3	4.5
Chhattisgarh	24,189	27,163	5.80	23.24	41.5	24.0
Delhi	97,525	110,780	6.37	97.5	14.6	10.4
Goa	95,320	129,397	15.28	62.17	21.0	15.7
Gujarat	49,168	56,634	7.07	42.58	27.8	13.3
Haryana	55,044	61,716	5.72	34.79	16.2	9.7
Himachal Pradesh	43,492	49,203	6.17	10.04	52.4	21.2
Jammu & Kashmir	26,518	28,833	4.18	27.21	25.5	11.7
Jharkhand	21,534	25,265	7.99	24.05	19.8	6.6
Karnataka	37,294	41,492	5.33	38.57	28.7	16.3
Kerala	47,360	52,808	5.44	47.72	22.1	19.1
Madhya Pradesh	20,959	23,272	5.23	27.63	23.9	11.5

Table 7.1 contd.

Table 7.1 contd.

States/Union Territories	NSDP per capita 2009–10	NSDP per capita 2011–12	Rate of Growth % p.a.	URBAN (%) 2011	FWFPR: NSS (R) 2011–12	FWFPR: NSS (U) 2011–12
Maharashtra	54,246	61,468	6.25	45.23	38.8	16.6
Manipur	21,810	22,169	0.82	30.21	26.2	18.2
Meghalaya	29,306	34,232	7.77	20.08	39.1	20.2
Mizoram	34,699	37,921	4.44	51.51	39.4	24.9
Nagaland	40,590	46,340	6.62	28.97	31.2	14.4
Odisha	22,846	24,542	3.58	16.68	24.6	15.5
Puducherry	80,363	80,517	0.10	68.31	22.1	14.7
Punjab	42,831	46,340	3.94	37.49	23.4	13.6
Rajasthan	24,304	29,612	9.88	24.89	34.7	14.1
Sikkim	60,774	73,704	9.64	24.97	48.7	27.3
Tamil Nadu	47,394	57,093	9.31	48.45	37.8	20.1
Tripura	34,544	39,608	6.84	26.18	22.8	11.3
Uttar Pradesh	16,390	18,014	4.72	22.28	17.7	10.2
Uttarakhand	44,557	52,606	8.30	30.55	30.8	8.6
West Bengal	29,799	32,164	3.82	31.89	18.9	17.4
All India	33,901	38,048	5.77	31.16	24.8	14.7

Source: National Sample Survey (2011–12), population census, 2011 (Government of India, 2011), Central Statistical Organisation.
Note: WFPR is worker (usual principal-cum-subsidiary status) to population ratio. NSDP per capita is in 2004–5 prices.

Effect of Urbanization

The effect of urbanization on the rural areas is important. With the exhaustion of further scope for expansion of the existing large cities, the nearby areas tend to get urbanized to some extent and operate as satellite towns, conducting activities by and large similar to what the large centres do. Towns emerging as mediums of a transformation process in the rural areas are indeed an important aspect of urbanization in India. Population growth and diversification of activities in the rural areas are an endemic part of this transformation process. However, there is ample evidence to suggest that a large component of the rural non-farm sector activities is not induced by demand-side factors. Agricultural stagnation and the lack of scope to enhance productive employment opportunities in the agriculture sector are some of the possible factors responsible for a residual absorption of labour in low productivity non-farm activities. The lack of rural industrialization seems to have aggravated the 'employment problem'.

From another angle, along with urbanization the rural (economic) growth is expected to rise, as urbanization is a concomitant of expansion in economic activities. Agglomeration benefits associated with urbanization are likely to result in enhanced productivity growth (Mitra, 1999) which can also get reflected in rural per capita income and consumption expenditure through the rural–urban inter-sectoral linkages. The increased work participation rate in the rural areas, change in the occupational structure away from farm towards non-farm prompted by rural diversification, and reduction in rural poverty are some of the expected outcomes. Based on the village-level data and countrywide NSS data, Himanshu and colleagues (2013) observed the growing importance and influence of the non-farm sector on the rural economy between the early 1980s and late 2000s. Besides, this non-farm diversification, although being quite a sluggish process, has been pro-poor in terms of distributional incidence. Further, they noted that the non-farm sector is not only increasing incomes and reducing poverty, but it also tends to break down barriers to mobility among the poorest segments of the rural society. This is again likely to raise urbanization through migration. Himanshu and colleagues (2011) also noted a close association between urban poverty reduction and rural non-farm growth (and accompanying rural poverty reduction). The beneficial effects were realized through an increase in both rural non-farm employment and wages. Lanjouw and Murgai (2010a, 2010b) brought out a clear-cut link between urban poverty decline and rural poverty decline in India which was not seen in the studies based on data for the pre-reform period. The association between urban development on the one hand and improvement in rural livelihoods on the other was envisaged through the impact of urban development on the rural non-farm diversification. So, in their conceptualization the causality runs from urbanization to rural poverty decline. One may further hypothesize that the demographic variables such as household size and child–woman ratio also decline with urbanization, which may be allowing women to participate in the labour market more explicitly.

Similarly, the effect of urbanization on women's labour market participation in the urban areas is expected to be positive. As urbanization increases labour demand may rise, and thus, the extra demand may be met by the female labour supplies. Also, urbanization helps women access education and job market information more intensely. General awareness improves which helps women overcome social and cultural barriers that hinder their participation in the labour market though education may delay the labour market participation of the younger ones. Second, with urbanization, if growth shoots up with an increase in wages for the male workers, females may drop out from the labour market explaining the backward sloping curve of the labour market. These standard textbook understandings of the link between urbanization and women's labour market participation based on industrial countries have been subjected to intense scrutiny by scholars. It may be interesting to state the experiences of late industrializing countries and how these understandings have contributed to the re-examining of the received theories. Often, it is seen that the employers prefer female workers as they have a lesser bargaining strength and also female wages are substantially lower than the male wages with a false belief that female workers are less productive. This has resulted in feminization in the labour market. In a number of activities the female-to-male worker ratio has steadily gone up over time (Banerjee, 1997). In fact, like contractualization, feminisation is an arrangement pursued to reduce labour cost sizeably. The other new change perceived in the recent years is the practice of subcontracting from the formal to the informal sector. Though it creates work opportunities in the informal sector, the business contractors follow the payment practice based on piece rate, reducing the remuneration of the workers. As many of the home-based workers are women, they are the ones who are worst hit (Patrick, 2001).

Keeping in view some of these interesting patterns, the analysis in this chapter is pursued at the district level. Most of the variables included in our analysis are for the year 2011 (taken from population census) and only poverty, inequality, and monthly per capita consumption expenditure are for the year 2011–12 (taken from NSS).

The variables considered in the factor analysis include the following:[4] HHSZ: household size; CHILD-WOM: proportion of children to women; WFPR: main workforce participation rate; LIT: literacy; SC: percentage of Scheduled Caste population; OTHERACT: percentage of workers engaged in non-household manufacturing and services; CUL: percentage of workforce engaged as cultivators; AGLAB: percentage of workforce engaged as agricultural labourers; MFGHH: percentage of workers in household industries; F/M: female–male ratio in the population, BPL: percentage of households below the poverty line; AVMPCE: average monthly per capita consumption expenditure; INEQ: inequality in terms of the difference between the minimum and maximum value of the consumption expenditure. In addition to the rural-specific variables, we have considered URBN which is the percentage of population in the urban areas in the district.

Empirical evidence however goes mostly against the view that urbanization would raise female work participation rate (factor 1 from Table 7.2). Though male work participation rate increases with urbanization, female participation declines in the rural areas. Several studies have confirmed that urbanization is highly unequal in India in the sense that a very large percentage of the total urban population resides in a couple of very large cities (Bhagat, 2011). Moreover, these cities are expanding further into the rural hinterland. Several new towns (census towns) have emerged between 2001 and 2011. This transformation process helps urban activities to spill out to the rural areas without really benefitting the rural population in terms of accessing productive work opportunities. Rural women in particular are worst affected as the skill mismatch is serious in their case (Mitra, 2013).

From our results literacy is seen to reduce work participation suggesting that women may be pursuing higher education, and thus participation of young women in the labour market may have declined. Micro-level studies exploring this phenomenon also suggest that young educated but married women are forced to withdraw for various social and cultural reasons (Jalan, 2000).

Poverty and women participation in the labour market are positively associated while growth reduces poverty and female work participation, both. Again, cultivation raises women work participation while other non-farm activities reduce it. This tends to suggest that in agriculture-dependent households there is a need for women to contribute in terms of their labour while the rural non-farm activities are not productive enough to attract women sizeably or these activities are not geared to absorbing women on

---

[4] See Mitra (2019).

Table 7.2 Results from Factor Analysis for Odisha (District: Rural)

Variables	Factor 1	Factor 2	Factor 3	Factor 4
RHHSZ	0.236	0.006	0.25	-0.29
RCHILD-WOM	-0.80	-0.26	0.03	-0.18
RWFPRM	0.16	0.47	0.05	0.17
RWFPRF	-0.51	-0.23	-0.05	0.43
RLITM	0.74	0.36	0.02	0.12
RLITF	0.75	0.35	0.04	0.08
RSCM	0.13	0.98	0.01	0.002
RSCF	0.18	0.97	0.01	0.004
ROTHERACTM	0.90	-0.05	0.31	0.05
ROTHERACTF	0.75	0.15	0.08	-0.21
RMFGHHM	0.28	0.22	-0.08	0.26
RMFGHHF	0.20	0.04	0.002	0.94
RCULM	-0.91	0.03	0.26	-0.09
RCULF	-0.84	-0.05	0.38	-0.10
RAGLABM	0.09	-0.02	-0.98	0.01
RAGLABF	-0.34	-0.18	-0.47	-0.11
RF/M	-0.59	-0.27	-0.02	-0.15
RBPL	-0.78	-0.31	-0.21	0.09
URBN	0.42	-0.18	0.35	0.24
RAVMPCE	0.76	0.27	0.07	0.32
RINEQ	0.10	-0.19	0.01	0.33
Eigenvalue	9.25	2.85	2.41	1.85
Explained Variation	0.47	0.15	0.12	0.10

Number of observations: 30

Source: Author's calculations based on population census, 2011 (Government of India, 2011).

Note: R represents rural areas, HHSZ: household size; CHILD-WOM: proportion of children to women; WFPR: main workforce participation rate; LIT: literacy; SC: percentage of Scheduled Caste population; OTHERACT: percentage of workers engaged in non-household manufacturing and services; CUL: percentage of workforce engaged as cultivators; AGLAB: percentage of work force engaged as agricultural labourers; MFGHH: percentage of workers in household manufacturing; F/M: female–male ratio in the population, BPL: percentage of households below the poverty line; URBN: percentage of population in the urban areas; AVMPCE: average monthly per capita consumption expenditure; INEQ: inequality in terms of the difference between the minimum and maximum value of the consumption expenditure. The variables are for 2011 or 2011–12 or 2010–11.

a large scale. Rise in rural female–male ratio again tends to reduce women work participation rate which is in fact quite against the popular views. On the other hand, a higher child–woman ratio raises the work participation implying that women from households with more children are, in fact, forced to join the labour market in order to meet the minimum consumption requirements.

However, in factor 2, urbanization and rural women work participation rate and in factor 4, which is also a statistically significant one (though much less significant than factor 1), urbanisation, economic growth and rural work participation rate of women, all show a positive association. Increased fertility (a higher child–woman ratio) and a large household size reduce participation (factor 4). These contrasting findings emerging from factor 1 and factor 4 can be rationalized on the ground that what factor 1 reveals is a much stronger and largely noticed phenomenon. But at the same time, the findings from factor 4 reveal that certain new features at par with theoretical underpinnings are emerging simultaneously though not so prevalently.

In the urban areas again, the higher level of urbanization reduces female work participation rate while economic growth reduces and poverty raises participation respectively (Table 7.3). With respect to child–woman ratio, female work participation rises as well as falls in factors 3 and 4 respectively, indicating that two groups of districts are present in Odisha with two different behavioural patterns. Possibly, in the poorer and tribal districts higher child–woman ratio compels women to participate in the job market while in relatively higher-income districts higher fertility reduces participation, as the theory would suggest. Higher female–male ratio shows a positive association with female participation in factor 3 whereas the association is negative in factor 4, indicating again the presence of two types of districts following two different types of patterns. Other activities including non-household manufacturing and services reduce the women work participation rate possibly because these activities are non-productive enough to motivate women to join the labour market. However, the inverse relationship between urbanization and poverty tends to suggest that the beneficial effects of urbanization reduce the compulsion-driven component of women's work participation. However, the positive effect of urbanization in raising women work participation is not distinct in the urban areas. Possibly, the cultural barriers are still so strong that the positive effects (in terms of enhanced level of urbanization) are not reaped. Literacy is seen to reduce participation while the presence of lower castes raises it.

Table 7.3 Results from Factor Analysis for Odisha (District: Urban)

Variables	Factor 1	Factor 2	Factor 3	Factor 4
UHHSZ	0.13	0.03	-0.23	0.02
UCHILD–WOM	-0.87	-0.12	0.23	0.20
UWFPRM	0.12	0.06	0.05	0.13
UWFPRF	-0.08	0.02	0.35	-0.52
ULITM	0.94	0.15	-0.06	0.23
ULITF	0.89	0.03	-0.25	0.22
USCM	-0.19	0.26	0.93	-0.07
USCF	-0.22	0.22	0.93	-0.07
UOTHERACTM	0.15	-0.67	-0.11	0.10
UOTHERACTF	0.06	-0.73	-0.24	0.38
UMFGHHM	0.26	0.90	0.16	0.05
UMFGHHF	0.13	0.93	0.23	0.01
UF/M	-0.22	0.07	0.07	-0.86
UBPL	-0.36	0.23	0.24	-0.16
URBN	0.13	-0.09	-0.33	0.23
UAVMPCE	0.24	-0.12	-0.23	0.38
UINEQ	0.08	-0.11	0.12	0.04
Eigenvalue	5.46	3.22	2.08	1.67
Explained Variation	0.36	0.21	0.14	0.11

Number of observations: 30

Source: Author's calculations based on population census, 2011 (Government of India, 2011).

Note: U represents urban areas; HHSZ: household size; CHILD–WOM: proportion of children to women; WFPR: main workforce participation rate; LIT: literacy; SC: percentage of Scheduled Caste population; OTHERACT: percentage of workers engaged in non-household manufacturing and services; MFGHH: percentage of workers in household manufacturing; F/M: female–male ratio in the population; BPL: percentage of households below the poverty line; URBN: percentage of population in the urban areas; AVMPCE: average monthly per capita consumption expenditure; INEQ: inequality in terms of the difference between the minimum and maximum values of the consumption expenditure.

The variables are for 2011 or 2011–12 or 2010–11.

The skill mismatch, in the case of women workers particularly, is a serious issue. Most of the economic activities being concentrated in very large cities, the medium-sized and small towns do not create much work opportunities. Hence, women in particular do not benefit and the urbanization level and women work participation rate do not show a positive relationship. Also, migration of women from rural to urban areas in India is mostly prompted by social factors such as marriage (Mitra and Murayama, 2008). Since these women do not necessarily participate in the urban labour market, urbanization and a reduced participation rate of women does not come as a surprise. A mere increase in literacy is not able to counter the cultural practices and the social backwardness that lead to the perception of women's participation in the labour market as a low-status phenomenon. Even among the educated lot this mindset is prevalent, forcing many educated and married women to withdraw from the job market (Jalan, 2000; Schultz, 1990). Also, household activities and domestic responsibilities involving children and the elderly are given higher priority over participation (Hirway, 2010). The disadvantaged classes, however, have different social norms: economic compulsions historically seem to have raised the participation of women in the job market alongside the males.

Evidence from District-Level Data across India

The negative effect of fertility and household size on rural female work participation comes out sharply from factor 1 (Table 7.4).[5] Greater domestic burdens in large households do not allow women to participate in the work force. Literacy raises participation (factor 1) though there are other districts forming a separate group in which literacy reduces participation (factor 2) possibly because enrolment of girls leads to labour market withdrawal. The positive association between tribal population and participation and the negative effect of low-caste population on participation are evident.

The visibility of women and urbanization level seem to be enhancing women participation in the rural areas. With increased level of urbanization, the rural–urban discontinuum tends to decline which brings in work opportunities even for rural women who do not migrate out. There is a cluster of districts which is indicative of women workers being engaged primarily as agricultural labour or cultivators (factor 2) though there are some other districts which tend to show increased participation

---

[5]   See Mitra and Okada (2018).

Table 7.4 Factor Analysis: Rural Female Work Participation Rate at the District
Level: All-India

Variables	Factor 1	Factor 2	Factor 3	Factor 4
HHSZ(R)	-0.6820	-0.0478	0.2315	-0.1173
CHILD(R)	-0.8783	0.1008	0.0717	0.1659
WPR(F,R)	0.4626	0.5607	-0.0051	0.2973
LIT(F,R)	0.7067	-0.3227	0.1442	-0.0066
SC(F,R)	0.1048	-0.0205	-0.2099	-0.7008
ST(F,R)	-0.0695	0.2442	0.2478	0.7081
F/M(R)	0.4101	0.1304	-0.0642	0.1631
URBAN	0.3592	-0.2852	-0.0290	0.0236
AGLAB(F,R)	0.0185	0.2679	-0.9526	-0.1024
CUL(F,R)	-0.1301	0.6514	0.6790	0.1662
MFGHH(F,R)	-0.0726	-0.1470	0.0037	-0.0821
OTHER(F,R)	0.1467	-0.9531	0.2402	-0.0518
CHILDSR(R)	0.0967	0.1167	-0.1530	0.4789
Eigenvalue	2.91318	2.49798	1.78244	1.05884
% Explained	0.3283	0.2815	0.2009	0.1193

N = 631

Source: Mitra and Okada (2018) based on population census, 2011 (Government of
India, 2011).

Note: The variables which are chosen are as follows: household size (HHSZ), literacy
rate (LIT), child–woman ratio (CHILD), female–male ratio in the population (F/M),
urbanization level (URBN), percentage of Scheduled Caste (SC) and Scheduled
Tribe population (ST), sex ratio among children (CHILDSR), shares of agricultural
labour (AGLAB), cultivators (CUL), household manufacturing (MFGHH) and
other activities (OTHER) in total work force. The child sex ratio may represent the
extent of gender discrimination at young age brackets. Districts with low levels of
child sex ratio would mean high degree of gender discrimination. The employment
composition is taken to assess how dynamic an area is.

R stands for rural and F for female.

with improvement in activities other than agriculture and household manufacturing. The non-household manufacturing and the services sector offer possibilities of better earnings, encouraging women—particularly the literate ones—to join the work force. Also, some of the jobs in the health sector, for example, are meant specifically for literate women. Unfortunately, rural diversification has been very sluggish in the Indian context with its limited impact on women work participation rate which can be seen from the low magnitude of the factor loading for the share of workers in non-household manufacturing and services in factor 1. Gender discrimination at early ages is reflective of its continuation even in the later years: an improvement in the gender ratio among children improves the work participation to a very limited extent.

Among the rural males the positive effect of urbanization on participation is evident (Table 7.5). Literacy raises the work participation rate while demographic pressure reduces it. Large families with large number of children are not able to generate better human capital formation, which in turn reduces the possibility of being absorbed in high productivity activities. Activities other than household manufacturing and agriculture have a positive effect on participation, suggesting the importance of rural diversification.

Among the urban females the findings are again quite similar to those for rural females except in relation to gender ratio, which does not have a positive effect on participation in the urban areas (Table 7.6). This is mainly because many educated women living in the urban areas remain confined to domestic activities. Even when the gender ratio rises due to migration of women after marriage—the biggest reason of female migration in India (Mitra and Murayama, 2008)—women do not necessarily participate in the labour market. Besides, women who accompany their husbands while migrating from rural to urban areas are not able to find employment in the urban labour market. At times there is skill mismatch and at times the labour demand for women is limited and transient. For example, in the construction sector demand for women labour is highly sporadic and when there is a decline in labour demand, the women workers are the first ones to be retrenched. So the discrimination issue is much wide and deep-rooted, it can exist even when at the time of birth it is not prevalent in the form of gender selective feticide. As Table 7.6 shows, the child sex ratio has a positive association with work participation but the overall gender ratio has a much stronger negative relationship with female work participation rate. With accessibility of women to job opportunities, female feticide seems to have declined, but rise in the women-to-men ratio has not resulted in enhanced participation due to cultural barriers. Urbanization and female work participation rate are, however, positively associated.

Table 7.5 Factor Analysis: Rural Male Work Participation Rate at the District
Level: All-India

Variables	Factor 1	Factor 2	Factor 3
HHSZ(R)	-0.7141	-0.1482	0.1723
CHILD(R)	-0.8742	-0.2242	-0.0524
WPR(M,R)	0.6612	-0.0179	-0.0679
LIT(M,R)	0.5956	0.2986	0.2413
SC(M,R)	0.1588	-0.0013	-0.2127
ST(M,R)	-0.0818	-0.2575	0.1938
URBAN	0.2565	0.3895	0.1347
AGLAB(M,R)	0.0228	0.0286	-0.9928
CUL(M,R)	-0.1644	-0.9483	0.2152
MFGHH(M,R)	-0.0853	0.1331	-0.0280
OTHER(M,R)	0.1338	0.8054	0.5778
CHILDSR(R)	0.1189	-0.0092	-0.1499
Eigenvalue	3.19995	1.97325	1.73938
% Explained	0.3785	0.2334	0.2057

N = 631

Source: Mitra and Okada (2018), based on population census, 2011 (Government
of India, 2011).

Note: The variables which are chosen are as follows: household size (HHSZ), literacy
rate (LIT), child–woman ratio (CHILD), female–male ratio in the population (F/M),
urbanization level (URBN), percentage of Scheduled Caste (SC) and Scheduled
Tribe population (ST), sex ratio among children (CHILDSR), shares of agricultural
labour (AGLAB), cultivators (CUL), household manufacturing (MFGHH) and
other activities (OTHER) in total work force. The child sex ratio may represent the
extent of gender discrimination at young age brackets. Districts with low levels of
child sex ratio would mean high degree of gender discrimination. The employment
composition is taken to assess how dynamic an area is.
R stands for rural and M for male.

Among the males the findings are again not different from what we noted in the
rural context (Table 7.7). However, the association between the share of activities
comprising non-household manufacturing and services and the work participation rate

is highly significant. Higher levels of urbanization are seen to raise the participation confirming the agglomeration effects. With greater concentration of infrastructure and activities, labour demand seems to have raised the participation rate.

Table 7.6 Factor Analysis: Urban Female Work Participation Rate at the District Level: All-India

Variables	Factor 1	Factor 2	Factor 3	Factor 4
HHSZ(U)	-0.7893	-0.0272	0.0657	0.0318
CHILD(U)	-0.8262	0.1174	0.2322	0.1146
WPR(F,U)	0.6137	0.1048	0.2320	0.4184
LIT(F,U)	0.7600	-0.2329	-0.0343	0.1495
SC(F,U)	0.1254	0.0876	-0.1199	-0.6222
ST(F,U)	0.0176	-0.0951	0.4184	0.7240
F/M(U)	-0.8262	0.1174	0.2322	0.1146
URBAN	0.3041	-0.1769	-0.1508	-0.0241
AGLAB(F,U)	-0.0445	0.9978	0.0138	-0.0404
CUL(F,U)	-0.0879	0.0914	0.9793	0.1661
MFGHH(F,U)	-0.1243	0.0239	-0.0724	-0.0562
OTHER(F,U)	0.1470	-0.6715	-0.4819	-0.0296
CHILDSR(U)	0.2846	0.1268	0.0424	0.5288
Eigenvalue	3.14689	2.37446	1.73720	1.01386
% Explained	0.3584	0.2705	0.1979	0.1155

N = 637

Source: Mitra and Okada (2018), based on population census, 2011 (Government of India, 2011).

Note: The variables which are chosen are as follows: household size (HHSZ), literacy rate (LIT), child–woman ratio (CHILD), female–male ratio in the population (F/M), urbanization level (URBN), percentage of Scheduled Caste (SC) and Scheduled Tribe population (ST), sex ratio among children (CHILDSR), shares of agricultural labour (AGLAB), cultivators (CUL), household manufacturing (MFGHH) and other activities (OTHER) in total work force. The child sex ratio may represent the extent of gender discrimination at young age brackets. Districts with low levels of child sex ratio would mean high degree of gender discrimination. The employment composition is taken to assess how dynamic an area is.

U stands for urban and F for female.

Table 7.7 Factor Analysis: Urban Male Work Participation Rate at the District Level: All-India

Variables	Factor 1	Factor 2	Factor 3
HHSZ(U)	-0.7569	0.0513	0.1070
CHILD(U)	-0.8366	0.1671	0.2077
WPR(M,U)	0.6008	-0.1819	-0.2105
LIT(M,U)	0.7096	-0.3451	-0.0913
SC(M,U)	0.1605	0.0831	-0.0248
ST(M,U)	-0.0642	-0.1414	0.2994
URBAN	0.2488	-0.1746	-0.1904
AGLAB(M,U)	-0.1520	0.9731	0.1671
CUL(M,U)	-0.1462	0.1956	0.9631
MFGHH(M,U)	-0.1539	0.0851	0.0186
OTHER(M,U)	0.2178	-0.6645	-0.6270
CHILDSR(M,U)	0.2600	0.1206	0.0630
Eigenvalue	3.94216	1.67724	1.27130
% Explained	0.4961	0.2111	0.1600

Source: Mitra and Okada (2018), based on population census, 2011 (Government of India, 2011).

Note: The variables which are chosen are as follows: household size (HHSZ), literacy rate (LIT), child–woman ratio (CHILD), female–male ratio in the population (F/M), urbanization level (URBN), percentage of Scheduled Caste (SC) and Scheduled Tribe population (ST), sex ratio among children (CHILDSR), shares of agricultural labour (AGLAB), cultivators (CUL), household manufacturing (MFGHH) and other activities (OTHER) in total work force. The child sex ratio may represent the extent of gender discrimination at young age brackets. Districts with low levels of child sex ratio would mean high degree of gender discrimination. The employment composition is taken to assess how dynamic an area is.

R stands for rural and F for female.

U stands for urban and M for male.

Productivity and Female Participation

In this section, based on the state-level data, we assess if female labour participation raises labour productivity or otherwise. On *a priori* basis the relationship between the variables can go in either direction—positive or negative. In ageing societies as the labour supply shrinks, the shortages can be mitigated by raising the female labour force participation. Also, given the fact that female labour is docile and sincere, labour productivity can actually rise with increased participation of women in the labour market. Besides, female wages being lower than the male wages the substitution of female labour for male labour can reduce the wage share (or labour cost) in value added. In other words, wage-to-labour productivity ratio can decline which means increased efficiency of the unit from the point of view of the employer. This can then contribute to overall growth.

However, from another angle, particularly in a typical neoclassical frame, female wages are lower because female productivity is believed to be lower than male productivity: the rationalization is derived from the proposition that each of the factors of production gets paid according to its marginal productivity under perfect competition. This postulation has led to the concern that increased participation of females in the labour market can actually reduce labour productivity and growth.

Further, as we say low productivity means low wages which in turn raises labour demand, there is a possibility of a causal relationship running from productivity to participation as well. In other words, to put in plainly, lower productivity would mean more manpower to complete the job. So the bi-directionality issue is quite important. In addition, productivity cannot be measured as a function of participation only. Other relevant variables representing technology, skill, and production structure, to cite a few, need to be controlled for. However, given the paucity of information and the lack of possibility of carrying out a rigorous quantitative exercise, we simply take overall labour productivity as a function of certain variables on which information is readily available. This is pursued basically to address the importance of certain policy options. For example, economic necessity may compel women to participate in the labour market and without adequate education and skill they may pursue petty activities. This sort of a situation will lead to increased participation but with low levels of productivity. On the other hand, with higher levels of education and skill when women participate in the labour market their productivity can be much higher. But with higher levels of education women may not necessarily participate in the labour market as the social factors may pose major hindrances. Hence, based on the observed association between productivity and participation certain broad inferences can only be drawn regarding the quality of jobs that women get absorbed into, and accordingly suggestions can be made in favour of strategies which can help attain the twin objectives of productivity growth and increased participation.

There are certain practical difficulties in assessing the relationship between female labour force participation rate and labour productivity. A highly capital-intensive technology which reduces the pace of labour absorption without reducing value added would mean higher labour productivity. Hence, there is difficulty in assessing the impact of labour force participation rate on labour productivity as lower employment levels would always mean higher labour productivity. So, this needs to be interpreted very carefully. Second, labour productivity is defined as value added per labour. But no information is available on how much of value added is contributed by the male and female workers separately. Hence, it becomes difficult to assess the association between female labour force participation and female labour productivity. Again, the information on rural and urban labour productivity is missing because value-added figures are given sector-wise. So, what is doable is as follows. We can only investigate whether there is a positive relationship between female labour force participation and overall labour productivity.

When we take labour productivity as a function of participation rate, the endogeneity problem arises because participation itself is an endogenous outcome which is determined in terms of certain variables. We have, therefore, presented two sets of results below (Table 7.8). One set gives the ordinary least square (OLS) results while the other corrects for endogeneity by considering an appropriate instrument for participation. The instrument is generated by estimating the participation equation first and then considering its predicted value. The results tend to indicate that the female participation rate is statistically insignificant in most of the equations with labour productivity as the dependent variable. It has a negative sign but that can be primarily because many women workers are engaged in petty activities in the informal sector, both in rural as well as urban areas.

What is striking from Table 7.8 is that, given participation, women's education (captured through enrolment), urbanization, and infrastructure availability are some of the most important determinants of productivity. Also, the social infrastructure covering health- and education- specific variables, and physical and financial infrastructure impact women's participation in the labour market significantly. Poor health conditions measured in terms of higher infant mortality rate reduce the participation. The panel data analysis also confirms that poor health reduces women participation. These findings are important from policy point of view because different infrastructure variables are seen to improve both women participation and labour productivity. Infrastructure (social, physical, and financial) can to a certain extent help break the social and cultural barriers and help women participate in the labour market thereby making productive contribution. For voicing the women's needs, overcoming the social constraints, and enhancing their bargaining power, their physical presence is essential as indicated by a positive association between female–male ratio and women participation, particularly in the rural areas where social barriers are strong.

Table 7.8 Effect of Female Participation on Labour Productivity

Variables	Dep var: Lab Prod (OLS)	Dep var: Lab Prod (OLS)	Dep var: WORK (E,R) (OLS)	Dep var: WORK (E,U) (OLS)	Dep var: LFPR (E,R) (OLS)	Dep var: LFPR (F,U) (OSLS)	Dep var: Lab Prod (2SLS)	Dep var: Lab Prod (2SLS)
WORK(E,R)	-9474.98 (-0.21)						-26709.8 (-0.26)	
WORK(E,U)	-185178.5 (-1.84)						-385561.6 (-1.35)	
LFPR(F,R)		-185115.6 (0-.57)						-103884.6 (-2.0)
LFPR(F,U)		-0.36783.7 (-0.76)						-190538.2 (-1.84)
SERDP	75500.8 (1.82)	80466.8 (1.71)					68489.8 (1.54)	64334.9 (1.55)
URBAN	78042.7 (3.43)*	62162.9 (2.52)*					100857 (3.14)*	92146.9 (3.59)*
ROAD		150.1 (0.16)	0.013 (3.99)*	0.005 (2.96)*	0.017 (2.71)*	0.009 (2.05)	1817.1 (1.23)	3335.0 (2.05)*
CR–DP			0.180 (3.95)*	0.05 (2.26)*	0.19 (2.13)*	-0.02 (-0.35)		
ENROL of girls	44694.7 (2.57)*	40649.1 (2.07)*	0.136 (2.30)*	0.107 (3.61)*	0.389 (3.46)*	0.26 (3.52)*	59537 (2.31)*	109144.9 (3.21)*

Table 7.8 contd.

Table 7.8 contd.

Variables	Dep var: Lab Prod (OLS)	Dep var: Lab Prod (OLS)	Dep var: WORK (E,R) (OLS)	Dep var: WORK (EU) (OLS)	Dep var: LFPR (E,R) (OLS)	Dep var: LFPR (EU) (OSLS)	Dep var: Lab Prod (2SLS)	Dep var: Lab Prod (2SLS)
IMR(F)				-0.12 (-2.62)*		0.28 (-2.47)*		
F/M			32.33 (1.78)		77.59 (2.24)*			
Constant	-8386365 (-2.89)*	-8751124 (-2.65)*	-43.35 (-2.42)*	0.51 (0.13)	96.22 (-2.81)*	2.58 (0.27)	-8347673 (-2.69)*	-1.10+e07 (-3.56)*
Adj R2	0.64	0.66	0.55	0.48	0.47	0.50	0.59	0.64
N	32	32	35	35	35	35	32	32

Source: Mitra and Okada (2018).

Note: R within parenthesis represents rural, U urban and F female.

WFPR and LFPR: work and labour force participation rate respectively; SERDP: percentage of services in total gross state domestic product; URBAN: percentage urban; CR–DP: credit–deposit ratio of scheduled commercial banks; IMR: infant mortality rate among girls; ENROL: gross enrolment rate in classes 1 to 8 among girls; F/M: female to male population and LAB PROD: labour productivity.

We also noted elsewhere (Mitra, 2019) the beneficial effect of female labour force participation rate (from the panel data analysis) on infant mortality of girls as well as boys after controlling for growth indicator which also has a very strong effect on infant mortality rate. Access of mothers to resources through labour market participation improves the health status of the children as their nutritional status also improves. Also, greater volume of resources is required for enhancing the provision of healthcare facilities which can be met through higher levels of growth.

Elsewhere it has been shown, based on data from a number of Asia-Pacific countries, that decline in gender inequality in the labour market through improvement in female labour force participation reduces inequality in many other spheres and eventually leads to greater participation of women in the decision making process, both within the households and at macro-level (Mitra, 2009). Particularly when it comes to fertility decisions working women are able to voice their preference better as compared to housewives. Similarly, working women could vouch for gender budgeting and participate in the political process as well. Refuting the view that increased participation of females in the labour market would reduce growth, the study also displayed evidence in favour of economic growth responding positively to a rise in female participation. Poor levels of skills resulting from gender discrimination, limited scope to undergo on-the-job training, information asymmetry aggravated by the inadequate access of women to job market information, inability to pursue job search on full-time basis due to domestic responsibilities, unavailability of productive jobs with flexi-hours, and weak bargaining power result in lower wages for women workers than their male counterparts. And this wage discrepancy has sent a wrong message about women being less productive.

Conclusion

Urbanization and women work participation based on district-level data from Odisha show a negative association. Districts with higher level of urbanization show a lower participation of women, both in rural and urban areas. Women from poor households seem to be working more as poverty and female work participation rate are positively associated.

Growth and urbanization are however positively associated while growth and poverty are inversely related. Also, growth and women's WFPR are negatively associated. This is indicative of either a backward sloping supply curve of women at higher levels of per capita income or growth being unable to create work opportunities, which in turn leads to the phenomenon of discouraged dropouts, that is, withdrawal of women from the labour market due to unavailability of jobs of desirable status. On the whole, the positive role of urbanization in removing the social and cultural barriers so as to release more women into the job market or to create more work opportunities for women in the growth process—by removing productivity differentials across sexes—is rather limited. Odisha at a comparatively lower level of urbanization registered a higher work participation rate for women but across districts the positive association between urbanization and work participation is not strongly evident, particularly in the urban areas though in the rural areas there is a subtle positive association lying beneath a predominantly negative association. In other words, the positive impact of urbanization on rural women and their participation in the job market is on the rise though the urban areas would still have to wait for urbanization to pick up further to experience an increased participation of women. The growth effect on women's work participation in the urban areas is mostly negative which did not possibly contribute to turn the relationship between urbanization and women's work participation into a positive one. Or we can say, employment opportunities emerging in the process of economic growth in the urban areas seem to have a gender bias. The new jobs in the high productivity segment are both technology- and skill-intensive. Either women do not possess the requisite skills to access these jobs or at times the social norms view women's participation in the job market as a low-status phenomenon despite the fact that educated women are likely to get absorbed in white-collar jobs, and not blue-collar ones. From the demand side, again, business firms tend to prefer male workers, viewing women workers as an expensive category (because of maternity benefits and leave, and so on).

Policy interventions to counter such distortions are essential so that women access higher levels of skill and education and subsequently participate in the job market instead of withdrawing from it. In the rural areas, diversification is important for women's absorption in productive activities if the low equilibrium situation of continuing in marginal activities in the agricultural sector is to be broken. The factors which constrain women's migration to urban areas to take advantage of better opportunities are mostly social and cultural but it is important to counteract them by improving the human resource component and the economic freedom of women. Biases against hiring women can partly be removed with gender sensitization programmes. Biases in favour of employing women so that labour cost is reduced by offering them lower wages need to be checked through strict legislations. Skill development and vocational training programmes, particularly in the urban areas, need to be implemented on a large scale and with the provision of flexi-hours so that the relationship between urbanization and women work participation can be made positive.

At the all-India level, based on district-level data, the visibility of women and urbanization level seem to be enhancing women participation in the rural areas. With increased level of urbanization the rural–urban discontinuum tends to decline which brings in work opportunities even for rural women who do not migrate out. There is a cluster of districts which is indicative of women workers being engaged primarily as agricultural labour or cultivators though there are some other districts which tend to show increased participation with improvement in activities other than agriculture and household manufacturing. The non-household manufacturing and the services sector offer possibilities of better earnings, encouraging women, particularly the literate ones, to join the workforce. In the urban areas, the findings are again quite similar to those for rural females. Urbanization and female work participation rate are positively associated. The panel data analysis also confirms that poor health reduces women participation. These findings are important from policy point of view because different infrastructure variables are seen to improve both women participation and labour productivity. Infrastructure (social, physical, and financial) can to a certain extent help break the social and cultural barriers and help women participate in the labour market thereby making productive contribution. For voicing women's needs, overcoming social constraints, and enhancing their bargaining power, their physical presence is essential as indicated by a positive association between female–male ratio and women participation, particularly in the rural areas where social barriers are strong.

Bibliography

Agarwal, B. (1988). 'Who Sows? Who Reaps? Women and Land Rights in India'. *The Journal of Peasant Studies* 15(4): 531–81.

——— (1985). 'Work Participation of Rural Women in the Third World: Some Data and Conceptual Biases'. *Economic and Political Weekly* 2(51–52): A155–A164.

Agrawal, T. and S. Chandrasekhar (2015). 'Short Term Migrants in India: Characteristics, Wages and Work Transition'. Working Paper No. 29, Indira Gandhi Institute of Development Research, Mumbai.

Ahrend, R., E. Farchy, I. Kaplanis, and A. C. Lembcke (2014). 'What Makes Cities More Productive? Evidence on the Role of Urban Governance from Five OECD Countries'. OECD Regional Development Working Papers, no. 2014/05. OECD, Paris.

Arshad, Sidra, Shougeng Hu, and Badar Nadeem Asraf (2018). 'Mini Review: Zipf's Law and City Size Distribution: A Survey of the Literature and Future Research Agenda'. *Physica A: Statistical Mechanics and Its Applications* 492(15 February): 75–92.

Baganha, I. B. M. (1991). 'The Social Mobility of Portuguese Immigrants in the United States at the Turn of the Nineteenth Century'. *International Migration Review* 25(2): 277–302.

Banerjee, B. (1986). *Rural to Urban Migration and the Urban Labour Market: A Case Study of Delhi*. Bombay: Himalaya Publishing House.

Banerjee, B. and G. A. Bucci (1994). 'On the Job Search after Entering Urban Employment: An Analysis Based on Indian Migrants'. *Oxford Bulletin of Economics and Statistics* 56: 33–47.

Banerjee, N. (1997). 'How Real Is the Bogy of Feminization?' *The Indian Journal of Labour Economics* 40(3): 427–38.

Basu, A. M., K. Basu, and R. Ray (1987). 'Migrants and the Native Bond: An Analysis of Micro-level Data from Delhi'. *Economic and Political Weekly* 22(19): 20–1.

Baulch, B. and J. Hoddinott (2000). 'Economic Mobility and Poverty Dynamics in Developing Countries'. *Journal of Development Studies* 36(1): 1–24.

Becker, C. M., and A. R. Morrison (1999). 'Urbanization in Transforming Economies'. In J. V. Henderson and J. F. Thisse (eds), *Handbook of Regional and Urban Economics*, vol. 3, 1673–1790. Amsterdam: Elsevier.

Behrman J. R. and Z. Zhang (1995). 'Gender Issues and Employment in Asia'. *Asian Development Review* 13(2): 1–49.

Beteille, A. (1969). 'Caste in a South Indian Village'. In A. Beteille (ed.), *Social Inequality*. Harmondsworth: Penguin Books.

Bhagat, R. B. (2011). 'Emerging Pattern of Urbanisation in India'. *Economic and Political Weekly* 46(34): 10–12.

Bhandari, G. and B. C. Reddy (2015). 'Impact of Out Migration on Agriculture and Women Work Load: An Economic Analysis of Hilly Regions of Uttrakhand, India'. *Indian Journal of Agricultural Economics* 70(3): 395–404.

Bhanumurthy, N. R. and A. Mitra (2010). 'Globalization, Growth and Poverty in India'. In M. Nissanke and Erik Thorbecke (eds), *The Poor under Globalisation in Asia, Latin America and Africa*, ch. 5. New York: Oxford University Press.

Bharadwaj, K. (1989). 'The Formation of Rural Labour Markets: An Analysis with Special Reference to Asia'. World Employment Research Programme Working Paper, WEP 10-6/WP 98. ILO, Geneva.

Bhattacharya, P. C. (2002). 'Rural-to-Urban Migration in LDCs: A Test of Two Rival Models'. *Journal of International Development* 14(7): 951–72.

Boserup, E. (1970). *Woman's Role in Economic Development*. New York: St. Martin's Press.

Breman, J. (1993). *Beyond Patronage and Exploitation*. Delhi: Oxford University Press.

——— (1990). 'Even Dogs Are Better Off: The Ongoing Battle between Capital and Labour in the Cane Fields of Gujarat'. *The Journal of Peasant Studies* 17: 546–608. DOI:10.1080/ 03066159008438436.

——— (1985). *Of Peasants, Migrants and Paupers: Rural Labour Circulation and Capitalist Production in West India*. Oxford: Oxford University Press.

Brenner, N. (2013). 'Theses on Urbanization'. *Public Culture* 25(1): 85–114. Available at http://www.urbantheorylab.net/site/assets/files/1015/public_ culture.pdf.

Burger, Martijn J. and Evert J. Meijers (2016). 'Agglomerations and the Rise of Urban Network Externalities'. *Regional Science* 95(1): 5–15.

Burte, H. (2014). 'The 'Smart City' Card'. *Economic and Political Weekly* 49(46): 22–5.

Cagatay, N. and S. Ozler (1995). 'Feminisation of the Labour Force: The Effects of Long-term Development and Structural Adjustment'. *World Development* 23(11): 1883–94.

Cali, M. (2008). 'Urbanisation, Inequality and Economic Growth: Evidence from Indian States and Towns'. Background Note for the World Development Report, 2009.

Cali, M. and Carlo Menon (2012). 'Does Urbanization Affect Rural Poverty? Evidence from Indian Districts'. *The World Bank Economic Review* 27(2): 171–201. DOI:10.1093/wber/lhs019.

Camagni, Roberto, Roberta Capello, and Andrea Caragliu (2016). 'Static vs. Dynamic Agglomeration Economies: Spatial Context and Structural Evolution behind Urban Growth'. *Regional Science* 95(1): 133–58.

Caragliu, A., C. Del Bo, and P. Nijkamp (2011). 'Smart Cities in Europe'. *Journal of Urban Technology* 18(2): 65–82.

Castaldo, A., P. Deshingkar, and A. Mckay (2012). 'Internal Migration, Remittances and Poverty: Evidence from Ghana and India, Migrating out of Poverty'. Research Programme Consortium, Working Paper 7 (September).

Castells-Quintana, David and Vicente Royuela (2014). 'Tracking Positive and Negative Effects of Income Inequality on Long-run Growth'. AQR-IREA Working Paper series 2014/1.

Chandrasekhar, S. and Arup Mitra (2019). 'Migration, Caste and Livelihood: Evidence from Indian City-Slums'. *Urban Research & Practice* 12(2): 156–72. Available at https://doi.org/10.1080/17535069.2018.1426781.

Chandrasekhar, S. and Ajay Sharma (2014). 'Urbanisation and Spatial Patterns of Internal Migration in India'. Working paper no. WP-2014-016. Indira Gandhi Institute of Development Research, Mumbai.

Chakravorty, Sanjoy (1993). 'The Distribution of Urban Population and Income: Explorations Using Six Asian Cases'. *Geo Journal* 29(2): 115–24.

Chatterjee, U., R. Murgai, A. Narayan, and M. Rama (2016). *Pathways to Reducing Poverty and Sharing Prosperity in India: Lessons from the Last Two Decades.* Washington, DC: The World Bank.

Chetty, R., N. Hendren, P. Kline, E. Saez, and N. Turner (2013). 'The Equality of Opportunity Project'. Available at http://www.equality-of-opportunity. org/ (accessed 30 January 2019).

Combes, Pierre-Philippe, Gilles Duranton, Laurent Gobillon, Diego Puga, and Sébastien Roux (2012). 'The Productivity Advantages of Large Cities: Distinguishing Agglomeration from Firm Selection'. *Econometrica* 80(6): 2543–94.

Corak, M. (2013). 'Income Inequality, Equality of Opportunity, and Intergenerational Mobility'. *Journal of Economic Perspectives* 27(3): 79–102.

CSDS-Lokniti (2014). 'State of Indian Farmers: A Report'. New Delhi. Available at https://www.lokniti.org/pdf/Farmers_Report_Final.pdf (accessed 29 January 2019).

Chant, S. (ed.) (1992). *Gender and Migration in Developing Countries.* London (UK) and New York (USA): Belhaven Press.

Chattopadhyay, B. (2005). 'Why Do Women Workers Migrate? Some Answers by Rural–Urban Female Migrants'. *Urban India* 15(1): 1–20.

Connell, J., B. Dasgupta, and R. Laishley (1976). *Migration from Rural Areas: The Evidence from Village Studies.* New Delhi: Oxford University Press.

Dandekar, V. M. and N. Rath (1971). *Urban Poverty in India.* Pune: Indian School of Political Economy.

Daniel, U. (2011). Update on National Workshop on Child Migration, Education and Protection, 29–30 November 2011, New Delhi. Presentation at the UNESCO–UNICEF National Workshop on Internal Migration and Human Development in India, 6–7 December, New Delhi.

Dasgupta, P. (2000). 'Overview: Economic Progress and the Idea of Social Capital'. In P. Dasgupta and I. Serageldin (eds), *Social Capital: A Multifaceted Perspective.* Washington, DC: The World Bank.

Dasgupta, P. and B. N. Goldar (2006). 'Female Labour Supply in Rural India: An Econometric Analysis'. *Indian Journal of Labour Economics* 49(2): 293–310.

Dasgupta, P. and I. Serageldin (2000). *Social Capital: A Multifaceted Perspective.* Washington, DC: The World Bank.

Davis, K. (1951). *The Population of India and Pakistan.* Princeton, USA: Princeton University Press.

Dayal, V., P. Kapuria, and A. Mitra (2012). 'Modes of Transport, Basic Amenities and Wellbeing, Findings from Delhi City'. *Journal of Urban Regeneration and Renewal* 5(3): 253–65.

de Haan, A. (2011). 'Inclusive Growth? Labour Migration and Poverty in India'. International Institute of Social Studies, Working Paper No.513.

——— (1994). *Unsettled Settlers, Migrant Workers and Industrial Capitalism in Calcutta.* Hilversum: Verloren.

Deaton, A. and J. Dreze (2002). 'Poverty and Inequality in India: A Re-Examination'. *Economic and Political Weekly* 37(36): 3729–48.

Desai, I. P. 1984. 'Should Caste Be the Basis for Recognizing Backwardness?' *Economic and Political Weekly* 19(28): 1106–16.

Deshingkar, P. (2010). 'Migration, Remote Rural Areas and Chronic Poverty in India'. Working Paper 323, CPRC Working Paper 163.

Deshingkar, P. and S. Akter (2009). 'Migration and Human Development in India, Human Development'. UNDP (Human Development Research Paper, 2009/13). Available at http://hdr.undp.org/en/reports/global/hdr2009/papers/HDRP_2009_13.pdf (accessed 1 February 2019).

Deshingkar, P. and J. Farrington (2006). 'Rural Labour Markets and Migration in South Asia: Evidence from Indian and Bangladesh'. Background paper for the World Development Report, India.

Deshpande, S. 2003. 'Caste Inequality and Indian Sociology: Notes on Questions of Disciplinary Location'. In M. Chaudhuri (ed.), *The Changing Contours of the Discipline*. New Delhi: Orient Longman.

Dupont, V. and A. Mitra (1995). 'Population Distribution, Growth and Socio-economic Spatial Patterns in Delhi. Findings from the 1991 Census Data', *Demography India* 24 (1–2): 101–32.

Durand, J. D. (1975). *The Labour Force in Economic Development*. Princeton, NJ: Princeton University Press.

Duranton, G. (2016). 'Determinants of "City Growth in Colombia"'. *Regional Science* 95(1): 101–31.

Duranton, G. and D. Puga (2001). 'Nursery Cities: Urban Diversity, Process Innovation, and the Life Cycle of Products'. *American Economic Review* 91(5): 1454–77.

Edelman, B. and A. Mitra (2006). 'Access to Basic Amenities: The Role of Political Contact, Its Determinants and Adverse Effects'. *Review of Urban and Regional Development Studies* 18(1): 25–40.

Elliott, J. (1999). 'Social Isolation and Labour Market Isolation: Network and Neighbourhood Effects on Less-educated Urban Workers'. *Sociological Quarterly* 40(2): 199–216.

Fawcett, J. T., S. E. Khoo, and P. C. Smith (eds) (1984). *Women in Cities of Asia: Migration and Urban Adaptation*. Boulder, USA: Westview Press.

Ferré, Céline, Francisco H.G. Ferreira, and Peter Lanjouw (2012). 'Is There a Metropolitan Bias? The Relationship between Poverty and City Size in a Selection of Developing Countries'. *World Bank Economic Review* 26(3): 351–82.

Fields, G. S. (2000). 'Income Mobility: Concepts and Measures'. In N. Birdsall and C. Graham (eds), *New Markers, New Opportunities? Economic and Social Mobility in a Changing World*. Washington, D.C.: Brookings Institution and Carnegie Endowment for International Peace.

Forhad S. (2019). 'Structural Change in Space: Employment Transition and Urbanization in Developing Countries'. Policy Research Talks, World Bank, 4 March. Available at https://www.worldbank.org/en/events/2019/03/04/structural-change-in-space-employment-transition-and-urbanization-in-developing-countries (accessed 2 February 2019).

Forsythe, N. R., P. Korzeniewicz, and V. Durrant (2000). 'Gender Inequalities and Economic Growth: A Longitudinal Evaluation'. *Economic Development and Cultural Change* 48(3): 573–617.

Frick, Susanne and Andrés Rodríguez-Pose (2017). 'Big or Small Cities? On City Size and Economic Growth'. *Growth and Change, a Journal of Urban and Regional Policy* 49(1): 4–32. DOI: 10.1111/grow.12232.

Fujita, M. and N. Hamaguchi (2016). 'Supply Chain Internationalization in East Asia: Inclusiveness and Risks'. *Regional Science* 95(1): 81–100.

——— (2008). 'Regional Integration in East Asia: Perspectives of Spatial and Neoclassical Economics'. In M. Fujita, S. Kumagai and K. Nishikimi (eds), *Economic Integration in East Asia: Perspectives from Spatial and Neoclassical Economics*, 13–42. Northampton, MA: Edward Elgar.

Fujita, M. and J. F. Thisse (2003). 'Does Geographical Agglomeration Foster Economic Growth? And Who Gains and Loses from It?' *The Japanese Economic Review* 54: 121–45.

Fox, T. and S. M. Mille (1965). 'Occupational Stratification and Mobility: Intra-Country Variations'. *Studies in Comparative International Development* 1: 1–10.

Gangopadhyay Shubhashis, Namrata Ghosh, and Purti Sharma (2010). 'Report on "Generating Poverty Maps for India"'. Submitted to the Planning Commission, Government of India, New Delhi.

Gangopadhyay Shubhashis, Namrata Ghosh, Purti Sharma, and Niloo Kumari (2011). 'Report on "Generating Poverty Estimates Using New Poverty Lines"'. Submitted to the Planning Commission, Government of India, New Delhi.

Glaeser, E. (2011). *Triumph of the City: How Urban Spaces Make Us Human*. Delhi: Pan Macmillan.

Glaeser, E. L. and M. E. Kahn (2004). 'Sprawl and Urban Growth'. In J. V. Henderson and J. F. Thisse (eds), *Handbook of Regional and Urban Economics*, vol. 4, 2120–171. Amsterdam: Elsevier B V.

Glaeser, E. L., Giacomo A. M. Ponzetto, and Yimei Zou (2016). 'Urban Networks: Connecting Markets, People, and Ideas'. *Regional Science* 95(1): 17–59.

Goldin. C. (1994). 'The U-shaped Female Labour Force Function in Economic Development and Economic History'. NBER Working Paper No. 4707. National Bureau of Economic Research, Cambridge.

Gong, X. and A. van Soest (2002). 'Wage Differentials and Mobility in the Urban Labour Market: A Panel Data Analysis for Mexico'. *Labour Economics* 9(4): 513–29.

Gong, X., A. van Soest, and E. Villagomez (2004). 'Mobility in the Urban Labour Market: A Panel Data Analysis for Mexico'. *Economic Development and Cultural Change* 53(1): 1–36.

Government of Delhi (2013). *Delhi Human Development Report 2013: Improving Lives, Promoting Inclusions.* New Delhi: Academic Foundations and Institute for Human Development.

Government of India (2013). 'Press Note on Poverty Estimates 2011–12'. Planning Commission, Government of India, New Delhi.

——— (2011). 'Primary Census Abstract'. In *Census of India 2011.* New Delhi: Registrar General & Census Commissioner, Ministry of Home Affairs, Government of India.

——— (2009). *Report of the Committee on Slum Statistics/Census (2009).* New Delhi: Ministry of Housing and Urban Poverty Alleviation, Government of India.

——— (2001). *Census of India 2001.* New Delhi: Registrar General & Census Commissioner, Ministry of Home Affairs, Government of India.

——— (1993). *Report of the Expert Group on Estimation of Proportion and Number of Poor.* New Delhi: Planning Commission, Government of India.

——— (n.d.). *Report of the Technical Group (11th Five-Year Plan: 2007–12) on the Estimation of Urban Housing Shortage.* New Delhi: Ministry of Housing and Urban Poverty Alleviation, National Buildings Organisation, Government of India.

Graham, S. and S. Marvin (2001). *Splintering Urbanism: Networked Infrastructures, Technological Mobilities and the Urban Condition.* London: Routledge.

Grusky, D. and R. Kanbur (2006). 'Conceptual Ferment in Poverty and Inequality Measurement: The View from Economics and Sociology'. Q-Squared Working Paper 21. Centre for International Studies, University of Toronto.

Gugler, J. (1988). 'Over-urbanisation Reconsidered'. In J. Gugler (ed.), *The Urbanisation of the Third World.* Oxford, UK: Oxford University Press.

Hardt, M. and A. Negri (2009). *Commonwealth.* Boston, MA: Harvard University Press.

Harman, H. H. (1967). *Modern Factor Analysis.* Chicago: University of Chicago Press.

Harris, J. R. and M. P. Todaro (1970). 'Migration, Unemployment and Development: A Two-sector Analysis'. *American Economic Review* 60(1): 126–42.

Hayase, Y. (2005). 'Gender Perspectives in Family Planning in Postwar Japan and Policy Implications from the Japanese Experience'. In M. Murayama (ed.), *Gender and Development: The Japanese Experience in Comparative Perspective.* New York: Palgrave-Macmillan, IDE-JETRO.

Head, K. and T. Mayer (2004). 'The Empirics of Agglomeration and Trade'. In V. Henderson and J. F. Thisse (eds), *Handbook of Regional and Urban Economics,* vol. 4, 2609–69. Amsterdam: North-Holland.

Henderson, J .V. (1974). 'The Sizes and Types of Cities'. *American Economic Review* 64(4): 640–56.

———— (1988). Urban Development: *Theory, Fact and Illusion*. New York: Oxford University Press.

Himanshu, H., Peter Lanjouw, Abhiroop Mukhopadhyay, and Rinku Murgai (2011). 'Non-Farm Diversification and Rural Poverty Decline: A Perspective from Indian Sample Survey and Village Study Data'. Asia Research Centre Working Paper 44, London School of Economics and Political Science, London.

Himanshu, H., Peter Lanjouw, Rinku Murgai, and Nicholas Stern (2013). 'Non-Farm Diversification, Poverty, Economic Mobility and Income Inequality: A Case Study in Village India'. Policy Research Working Paper, no. 6451. World Bank, Washington, DC.

Hirway, I. (2010). 'Time-Use Surveys in Developing Countries: An Assessment'. In R. Antonopoulos and I. Hirway (eds), *Unpaid Work and the Economy: Gender, Time Use and Poverty in Developing Countries*. London, UK: Palgrave Macmillan.

———— (2005). 'Measurements Based on Time Use Statistics Some Issues'. Paper prepared for the Conference on 'Unpaid Work and Economy: Gender, Poverty and Millennium Development Goals' organized at Levy Economics Institute, New York, 1–3 October. Available at http://www.levyinstitute.org/undp-levy-conference/papers/paper_Hirway-Session7 (accessed 1 March 2019).

Hollands, R.G. (2013). 'Is an "Alternative" Smart City Possible? Critically Revisiting the Smart City Debate'. Paper presented at the conference on 'Smart Urbanism: Utopian Vision or False Dawn?' Durham University, Durham.

Holmstrom, M. (1985). Industry and Inequality: *The Social Anthropology of Indian Labour*. Bombay: Orient Longman.

———— (1976). *South Indian Factory Workers: Their Life and Their World*. Cambridge: Cambridge University Press.

Holzer, Marc, John Fry, Etienne Charbonneau, Gregg Van Ryzin, Etienne Charbonneau, Tiankai Wang, and Eileen Burnash (2009). 'Literature Review and Analysis Related to Optimal Municipal Size and Efficiency'. Local Unit Alignment, Reorganization, and Consolidation Commission, 6 May, School of Public Affairs and Administration, Rutgers Network.

Hoselitz, B. (1953). 'The Role of Cities in the Economic Growth of Underdeveloped Countries'. *Journal of Political Economy* 61(3): 195–208.

HPEC (2011). 'Report on Indian Urban Infrastructure and Services'. New Delhi: MoUD. Available at http://icrier.org/pdf/FinalReport-hpec.pdf (accessed 1 February 2019).

Huwart, J. Y. and L. Verdier (2013). 'Economic Globalisation: Origins and Consequences'. OECD Insights, OECD Publishing. Available at http://dx.doi.org/10.1787/ 9789264111899-en (accessed 1 February 2019).

Ioannides, Y. M. and L. Datcher Loury (2004). 'Job Information Networks, Neighbourhood Effects and Inequality'. *Journal of Economic Literature* 42: 1056–93.

ILO (2002). *Women and Men in the Informal Economy: A Statistical Picture.* Geneva: Employment Sector, International Labour Office.

Jalan, J. (2000). 'Does Economic Progress close the Gender Gap in Human Resource Development'. *Journal of Quantitative Economics* 18(1): 19–32.

Jayaraj, D. (2013). 'Family Migration in India "Push" or "Pull" or Both or What?' *Economic and Political Weekly* 48(42): 44–52.

Jeffrey, Craig (2001). '"A Fist Is Stronger than Five Fingers": Caste and Dominance in Rural North India'. *Transactions of the Institute of British Geographers* 25(2): 1–30.

Jeffery, R. and P. Jeffery (1997). *Population, Gender and Politics: Demographic Change in Rural North India.* Cambridge: Cambridge University Press.

Jha, R. (2002). 'Reducing Poverty and Inequality in India: Has Liberalization Helped?' Departmental Working Papers 2002–04, The Australian National University, Arndt-Corden Department of Economics. Available at https://crawford.anu.edu.au/acde/publications/publish/papers/wp2002/wp-econ-2002-04.pdf (accessed 30 January 2019).

Joshi, Heather and Vijay Joshi (1976). *Surplus Labour and the City: A Study of Bombay.* Delhi: Oxford University Press.

Kakwani, N. N., B. Prakash, and H. H. Son (2000). 'Growth, Inequality and Poverty: An Introduction'. *Asian Development Review* 18(2): 1–21.

Kannappan, S. (1985). 'Urban Employment and the labour Market in Developing Nations'. *Economic Development and Cultural Change* 33(4): 699–730.

Karlekar, M. (1995). 'Gender Dimensions in Labour Migration: An Overview'. In L. Schenk-Sandbergen (ed.), *Women and Seasonal Labour Migration.* New Delhi (India), Thousand Oaks (USA) and London (UK): Sage Publications.

Kasturi, L. (1990). 'Poverty, Migration and Women's Status'. In V. Majumdar (ed.), *Women Workers in India: Studies in Employment and Status.* New Delhi, India: Chanakya Publication.

Kaur, G. (1996). *Migration Geography.* New Delhi, India: Anmol Publications.

Kaur, R. (2006). 'Migrating for Work: Rewriting Gender Relations'. In S. Arya and A. Roy (eds), *Poverty, Gender and Migration.* New Delhi (India), Thousand Oaks (USA) & London (UK): Sage Publications.

Khera, Reetika (2006). 'Employment Guarantee and Migration'. *The Hindu*, 13 July.

Komninos, N. (2002). *Intelligent Cities: Innovation, Knowledge Systems and Digital Spaces*. London: Spon Press.

Kono, H. (2006). 'Employment with Connections: Negative Network Effects'. *Journal of Development Economics* 81: 244–58.

Krishna, Anirudh (2017). *The Broken Ladder: The Paradox and Potential of India's One-Billion*. New Delhi: Penguin Random House and New York: Cambridge University Press.

——— (2012). 'Escaping Poverty and Becoming Poor in Three States of India, with Additional Evidence from Kenya, Uganda and Peru'. In D. Narayan and P. Petesch (eds), *Moving out of Poverty: Cross Disciplinary Perspectives on Mobility*. Washington, DC: World Bank and New Delhi: Academic Foundation.

Krueger, A. B. (2012). 'The Rise and Consequences of Inequality in the United States'. Speech at the Center for American Progress, 12 January. Available at http://www.americanprogress.org/events/2012/01/pdf/krueger.pdf (accessed 5 February 2014).

Krugman, P. (1991). 'Increasing Returns and Economic-Geography'. *Journal of Political Economy* 99(3): 483–99.

Kumar, R., S. Kumar, and A. Mitra (2009). 'Social and Economic Inequalities: Contemporary Significance of Caste in India'. *Economic and Political Weekly* 44(50): 55–63.

Kumar, S. (2008). 'Strategic Transformation in Lower Caste Labour in Western Uttar Pradesh'. Presented at Seventh International Conference of the Association of Indian Labour Historians, Noida, India.

Kundu, A. (2009). 'Exclusionary Urbanisation: A Macro Overview'. *Economic and Political Weekly* 44(48): 48–58.

——— (2006). 'Urbanisation and Urban Governance: Search for a Perspective beyond Neo-liberalism'. In A. Shaw (ed.), *Indian Cities in Transition*. Hyderabad: Orient Longman.

——— (1989). 'National Commission on Urbanisation: Issues and Non-Issues'. *Economic and Political Weekly* 24(21): 1185–8.

Kundu, A. and N. Sarangi (2007). 'Migration, Employment Status and Poverty: An Analysis across Urban Centers'. *Economic and Political Weekly* 42(4), 27 January–2 February: 299–306.

Kundu, A. and P. C. Mohanan (2009). 'Poverty and Inequality Outcomes of Economic Growth in India: Focus on Employment Pattern during the Period of Structural Adjustment'. OECD Seminar on 'Employment Outcomes and Inequality: New Evidence, Links and Policy Responses in Brazil, China and India', 8 April, Paris.

Kundu, K. K. (2013). 'India Has a Problem with Inequality, and It Won't Be Solved Easily'. *Business Standard*, 25 May. Available at http://www.business-standard.com/article/opinion/india-has-a-problem-with-inequality-and-it-won-t-be-solved-easily-113052500705_1.html (accessed 6 February 2014).

Kuznets, S. (1966). *Modern Economic Growth: Rate, Structure and Spread.* New Haven: Yale University Press.

Lall, S.V., Harris Selod, and Z. Shalizi (2006). *Rural–Urban Migration in Developing Countries: A Survey of Theoretical Predictions and Empirical Finding.* Development Research Group, World Bank.

Lanjouw, Peter and Rinku Murgai (2010a). 'Size Matters: Urban Growth and Poverty in India, 1983–2005'. Development Economics Research Group Working Paper, World Bank, Washington DC.

——— (2010b). 'Urban Growth and Rural Poverty in India'. Paper prepared for the International Conference on Dynamics of Rural Transformation, 14–16 April, Delhi. Available at http://www.rimisp.org/wp-content/uploads/2013/05/Ppt_Lanjouw-and-Murgai-4.1.pdf (accessed 7 February 2014).

Leonhardt, D. (2013). 'In Climbing Income Ladder Location Matters', *New York Times*, July 22. Available at http://www.nytimes.com/2013/07/22/business/in-climbing-income-ladder-location-matters.html?_r=0 (accessed 7 February 2014).

Lewis, Arthur (1954). 'Economic Development with Unlimited Supplies of Labour', *The Manchester School 22*(2).

Luke, N. and K. Munshi (2006). 'New Roles for Marriage in Urban Africa: Kinship Networks and the Labour Market in Kenya'. *The Review of Economics and Statistics* 88(2): 264–82.

Mathur, A. (1994). 'Work Participation, Gender and Economic Development: A Quantitative Anatomy of the Indian Scenario'. *The Journal of Development Studies 30*(2): 466–504.

Mathur, O. P. (2014). 'City-Size Distributions in a Quasi-Open Economy: The India Evidence'. Asian Development Bank, Manila.

McAllister, I. (1995). 'Occupational Mobility among Immigrants: The Impact of Migration on Economic Success in Australia'. *International Migration Review* 29(2): 441–68.

McKinsey Global Institute (2010). 'India's Urban Awakening: Building Inclusive Cities, Sustaining Economic Growth'. Available at http://www.mckinsey.com/mgi/reports/freepass_pdfs/india_urbanisation/MGI_india_urbanization_fullreport.pdf (accessed 10 March 2013).

Mahadevia, D. and S. Sarkar (2012). *Handbook of Urban Inequalities.* New Delhi: Oxford University Press.

Melendez, E. (1994). 'Puerto Rican Migration and Occupational Selectivity, 1982–1988'. *International Migration Review* 28(1): 49–67.

Mills, E. S. and Arup Mitra (1997). *Urban Development and Urban Ills.* Delhi: Commonwealth Publishers.

Mills, E. S. and C. M. Becker (1986). *Studies in Indian Urban Development.* Oxford: Oxford University Press, World Bank Research Publication.

Ministry of Urban Development (2015). 'Smart Cities Mission'. New Delhi: Government of India. Available at http://smartcities.gov.in/ (accessed 10 February 2019).

Mitra, Arup (2019). 'Women's Work in Response to Urbanization: Evidence from Odisha'. *Indian Journal of Women and Social Change* 4(1): 92–106.

——— (2014). 'Agglomeration Economies and Wellbeing: Evidence from India'. *Athens Journal of Health* 1(1), March: 23–36.

——— (2013). *Insights into Inclusive Growth, Employment and Wellbeing in India.* Heidelberg: Springer.

——— (2010a). 'Migration, Livelihood and Well-being: Evidence from Indian City Slums'. *Urban Studies* 47(7): 1371–90.

——— (2010b). 'Women's Employment in Asia-Pacific'. Asia-Pacific Human Development Report, Background Papers Series 2010/07, UNDP.

——— (2009). 'Technology Import and Industrial Employment: Evidence from Developing Countries'. *Labour* 23(4): 697–718.

——— (2008). 'Social Capital, Livelihood and Upward Mobility'. *Habitat International* 32(2): 261–9.

——— (2006). 'Labour Market Mobility of Low Income Households'. *Economic and Political Weekly* 41: 2123–30.

——— (2005). 'Women in the Urban Informal Sector: Perpetuation of Meagre Earnings'. *Development and Change* 36(2): 291–316.

——— (2004). 'Informal Sector, Networks and Intra-city Variations in Activities: Findings from Delhi Slums'. *Review of Urban and Regional Development Studies* 16(2): 154–69.

——— (2003). *Occupational Choices, Networks and Transfers: An Exegesis Based on Micro Data from Delhi Slums.* New Delhi: Manohar Publishers.

——— (2001). 'Employment in the Informal Sector'. In A. Kundu and A. N. Sharma (eds), *Informal Sector in India: Perspectives and Policies*, 85–92. New Delhi: Institute for Human Development and Institute of Applied Manpower Research.

——— (1999). 'Agglomeration Economies as Manifested in Technical Efficiency at the Firm Level'. *Journal of Urban Economics* 45(3): 490–500.

——— (1988). 'Spread of Urban Slums: The Rural-Spill-Over?' *Demography India* 17(1): 29–42.

——— (1994). *Urbanisation, Slums, Informal Sector Employment and Poverty: An Exploratory Study.* Delhi: B.R. Pub. Corp. (D.K. Pub. and Dist.).

Mitra, Arup and Aviral Pandey (2016). 'Unorganized Sector in India: Employment Elasticity and Wage Production Nexus'. In K. P. Kannan,

Rajendra P. Mamgain, and Preet Rustagi (eds), Labour and Development: Essays in Honour of Prof. T. S. Papola. New Delhi: Academic Foundation.

Mitra, Arup and Aya Okada (2018). *Labour Market Participation in India: A Region-and Gender-Specific Study.* Singapore: Springer.

Mitra, Arup and Yuko Tsujita (2016). 'Issues in Upward Mobility: Study Based on Longitudinal Data from Delhi Slums'. *Habitat International* 53: 320–30.

———— (2014). 'Dimensions and Determinants of Upward Mobility: A Study based on Longitudinal Data from Delhi Slums'. IDE Discussion Papers, No. 448, March. Available at https://www.ide.go.jp/English/Publish/Download/Dp/448.html.

———— (2008) 'Migration and Wellbeing at the Lower Echelons of the Economy: A Study of Delhi Slums'. In H. Sato and M. Murayama (eds), *Globalization, Employment and Mobility: The South Asian Experience.* Basingstoke and New York: Palgrave Macmillan.

Mitra, A. and R. Kumar (2015). 'New Patterns in Indian Urbanization: Emergence of Census Towns'. *Environment and Urbanization ASIA* 6(1): 1–9.

Mitra, A. and B. Mehta (2011). 'Cities as the Engine of Growth: Evidence from India'. *Journal of Urban Planning and Development* 137(2): 171–83.

Mitra, A. and J. P. Nagar (2018a). 'City Size, Deprivation and Other Indicators of Development: Evidence from India'. *World Development* 106: 273–83.

———— (2018b). 'Smart Cities in India: Existing Facilities and Indicators of Development'. *Urban India* 38(2), July–December.

Mitra, A. and M. Murayama (2009). 'Rural to Urban Migration: A District Level Analysis for India'. *International Journal of Migration, Health and Social Care* 5(2), September: 35–52.

———— (2008). 'Rural to Urban Migration: A District Level Analysis for India'. IDE Discussion Paper No. 137, Institute of Developing Economies, Japan External Trade Organization (JETRO), Chiba, Japan.

Mehta, Aasha Kapur, Shashanka Bhide, Anand Kumar, and Amita Shah (eds) (2018). *Poverty, Chronic Poverty and Poverty Dynamics:* Policy Imperatives. Singapore: Springer.

Mohan, R. (1993). 'Industrial Location Policies and Their Implications for India'. Paper No. 9, Ministry of Industry, Office of the Economic Adviser, Government Of India.

Mohanty, K. S., S. Mahapatro, A. Kastor, and B. Mahapatra (2015). 'Does Employment-related Migration Reduce Poverty in India'. *Journal of International Migration and Integration* (online), May.

Montgomery, J. D. (1991). 'Social Networks and Labour Market Outcomes: Towards an Economic Analysis'. *American Economic Review* 81(5): 1408–18.

Montgomery, M. R., R. Stren, B. Cohen, and H. E. Reed (2013). *Cities Transformed: Demographic Change and Its Implications in the Developing World*. Oxfordshire: Routledge.

Mortensen, D. (1986). 'Job Search and Labour Market Analysis'. In O. Ashenfelter and R. Layard (eds), *Handbook of Labour Economics*. Amsterdam: North-Holland.

Mukherjee, P., B. Paul, and J. I. Pathan (2010). 'Migrant Workers in Informal Sector: A Probe into Working Conditions'. ATLMRI Discussion Paper Series Discussion, Paper 9. Tata Institute of Social Sciences, Mumbai.

Mukhopadhyay, P., M. H. Zerah, G. Samanta, and A. Maria (2016). 'Understanding India's Urban Frontier: What Is behind the Emergence of Census Towns in India?' Policy Research Working Paper No. WPS 7923. World Bank, Washington, DC.

Munshi, K. (2003). 'Networks in the Modern Economy: Mexican Migrants in the U.S. Labour Market'. *Quarterly Journal of Economics* 118(2): 549–99.

Munshi, K. and M. Rosenzweig (2006). 'Traditional Institutions meet the Modern World: Caste, Gender, and Schooling Choice in a Globalizing Economy'. *The American Economic Review* 96(4): 1225–52.

Murayama, M. (ed.) (2005). *Gender and Development: The Japanese Experience in Comparative Perspective*. IDE-JETRO: Palgrave-Macmillan.

Narayan, D. and P. Petesch (2012). 'Agency, Opportunity Structure and Poverty Escapes'. In D. Narayan and P. Petesch (eds), *Moving out of Poverty: Cross Disciplinary Perspectives on Mobility*, 1–44. Washington, D.C.: World Bank and New Delhi: Academic Foundation.

Navlakha, S. (1989). Elite and Social Change: *A Study of Elite Formation in India*. New Delhi: Sage Publications.

Neetha, N (2004). 'Making of Female Breadwinners: Migration and Social Networking of Women Domestics in Delhi'. *Economic and Political Weekly* 39(17).

Neirotti, P., A. De Marco, A. C. Cagliano, G. Mangano, and F. Scorrano (2014). 'Current Trends in Smart City Initiatives: Some Stylised Facts'. *Cities* 38: 25–36.

Nguyen, L. (2005). 'Pattern and Determinants of Occupational Mobility of Adult Ghanaian In-migrants in the Central Region'. Population Association of America, Annual Meeting Programme. Available at http://paa2005.princeton.edu/abstracts/50333 (accessed 30 November 2013).

Nishikimi, K. (2008). 'Specialisation and Agglomeration Forces of Economic Integration'. In M. Fujita, S. Kumagai and K. Nishikimi (eds), *Economic Integration in East Asia: Perspectives from Spatial and Neoclassical Economics*, 43–73. Northampton, MA: Edward Elgar.

Nord, S. (1989). 'The Relationship among Labour Force Participation and Service Sector Employment and Underemployment'. *Journal of Regional Science* 29(3): 407–21.

Oberai, A. S. and H. K. Manmohan Singh (1983). *Causes and Consequences of Internal Migration: A Study of Indian Punjab.* New Delhi, India: Oxford University Press.

Oberai, A. S., H. P. Prasad, and M. G. Sardana (1989). *Determinants and Consequences of Internal Migration in India: Studies in Bihar, Kerala and Uttar Pradesh.* Delhi, India: Oxford University Press.

Oppenheimer, V. (1970). *The Female Labour Force in the United States.* Berkeley, CA: Institute for International Studies.

Ottaviano, G. and J. F. Thisse (2004). 'Agglomeration and Economic Geography'. In J. V. Henderson and J. F. Thisse (eds), *Handbook of Regional and Urban Economics*, vol. 4, 2120–71. Amsterdam: Elsevier B V.

Papola, T. S. (1981). *Urban Informal Sector in a Developing Economy.* New Delhi: Vikas Publishing House.

Patrick, M. (2001). 'Unorganized Women in an Urban Setting: Opportunities and Challenges'. In A. Kundu and A. N. Sharma (eds), *Informal Sector in India: Perspectives and Policies*, 349–60. New Delhi: Institute for Human Development and Institute of Applied Manpower Research.

Portes, A. (1998). 'Social Capital: Its Origins and Applications in Modern Sociology'. *Annual Review of Sociology* 24: 1–24.

Putnam, R. D. (1993). *Making Democracy Work: Civic Traditions in Modern Italy.* Princeton: Princeton University Press.

Pradhan, Basanta K., Shalabh K. Singh, and Arup Mitra (2015). 'Female Labour Supply in a Developing Economy: A Tale from a Primary Survey'. *Journal of International Development* 27: 99–111.

Raijman, R. and M. Semyonov (1995). 'Modes of Labor Market Incorporation and Occupational Cost among New Immigrants to Israel'. *International Migration Review* 29(2): 375–94.

Rajan, S. I. (2013). *Internal Migration and Youth in India: Main Features, Trends and Emerging Challenges.* New Delhi: UNESCO.

Rakshit, M. (2007). 'Services-led Growth: The Indian Experience'. *Money and Finance* 3(February): 91–126.

Ravallion, M. and G. Datt (2002). 'Why Has Economic Growth Been More Pro-Poor in Some States of India Than Others?' *Journal of Development Economics* 68(2): 381–400.

Ravi, S., A. Tomer, A. Bhatia, and, J. Kane (2016). *Building Smart Cities in India: Allahabad, Ajmer and Visakhapatnam.* Brookings India and Bookings Institution, Washington, DC.

Rosenthal, S. S. and W. C. Strange (2004). 'Evidence on the Nature and Sources of Agglomeration Economies'. In J. V. Henderson and J. F. Thisse (eds), *Handbook of Regional and Urban Economics*, vol. 4, 2120–71. Amsterdam: Elsevier B V.

Rosenzweig, Mark R. (2013). 'Payoffs from Panels in Low-Income Countries: Economic Development and Economic Mobility'. *American Economic Review* 93(2): 112–17.

Sachs, J. D., N. Bajpai, and A. Ramiah (2002). 'Understanding Regional Economic Growth in India'. CID Working Paper No. 88, March. Center for International Development at Harvard University, Cambridge, MA.

Sastry, N. S. (2004). 'Estimating Informal Employment and Poverty in India'. United Nations Development Programme India, Discussion Paper Series-7, December.

Schultz, T. P. (1990). 'Women's Changing Participation in the Labour Force: A World Perspective'. *Economic Development and Cultural Change* 38: 457–88.

Sen, A. (1981). 'Market Failure and Control of Labour Power: Towards an Explanation of "Structure" and Change in Indian Agriculture (Part 2)'. *Cambridge Journal of Economics* 5(4): 327–50.

Sen, P. (2017). 'The Puzzle of Indian Urbanisation, Ideas for India'. *Ideas for India*, 12 April. Available at http://www.ideasforindia.in/topics/urbanisation/the-puzzle-of-indian-urbanisation.html (accessed 30 January 2019).

Sethuraman, S. V. (1976). 'The Urban Informal Sector: Concept, Measurement and Policy'. *International Labour Review* 114(1): 69–81.

Shah, A. M. (2007). 'Caste in the 21st Century: From System to Elements'. *Economic and Political Weekly* 42: 109–16.

Shah, Amita (2009). 'Land Degradation and Migration in a Dry Land Region in India: Extent, Nature, and Determinants'. *Environment and Development Economics* 15(2): 1–24. DOI: https://doi.org/10.1017/S1355770X09990131.

Shah, Amita and Anand Kumar (2011). 'Migration and Poverty in India: A Multi-patterned and Complex reality'. CPRC–IIPA, Working Paper 45, New Delhi.

Shah, Amita, Itishree Pattnaik, and Animesh Kumar (2018). 'Changing Scenario of Migration and Poverty in India: Reflections and Issues'. In Aasha Kapur Mehta, Shashanka Bhide, Anand Kumar, and Amita Shah (eds), *Poverty, Chronic Poverty and Poverty Dynamics: Policy Imperatives*, 127–52. Singapore: Springer.

Sharma, U. (1986). *Women's Work, Class and the Urban Household: A Study of Shimla, North India*. London (UK) and New York (USA): Tavistock Publications.

Sharma, P. and N. Kumari (2012). 'Location as a Poverty Trap'. Available at https://www.google.co.in/webhp?sourceid=chrome-instant&ion=1&espv=2&ie=UTF-8#q=SHARMA+AND+KUMARI+ON+POVERTY.

Shaw, A. (1990). 'Linkages of Large Scale, Small Scale and Informal Sector Industries: A Study of Thane-Belapur'. *Economic and Political Weekly* 25(7–8): M17–M22.

Singh, A. M. (1984). 'Rural-to-urban Migration of Women in India: Patterns and Implications'. In J. T. Fawcett, S. E. Khoo, and P. C. Smith (eds), *Women in the Cities of Asia: Migration and Urban Adaptation*. Boulder, USA: Westview Press.

Singh, A. M. and A. D'Souza. 1980. *The Urban Poor: Slum and Pavement Dwellers in the Major Cities of India*. Delhi: Manohar Publishers.

Singh, D. P. (2009). 'Poverty and Migration: Does Moving Help?' In *India Urban Poverty Report*, 50–75. New Delhi: Oxford University Press.

Sinha, J. N. (1965). 'Dynamics of Female Participation in Economic Activity in a Developing Economy'. World Population Conference, Belgrade, vol. IV, UN Publication no. 66, XIII 8.

Sinha, S. K. (1986). *Internal Migration in India 1961–81*. New Delhi, India: Office of the Registrar General, Ministry of Home Affairs.

Skeldon, R. (1986). 'On Migration Patterns in India during the 1970s'. *Population and Development Review* 12(4): 759–79.

Söderström, O., T. Paasche, and F. Klauser (2014). 'Smart Cities as Corporate Storytelling'. *City* 18(3): 307–20.

Spence, Michael, Patricia Clarke Annez, and Robert M. Buckley, eds (2009). *Urbanization and Growth: Commission on Growth and Development*. World Bank Publications. Available at https://openknowledge.worldbank.org/handle/10986/2582.

Srinivas, M. N. (1969). 'The Caste System in India'. In A. Beteille (ed.), *Social Inequality*. Harmondsworth: Penguin Books.

Srivastava, R. (2011). 'Labour Migration in India: Recent Trends, Patterns and Policy Issues'. *The Indian Journal of Labour Economics* 54(3): 411–40.

Stark, O. (1984). 'Rural-to-Urban Migration in LDCs: A Relative Deprivation Approach'. *Economic Development and Cultural Change* 32(3): 475–86.

——— (1995). *Altruism and Beyond: An Economic Analysis of Transfers and Exchanges within Families and Groups*. Cambridge: Cambridge University Press.

Sundaram, K. (1986/1989). 'Agriculture–Industry Inter-relations: Issues of Migration'. In S. Chakravarty (ed.), *World Congress of the International Economic Association 1986, Proceedings: Balance between Industry and Agriculture in Economic Development, Manpower and Transfers*, vol. 3. London: Macmillan.

Sundaram, K. and S. D. Tendulkar (2003). 'Poverty among Social and Economic Groups in India in 1990s'. *Economic and Political Weekly* 38(50): 5263–76.

Sveikauskas, L. (1975). 'Productivity of Cities'. *Quarterly Journal of Economics* 89(3): 393–413.

Thorat, S. 1993. 'Economic Development Policies and Change: Emerging Status of Scheduled Castes after Independence'. Paper presented at the Seminar on Social Composition of Limited Elite, Centre for the Study of Social Systems, School of Social Sciences, Jawaharlal Nehru University, New Delhi.

Todaro, M. P. (1969). 'A Model of Labor Migration and Urban Unemployment in Less Developed Countries'. *American Economic Review* 59(1): 138–48.

Tripathy, S. (2013). 'Does Higher Economic Growth Reduce Poverty and Increase Inequality? Evidence from Urban India', *Indian Journal of Human Development* 7(1): 109–37.

Ugur, Mehmet and Arup Mitra (2017). 'Technology Adoption and Employment in Less Developed Countries: A Mixed-Method Systematic Review'. *World Development* 96(C): 1–18.

Udall, A. T. (1976). 'The Effects of Rapid Increases in Labour Supply on Service Employment in Developing Countries'. *Economic Development and Cultural Changes* 24(4): 765–85.

UNESCO (2013). *Social Inclusion of Internal Migrants in India*. New Delhi: UNESCO.

UNICEF and UNESCO (2012). *Internal Migration in India Initiative: Policy Briefs for a Better Inclusion of Internal Migrants in India*. New Delhi: UNESCO and UNICEF.

United Nations (2018). 'Revision of World Urbanization Prospects'. Department of Economic and Social Affairs, 16 May. Available at https://www.un.org/development/desa/publications/2018-revision-of-world-urbanization-prospects.html (accessed 30 January 2019).

——— (2014). *World Urbanization Prospects: The 2014 Revision*. Geneva, Switzerland: United Nations.

——— (2001a). *Reducing Disparities: Balanced Development of Urban and Rural Areas and Regions within the Countries of Asia and the Pacific*. Economic and Social Commission for Asia and the Pacific.

——— (2001b). *World Population Monitoring 2000: Population, Gender and Development*. New York.

Weber, M. ([1922] 1968). *Economy and Society: An Outline of Interpretive Sociology*. Translated by G. Roth and G. Wittich, originally published as *Wirstschaft and Gesellschaft*. New York: Bedminster Press.

Williamson, J. G. (1988). 'Migration and Urbanisation'. In H. Chenery and T. N. Srinivasan (eds.), *Handbook of Development Economics*, vol. I. Amsterdam: Elsevier Science Publishers, B.V.

———— (1965). 'Regional Inequality and the Process of National Development'. *Economic Development and Cultural Change* 13: 3–45.

Wood, A. (1997). 'Openness and Wage Inequality in Developing Countries: The Latin American Challenge to East Asian Conventional Wisdom'. *World Bank Economic Review* 11(1): 33–57.

World Bank (2011). *Perspectives on Poverty in India: Stylized Facts from Survey Data.* Washington, D.C.

Index